READING KAFKA

READING
KAFKA
PRAGUE, POLITICS,
and the
FIN DE SIÈCLE

edited by
MARK ANDERSON

SCHOCKEN BOOKS
New York

Permission acknowledgments can be found on page 285.

Library of Congress Cataloging-in-Publication Data

Reading Kafka : Prague, politics, and the fin de siècle / edited by Mark Anderson.
   p.   cm.
  Includes bibliographical references.
  ISBN 0-8052-4050-0.—ISBN 0-8052-0945-X (pbk.)
  1. Kafka, Franz. 1883–1924—Criticism and interpretation.
I. Anderson, Mark, 1955–
PT2621.A26Z8266 1990
833′.912—dc20   88-42592

Book Design by Glen Edelstein
Manufactured in the United States of America
First Edition

For Fred

CONTENTS

III. TEXTS, LETTERS, AND AUTOBIOGRAPHY

APPENDICES

ABBREVIATIONS

Originally written in four different languages and widely divergent circumstances, the following essays have been slightly altered to fit as independent essays in this volume. All quotations from Kafka's works have been changed to conform to the following widely available editions and are noted in parentheses in the text. On rare occasions, the translations have been silently emended.

CS *Complete Stories*, ed. Nahum Glatzer (New York: Schocken Books, 1976).

A   *Amerika*, trans. Willa and Edwin Muir (New York: Schocken Books, 1962).

T   *The Trial*, trans. Willa and Edwin Muir (New York: Schocken Books, 1968).

C   *The Castle*, trans. Willa and Edwin Muir (New York: Schocken Books, 1974).

D   *Diaries* (one volume), ed. Max Brod; 1910–1913 trans. Joseph Kresh, 1914–1923 trans. Martin Greenberg and Hannah Arendt (New York: Schocken Books, 1988).

DF   *Dearest Father,* trans. Ernst Kaiser and Eithne Wilkins (New York: Schocken Books, 1954).

L   *Letters to Friends, Family, and Editors,* trans. Richard and Clara Winston (New York: Schocken Books, 1977).

F   *Letters to Felice,* eds. Erich Heller and Jürgen Born; trans. James Stern and Elisabeth Duckworth (New York: Schocken Books, 1973).

M   *Letters to Milena,* ed. Willy Haas; trans. Tania and James Stern (New York: Schocken Books, 1962).

O   *Letters to Ottla and the Family,* ed. Nahum Glatzer; trans. Richard and Clara Winston (New York: Schocken Books, 1982).

J   Gustav Janouch, *Conversations with Kafka,* 2nd ed., trans. Goronwy Rees (New York: New Directions Books, 1971).

READING KAFKA

INTRODUCTION

Mark Anderson

The poem is not timeless. Certainly, it raises a claim to infinity, it attempts to grasp its way through time—through it, not over and above it.

—Paul Celan

IF YET ANOTHER BOOK is to be added to the body of secondary literature about Kafka, a body that has long since outweighed Kafka's own slender corpus of writings, it is because the scholarship of the last twenty years has formed a substantially different image of an author whose writing continues to intrigue the twentieth-century imagination. For the most part this work has been done by Europeans and has not been available in this country or in English translation. And for the most part this work has been historically oriented, aiming to reconstruct what Kafka deliberately removed, effaced, or covered over in his own texts. Working on two different planes, the "macro" level of intellectual or social history and the "micro" level of textual analysis, this work challenges the conventional image of Kafka as the isolated, alienated, "negative" genius of the modern age, seeking instead to map out the historical context of his isolation: Prague at the turn of the century.

3

This is not the place to detail the history of Kafka's reception since his death in 1924, a history that in itself, comprising such names as Walter Benjamin and Theodor Adorno, Albert Camus and Jean-Paul Sartre, Harold Bloom and Jacques Derrida, would constitute an intellectual biography of this century. But it is worth noting that few modern authors have received the same degree of international attention as Kafka. To a remarkable extent, his work has been appropriated by different foreign cultures as if he were a native author. Joyce's linguistic experimentalism ties his texts to their original language and makes translation a questionable enterprise. Proust's work is tied not only to the rhythm, length, and sculpted beauty of his French sentences but also to a specific cultural milieu and historical period, so that translations have not achieved the same centrality in foreign cultures that the original has in France. By contrast, Kafka's writings are (or at least have seemed to be) tied to no culture or period—and have therefore proved eminently translatable. In their strange and otherworldly purity, with barely a reference to a particular date or place, they appeared to his first readers already to be a distillation of some other language that could be rendered without appreciable loss in any and all languages. In fact, Kafka's first success was in France, England, and the United States, in translation. It was only after the Second World War that he re-entered Germany and Austria (neither of which could be considered his native country) in his original German, more or less as an imported fashion.

What this means is that Kafka has been read to an overwhelming extent in isolation from the material context in which he lived and wrote. Most readers know that Kafka wrote in German, but few could say how his German relates to High German or to the particular version of German spoken in Prague at the beginning of this century. For that matter, few know much about Prague itself—its population, languages, or political and cultural history. And while most readers know generally that Kafka was Jewish, few are familiar with the specific, complex historical issues such as assimilation, anti-Semitism, Zionism, Yiddish culture, and the political revival of Eastern Judaism that formed his perception of Judaism. As a result, many readers have tended to assume that Kafka had no literary predecessors, that his "foreign" and "otherworldly" texts were the anomalous creations of his powerful imagination. In 1938, as acute and sympathetic an observer as Walter Benjamin judged Kafka to be "essentially *isolated* in literature," much as Paul Klee was in painting.[1]

Of course, Kafka had done everything to encourage such an allegorical reception of his writing. The root content of all his writings was (to put it in terms that have since become clichéd) the isolation of the individual, an alien without relations, alone, "completely unsure of my footing in this world, in this town, in my family."[2] To produce this effect of isolation *in the reader*, Kafka eliminated the specific cultural signs that had traditionally served to locate a literary text in a particular place and time. Almost all place names, dates, proper names, and other references to a world outside the text were effaced. Moreover, the physical laws and social norms of this external world were also suspended: salesmen could turn into giant vermin overnight, law-abiding bank officials could be arrested in their beds, country doctors could wander eternally through an empty winter landscape, "exposed to the frost of this most unhappy of ages." Still more unsettling was Kafka's apparent disappearance from his own text. Throughout these bizarre, cruel, unjust events, the author himself seemed strangely absent, never pronouncing judgment or expressing the least surprise, maintaining instead a rigorously neutral, impersonal narrative style. Kafka's only claim for the general validity and importance of his work was that it represented, as he put it in an oft-cited phrase, "*das Negative meiner Zeit*"—the negativity of his time.[3] His relation to the world was not one of representation but, rather, one of refutation or a breakdown of representation; his poetic world was an antiworld, the negative mirror of history.[4]

Historical factors reinforced the negative, essentially ahistorical reception of his texts. For an entire generation of early readers marked by the experience of the Second World War, National Socialism, and the Holocaust, Kafka's work could not be separated from what came after it: for them, Joseph K.'s arrest at the beginning of *The Trial* (written in 1914) was not a fantastic event on the order of Gregor Samsa's metamorphosis, but a prophetic anticipation of the fate awaiting Hitler's victims. If Kafka had a relation to history it was not to the specific milieu of his own period but a prophetic, visionary relation to an event that would soon overshadow all others. In this teleological, even eschatological view, the negative existence of Kafka's protagonists made his work exemplary for the later negativity of

modern Europe, for the fate of European Jewry and for Western culture as a whole. It is for this reason that Auden could claim for Kafka
the same symbolic relation to his age that Dante, Shakespeare, and
Goethe had for theirs: in 1945 we were all pariahs like Joseph K. or
Gregor Samsa, exposed to the terrifying and absurd injustice "of this
most unhappy of ages."[5]

However understandable and significant these allegorizations may
be, they have consistently obscured the fact that Kafka himself
understood his negative relation to history and tradition as just
that—a *relation,* and as such, a product of historical forces. As the
Italian literary scholar Giuliano Baioni has noted, the only historical
category Kafka ever explicitly employed was that of a "Western Jewish
age" between emancipation and Zionism.[6] For the Jews of Kafka's
generation, born in the last decades of the nineteenth century, this
age was one of failed assimilation, a period of transition "whose end
is clearly unpredictable" (D 147).* Unlike the East European Jews
with their communal religious life, Western Jews were cut off from
their own past, not yet integrated in the national states; severed from
their historical traditions and traditional history, more alienated than
in exile, they inhabited a world where "everything has to be earned."
In 1920 Kafka expressed the negativity of his historical position thus,
in a letter to Milena Jesenská, a gentile:

> I have one peculiarity which in essence doesn't distinguish me much
> from my acquaintances, but in degree a great deal. We both know, after
> all, enough typical examples of Western Jews, I am as far as I know the
> most typical Western Jew among them. This means, expressed with ex-
> aggeration, that not one calm second is granted me, nothing is granted
> me, everything has to be earned, not only the present and the future,
> but the past too—something after all which perhaps every human being
> has inherited, this too must be earned, it is perhaps the hardest work.
> (M 218–19)

In this letter, Kafka sees himself not as a paradigm of the human
condition but, rather, as an extreme example of Western Judaism at
a particular moment in history. "I have not been guided into life by

---

* See list of Abbreviations on page ix.

the hand of Christianity," he had noted in the Zürau notebooks two years earlier, "and have not caught the hem of the Jewish prayer shawl—now flying away from us—as the Zionists have. I am an end or a beginning" (DF 99–100).

PRAGUE, JUDAISM, POLITICS

The essays in this anthology all seek to understand the ahistorical, negative quality of Kafka's life and writings as a function of particular historical and cultural forces in his time. In the last twenty years much research has been done to improve our knowledge of Prague, Kafka's predecessors, and the genesis of his writings. In many cases the results of this work have been startling: his texts, which had been taken for a blank, or nearly blank canvas of the modern age, turn out to be a palimpsest, texts that have been written over earlier layers of inscription, corrections, and partial effacements. Beneath the seamless, unified surface, readers have discovered surprisingly direct quotations from other authors, relations to key figures of the period, literal details from his personal biography. In certain cases, despite Kafka's habit of destroying all notes and preparatory material for his writing, scholars have been able to map out the genesis of his texts as they took shape on the page, thus giving us graphic details of his conception and execution of a literary idea.

One of the earliest and most important historical studies was Klaus Wagenbach's biography of Kafka's youth, first published in German in 1958 but unfortunately never translated into English.[7] Originally a dissertation, Wagenbach's meticulously researched critical study places Kafka and his work in a broad social and cultural context. Particularly the central chapter, which is presented here, "Prague at the Turn of the Century," deals with political, religious, and linguistic aspects of Kafka's environment that previously had been neglected. To characterize the isolation of German-speaking Jews in Prague around 1900, Wagenbach takes up the notion of a "sociological ghetto" that had replaced the actual ghetto (razed in 1896), and offers a historical explanation for Kafka's "foreignness": "shunned by the Czechs as 'German' and by the Germans as Jews," separated from the working and lower-middle classes for their economic superiority, these assimilated Jews had also lost the bonds of a common religion practiced in the ghetto. "The resulting foreignness," Wagenbach notes, appears in Kafka's works "in its exact and dangerous proportions."

Kafka's relation to Judaism—whether mediated through the Yiddish theater, Martin Buber's "cultural Zionism," or the Zionist activism of his friends Max Brod and Hugo Bergmann—has been a central issue in many recent studies.[8] Kafka's closest friends were directly involved in founding and running Prague's Zionist newspaper, the *Selbstwehr* ("Self-Defense"). With them he attended political and cultural meetings, took part in discussions sponsored by the Bar Kokhba (the Zionist student organization), attended the Eleventh Zionist Congress in Vienna in September 1913, studied Hebrew, planned to travel, and perhaps even to settle, in Palestine. Although suspicious of Buber's belief in a Zionist utopia, and (unlike Brod and Bergmann) never fully convinced by Theodor Herzl's political program, Kafka nonetheless worked and wrote in an intellectual and political landscape largely shaped by Zionism. Many of his writings— "The Investigations of a Dog," "Josephine the Singer, or the Mouse Folk," "The Great Wall of China," "Jackals and Arabs," "A Report to an Academy"—were conceived in an oblique dialogue with debates then current in Zionist circles and were first published for a Zionist audience.[9]

One of the most fruitful and influential studies of Kafka's Judaism is Christoph Stölzl's *Kafka's Nasty Bohemia*, which took up and expanded upon Wagenbach's thesis of a sociological ghetto maintained by Czech nationalism and anti-Semitism in Bohemia during the nineteenth century.[10] A historian of Central Europe, Stölzl makes no claim to literary analysis. Like Wagenbach, he offers a historical reading for what had previously been explained in metaphysical or psychological terms. Kafka's "torment," his tendency toward ironic and masochistic self-deprecation, his "fragmented" personality, are juxtaposed against contemporary "Jewish self-hatred," then a common phenomenon in central Europe at that time.[11] As the *Selbstwehr* reported in 1910 of Western Bohemian Jews: "When you hear how they talk among themselves about their fellow Jews, you would think you were in the best anti-Semitic company." That Kafka was not immune to such tendencies emerges all too clearly from the disturbing pas-

sages of his letters and diaries quoted by Stölzl. His self-critical attitude was a common feature of Western European Jews in a period of
extreme collective self-doubt—a period in which they were still subject to allegations of ritual murder and physical assault (one of Kafka's
closest friends lost his eyesight as a child after being attacked by anti-
Semites), were vilified as "bedbugs," "dogs," "apes," and "rats" by the
Czech nationalist majority—but were without the support of a vital
religious community. Assimilation, conversion to Christianity, and
suicide were all too common reactions. "There were perhaps only two
Jews in my class possessed of courage," Kafka once recalled, "and both
shot themselves while still at school or shortly after" (D 400).

Both Wagenbach and Stölzl focus on the central question of language in Prague. Drawing on Fritz Mauthner's linguistic studies, Wagenbach speaks of a "paper German" (*papiernes Deutsch*) that was used
for official, written transactions but which lacked the "fullness of organic expressions and spoken forms. The melody of the spoken language is also lost." Wagenbach sometimes uncritically accepts the
racial bias of these contemporary theories (which go back to Herder
and the German Romantics who had posited an organic relation between the *Volk* and its linguistic expression), but he rightly points to
the particularity of Prague German—its susceptibility to Czech influence, its distorted syntax, its relative poverty of expression, and its
abstract, official nature as an administrative language.

Stölzl focuses on the "Jewishness" of the German spoken in Kafka's
circle: the particular accent, intonation, and Yiddishisms that in
German were called *mauscheln* and that Jewish-German writers often
felt they had to "overcome." Kafka objected to *mauscheln* as a "bumptious, tacit, or self-pitying appropriation of someone else's property,
something not earned, but stolen" (L 288), and avoided in his own
writing any overt departure from the vocabulary, syntax, and grammar of High German; when he used Yiddish, he was almost invariably
quoting his father. Karl Kraus, the noted Viennese satirist whom
Kafka regarded as the spiritual leader of "German-Jewish writing"
(L 288), also objected to encroachments of High German. A Jew
who converted to Catholicism, Kraus defended the literary classicism
of Goethe and Schiller. However, he did so with the puns and linguistic brilliance of "Jewish" wit. And his own journalism and literary
sketches were informed by the same *mauscheln* that he castigated in

the writing of his fellow Jews. (As Kafka once noted in a letter to Max Brod, "no one can *mauscheln* like Kraus" [L 288].) Typically, Kraus directed most of his diatribes against Jewish writers, whom he accused of degrading the "purity" of High German. Many were journalists, but he also attacked Heinrich Heine on similar grounds in a famous essay that Kafka heard as a public lecture in Prague in 1911.[12] Kafka lacks Kraus's polemical edge, but their positions are not dissimilar. In a characteristic use of an animal metaphor to describe the predicament of Jewish writers between two different historical epochs, he notes:

> Most young Jews who began to write German wanted to leave Jewishness behind them, and their fathers approved of this, but vaguely (this vagueness was what was outrageous to them). But with their hind legs they were still glued to their father's Jewishness and with their waving front legs they found no new ground. The ensuing despair became their inspiration. (L 289)

In their essay "What Is a Minor Literature?" the French philosophers Gilles Deleuze and Félix Guattari take a quite different approach to the same language problem. Rather than as a linguistic assimilationist trying to inhabit a "pure" High German, they interpret Kafka as a subversive, "minority" writer within the major German literary tradition. The subtext for their theory is Kafka's own diary entry for December 25, 1911, in which he reflects on the advantages of "small" literatures written in "minor" languages like Yiddish or Czech (see the Appendix). These reflections stem from the Yiddish plays Kafka had been attending in Prague earlier that year and his discussions with one of the principal actors, Yitzhak Löwy:

> What I understand of contemporary Jewish literature in Warsaw through Löwy, and of contemporary Czech literature partly through my own insight, points to the fact that many of the benefits of literature . . . can be produced even by a literature whose development is not in actual fact unusually broad in scope [but which] lacks outstanding talents. The liveliness of such a literature exceeds even that of one rich in talent. . . . (D 148–49)

Deleuze and Guattari base their analysis on a flagrant but insightful misreading of this passage. Whereas Kafka uses the term minor literature to differentiate Löwy's Yiddish theater from his own German tradition, Deleuze and Guattari mean something quite different: "A minor literature doesn't come from a minor language; it is rather that which a minority constructs within a major language." Their argument is that Kafka, as a Prague Jew writing on the margin of the German literary establishment, creates a minor idiom *in* German without overtly challenging the rules of grammar and vocabulary. The advantage of this reading is that it exposes a political, nonconformist dimension to Kafka's writing that has often been found lacking. Although Deleuze and Guattari are not always immune to a political romanticism in their rereading, they address the problem of how Kafka's scrupulously neutral, sober prose style achieves such intense emotional registers. Through subtle displacements and deformations, Kafka's "correct" German opens up a realm of ungrammatical, "deterritorialized" freedom for the minority victims of linguistic hegemony. Championing the political force represented by the Yiddish actors, Deleuze and Guattari interpret the "poverty" of Kafka's German as the source of its subversive strength:

> Kafka does not opt for a reterritorialization through the Czech language. Nor toward a hypercultural usage of German with all sorts of oneiric or symbolic or mythic flights. . . . Nor toward an oral, popular Yiddish. Instead, using the path that Yiddish opens up to him, he takes it in such a way as to convert it into a unique and solitary form of writing. [Kafka] will tear out of Prague German all the qualities of underdevelopment that it has tried to hide; he will make it cry with an extremely sober and rigorous cry.

Giuliano Baioni also focuses on the encounter with the "actors from Lemberg," which he sees as the basis for the important distinction that Kafka drew between the communal unity of Eastern Judaism and the rootless, "alienated" condition of assimilated Western Jews. The awakening of Kafka's religious conscience ("In Hebrew my name is Amschel," he writes on Christmas Day, 1911) is unambiguously documented in the extensive diary entries he wrote in late 1911 and early 1912, the period in which the Yiddish actors were performing in Prague. At that time he read Heinrich Graetz's *History of the Jews* and a history of Jewish-German literature by the French scholar Meyer Isser Pines, attended numerous Yiddish plays which he scrupulously recorded in his diary, and above all conversed with Löwy about the everyday conditions of Jewish life in the *shtetlech* of Eastern Europe. Kafka sought to introduce Löwy's writings to the assimilated Jewish bourgeoisie in Prague with his early lecture "Introductory Talk on the Yiddish Language," an important but neglected text that Baioni analyzes in detail (it is included in an appendix to this anthology). With uncharacteristic enthusiasm, Kafka told his audience,

> once Yiddish has taken hold of you and moved you—and Yiddish is everything, the words, the Hassidic melody, and the essential character of this East European Jewish actor himself—you will have forgotten your former reserve. Then you will come to feel the true unity of Yiddish, and so strongly that it will frighten you. . . . (DF 385–86)

As Baioni notes, Kafka sees the source of Löwy's artistic vitality in the unity of the Eastern religious community, a quality he finds sorely lacking in his own German writing. At once an effective artist and a member of a cultural "family," Löwy had resolved the dilemma between art and life that, Kafka believed, plagued his own "Western Jewish" existence. "Kafka's birth as a writer," Baioni continues, "occurs through his encounter with a form of Judaism that, thanks to the Yiddish actors, reveals *through literature* his own most Western and assimilated characteristics." In fact, Kafka's literary breakthrough takes place shortly after this encounter; his earliest texts, "The Judgment," *The Metamorphosis* and the first six chapters of *Amerika* (written in late 1912), all bear the imprint of gestures, themes, and dramatic reversals from the Yiddish plays.[13]

YOUNG KAFKA AND THE *FIN DE SIÈCLE*

Part of Kafka's undeniable strength as a writer derives from his ability to hide his sources, and for many years readers thought that he either had none or that, if he did, they were too remote or general to be of any interest. Thus, the simple discovery that he had borrowed heavily from specific texts came as a revelation, especially because many of these sources stemmed from the "decadent" literature of the *fin de siècle* and Kafka's youth. His early fascination with Hugo von Hofmannsthal, the Jugendstil poet whose evocative and wistful verse had caused a literary sensation in the last decade of the century, is well known. Several passages in *Description of a Struggle* (1904–6), an early work written in a highly ornamental style unlike Kafka's later work, are almost literal quotations of Hofmannsthal and reveal the "young Kafka" in a phase of literary experimentation and self-searching.[14] But it was generally thought that, like Hofmannsthal, Kafka had rejected his early aestheticism and Jugendstil ornament for the sober, modern lines of his later prose style, modeled after the classical examples of Goethe, Kleist, Stifter, and Flaubert. In fact, a number of key works from this later period reveal a debt to rather minor, less canonical sources.[15]

Thus, as Michael Müller shows in the essay presented here, Casanova's account of his escape from prison (a popular bestseller during Kafka's lifetime) is closely related to Joseph K.'s arrest and imprisonment in *The Trial*. Scholars have also discovered that Octave Mirbeau's *Le Jardin des supplices* (1899), with its eroticized spectacle of torture on an oriental island, informs key details of "In the Penal Colony" and that Leopold von Sacher-Masoch's novel of sexual submission, *Venus in Furs* (1870), plays a direct role in Gregor Samsa's metamorphosis.[16] Immensely popular in their time, Mirbeau and Sacher-Masoch both have been disdained by literary critics for much of this century, in part because of the connection between violence and eroticism in their work. In her reading of "In the Penal Colony" and "A Hunger Artist," Margot Norris takes these references to the "decadent" literature of the *fin de siècle* as the starting points for her discussion of sadism and masochism. Execution and fasting in these two stories turn out to be complementary "punishment fantasies" of an erotic kind, both texts harboring a repressed fear of the "nurturing, oral mother."

Kafka scrupulously refrained from mentioning these works in his letters and diaries, just as he generally refrained from disclosing any details about the origin or meaning of his writings. Yet the parallels are striking and suggest that many of Kafka's late works go back to

readings and impressions from his youth. Of course, the mere discovery of a source is, in itself, just a beginning: it is precisely in deline-
ating the peculiar transformations Kafka effects on a "source" in
appropriating it for his own writing that one can begin to judge its
significance for him. Here, too, omissions and oblique references are
as important as actual quotations.

Kafka's relation to Prague political life at the turn of the century
was undogmatic and rather cautious; although an avid newspaper
reader, he always kept himself informed of political events. Zionism
constituted without doubt the central point of reference for his political orientation after his encounter with the Yiddish actors in 1911
and 1912. But before that the young Kafka also frequented Czech
anarchist circles and, if we are to believe Gustav Janouch, regarded
highly the writings of Max Stirner (author of the libertarian polemic
The Individual and His Property), of the Russian anarchists Kropotkin and Bakunin, and of his contemporary Gustav Landauer. As Michael Löwy points out in his essay, The Trial and Amerika display an
acute sensitivity to the alienating conditions of modern industrial,
capitalist society. And whether one labels Kafka anarchist or libertarian or utopian socialist, all of his writings testify to his passionate
commitment to individual freedom and "selfhood" (what he referred
to as each person's Eigentümlichkeit[17]) against the hierarchical restric-
tions of family, society, and state.

It has often been pointed out that Kafka preferred the diaries and
personal correspondence of canonical writers like Goethe, Hebbel,
Flaubert, and Kleist to their literary works proper. Whatever the
truth of this claim, it overlooks his penchant for the memoirs of less
famous, nonliterary figures who, curiously enough, were often women
and came from widely diverse social and political backgrounds. For
instance, Kafka intensely admired the spirit of Lily Braun's Memoirs
of a Socialist Woman (1909–1911), claiming that it was "more appropriate for this day and age and more to the point than anything else I
know, as well as being the liveliest encouragement" (F 499). But he
also valued the Pietist autobiography of Dorothea Erdmuthe, Countess von Zinzendorf, and frequently quoted it in his letters to Felice,
remarking that "the whole book" had a "special importance" for them
(F 484). What Kafka liked in these personal narratives was the authors' Menschenkenntnis, their direct, unpretentious, probing insight

into human affairs. It mattered little to him where he found it, although, characteristically, critics have almost completely neglected these nonliterary interests.

Such interests, of course, do not rule out Kafka's affinity with the preeminent intellectual figures of his period: Friedrich Nietzsche and Sigmund Freud. Like most other writers of his generation, Kafka read Nietzsche while he was still in the Gymnasium and never lost sight of him. Texts like "In the Penal Colony" (1914) and "A Hunger Artist" (1922) clearly reveal a debt to the notion of asceticism that Nietzsche advanced in *The Genealogy of Morals*. Kafka's relationship to Freud was more problematic, however. He followed Freud's work closely, and wrote in his diary, after finishing "The Judgment," "thoughts about Freud, of course" (D1 276). At one point, he planned to collaborate on an anti-patriarchal journal with one of Freud's disciples, Otto Gross. But like Rilke, Musil, Wittgenstein, and others, he distrusted psychoanalysis and felt that therapy would destroy the conflict basic to his writing. He also favored a cultural or sociological explanation of certain psychic disorders. "Psychoanalysis lays stress on the father-complex and many find the concept intellectually fruitful," he wrote to Max Brod in 1921. "In this case I prefer another version, where the issue revolves not around the innocent father but around the father's Jewishness."

What Kafka shares with both Freud and Nietzsche, as Gerhard Kurz stresses in his essay, is an "archaeological" impulse to dig beneath the surface of social convention, to discover the multiplicity of selves and fictional truths in the human psyche. Kafka's expressive use of gesture, which Walter Benjamin noted in an earlier essay and which Kurz develops further, links his work to depth psychology and its recognition of "the body's expressive force." Kafka's notion of the self as an unstable multiplicity of selves, a "swarm" of others, also bears a crucial relationship to Nietzsche and Freud, themselves indebted to the literary intuitions of German Romanticism.

Curiously, Kafka's personal antagonism to his father has obscured his political opposition to patriarchal authority. Like many in his generation, Kafka was influenced by the Swiss historian Johann Bachofen, whose belief in the matriarchal origin of Western cultures appears to have informed portions of *The Castle*. And, as Michael Löwy notes, Kafka was sympathetic to Otto Gross's struggle against paternal, institutional tyranny and his dream of founding a matriarchal utopia. Feminist critics have often objected to Kafka's depiction of women as degraded, subaltern, "animal" servants to the male authority figures, thus overlooking his polemical intent. But Kafka's vision of sexual relations was undoubtedly crippled by the profoundly misogynist prejudices of his culture. Reiner Stach furnishes an additional, important piece to this puzzle in documenting Kafka's debt to Otto Weininger, the brilliant author of *Sex and Character* (1903), whose socio-sexual theories were, at that time, more widely known than Freud's.[18] The impact of Weininger's book is hard to fathom today. A deeply misogynist, anti-Semitic treatise, it postulated a fundamental dualism between a "male" principle of creativity and form, and a "female" principle of passive, amorphous receptivity. Weininger, who asserted that all human beings are bisexual and combine these principles in differing proportions, was a common topic in Kafka's circle. His friend Oskar Baum delivered a lecture on *Sex and Character* in February 1921 that Johannes Urzidil reviewed for the *Selbstwehr*. As Stach observes, Kafka's depiction of the female "horde" clustered around Titorelli, or of Leni with her amphibian, webbed hand in *The Trial*, owes much to Weininger's wildly misconceived, but influential theories.

Finally, a word about Vienna. Although Kafka lived in Prague almost all his life, one should not forget that Vienna was the political and cultural capital of the Hapsburg Monarchy and that a constant stream of information flowed between the two cities. Critics have rarely brought Kafka and Vienna into the same cultural orbit, but the explosion of modern thought and art in Vienna at the turn of the century left unmistakable traces in his work. Apart from the figures whose work he knew and admired—Hofmannsthal, Musil, Kraus, Schnitzler, Freud, Weininger—one can add others with whom he had an intellectual and aesthetic affinity: Schönberg, Berg, Wittgenstein, Klimt, Schiele, Loos, to name a few. For instance, Adolf Loos's brilliant and polemical attack on ornament in Vienna at the time of the Secession ("Ornament and Crime," 1908) parallels Kafka's own stylistic break with Impressionist and Symbolist models in the same period and his later development of a modernist, "constructed" prose idiom. Alban Berg's use of silence and atonality involves a rhetorical strategy not unlike that of Kafka's "negative" aesthetics; and Wittgenstein's aphorisms and "language games" recall elements of Kafka's diaries and notebooks. These areas of Viennese *fin-de-siècle* culture, and others, remain to be explored.

TEXTS, LETTERS, AUTOBIOGRAPHY

American literary critics, marked by the successive methodologies of New Criticism, Structuralism and Deconstruction, have been particularly adverse to using an author's biography to interpret a literary text. The apparent irrelevance of Kafka's unspectacular life as an insurance official in Prague to the bizarre world of his writings allowed this facile separation between life and work to be maintained. The absence until 1982 of a single biography of Kafka in English (other than Max Brod's invaluable but uncritical account) among thousands of academic studies is indicative of this specific critical prejudice.[19] Certainly there are good reasons for avoiding biographical criticism, which all too often reduces the meaning of a literary text to particular events in the author's life. However, this prejudice has resulted in an excessive attention to a few of Kafka's canonical texts (the novels and stories) at the expense of what is, after all, the bulk of his writing: the diaries (including numerous literary sketches and fragments never published as "stories"), the notebooks and aphorism collections, and the letters, especially to Felice Bauer and Milena Jesenská. Moreover, it risks overlooking Kafka's radical inversion of the writing process, which calls into question the distinction between life and work. A new, more historical look at Kafka needs to take these "biographical" writings into account, not because they give us a detailed image of his life, nor simply because they have been neglected, but because they often embody most fully his own ideal of literature as a spontaneous act of searching and creation.

The relatively late publication in 1967 of the correspondence with Felice Bauer has significantly altered our image of Kafka and his writing in several ways. First, the more than five hundred cards and letters written between 1912 and 1917 provided unprecedented, detailed access into Kafka's personal preoccupations, literary ambitions, and daily activities during what must be counted as the most prolific, fateful period of his life. Second, the edition of the *Letters to Felice* was the first edition to maintain the original spellings, grammatical unorthodoxies and Praguisms that give Kafka's German an unmistakably regional character. Unlike the more polished, "correct" High German of the literary texts, the unaltered version of these letters lets us "hear" Kafka's southern German accent, the intonation, regional inflections, and vocabulary that situate his language in a particular place and time.

From a literary point of view, the correspondence has proved equally significant. When the *Letters to Felice* were published, Elias Canetti quickly noted the extent to which biography and literature are intertwined, the letters constituting a textual counterpart to his novel *The Trial*. In no way, Canetti noted, are the letters inferior to the novel *as literature*. Indeed, they revealed Kafka's radical ambition to transform everything he wrote into literature, to turn himself into literature. "I have no literary interests, but am made of literature, I am nothing else, and cannot be anything else," he wrote in an oft-cited letter to Felice (F 304). Moreover, these letters are animated by an emotional intensity and vision as strong as in any of his stories and novels. As Erich Heller remarks in his introduction to the correspondence,

> Kafka is not altogether wrong in saying to Felice that he is nothing but literature—"real" literature. For almost everything he has written possesses the indisputable "reality" and "being" that are rare in modern writing and transcend most "realities" of the age. In this sense too these letters are, like himself, "literature." (F xxii)

Kafka's urge to turn himself into the substance of his writing, essentially an extreme expression of *fin-de-siècle* aestheticism, allows us to situate the question of history in Kafka's work from another perspective. By withdrawing from the world and taking refuge "inside" his writings, Kafka imbues the very process of writing with its own spatiality and temporality: Writing becomes for him an independent world, subject to its own norms and modalities. Literature becomes an act, an event in time and place, a process rather than a finished "work." For the reader, access to this other world is of course facilitated by the manuscripts, and it is no coincidence that this view has recently been put forward by the editors of the first critical edition of

Kafka's works. As the editor traces the movements of Kafka's hand across the page, noting the progress of his imagination as it takes material shape in writing, noting also the changes in paper, writing instrument, clarity of penmanship, and other literal details, the writer's life at his desk gradually materializes before us. The tangible remnants of this world, the only one Kafka considered "real," allow us to view yet another stratum of his life of writing.

In a key essay, Malcolm Pasley, editor of critical editions of *The Castle* (1982) and *The Trial* (1990), establishes the basis for this historicization of the "act of writing." Pasley notes first of all a number of striking parallels between manuscripts and texts. For instance, at the point in *Amerika* where Karl Rossmann is given a new pen, the editor of the manuscript can see that Kafka himself "clearly had to struggle with, and replace, a poorly functioning fountain pen." Drawing on similar examples from "The Burrow" and *The Castle*, Pasley theorizes that these narratives

> simultaneously *represent* and *embody* a process of searching and researching. The story's tentative progress forward, in which it takes material shape as Kafka writes, does not *represent* the fictional hero's tentative progress but runs parallel to it: there are two related, ongoing searches and we become aware of both while reading. (Pasley's emphasis)

Kafka's rejection of "history" in the conventional sense reinforces the *hic et nunc* of the writing process, its material, "manual" nature: "Precisely because Kafka's works shut themselves off so emphatically from the empirical realities of life . . . they often get caught up (as paradoxical as this may sound) in the *manual* conditions of their creation."

Of course, an editor's privileged relation to Kafka's manuscripts does not fully coincide with the reader's experience of the published works. However engaging and theoretically significant, Pasley's reconstruction of the "act of writing" necessarily remains the experience of the happy few, which the common reader can appreciate only at a distance. Kafka's letters, however, permit us to see the act of writing that Pasley describes for the literary texts. More directly than the stories and novels, they transport the reader to the scene of writing, to Kafka sitting at his desk, in dialogue with Felice Bauer, Milena

Jesenská, or Max Brod, but also with the linguistic possibilities that each new sentence presents as it appears on the page. Consider, for example, the opening letter to Felice of September 1912, in which the material circumstances of the act of writing blend with Kafka's memory of their encounter:

> My dear Fräulein Bauer,
>   In the likelihood that you no longer have even the remotest recollection of me, I am introducing myself once more: my name is Franz Kafka, and I am the person who greeted you for the first time that evening at Director Brod's in Prague, the one who subsequently handed you across the table, one by one, photographs of a Thalia trip, and who finally, *with the very hand now striking the keys,* held your hand, the one which confirmed a promise to accompany him next year to Palestine. (Emphasis added.)

Here Kafka merges past, present, and future into the act of his hand striking the typewriter keys, the historical "event" that is relived and recreated each time the letter is read.

The three essays devoted to Kafka's major epistolary writings explore this notion of the history "inside" the act of writing letters, an internal history generated by Kafka's impulse to shut himself off from the "empirical realities of life." Elias Canetti notes how the letters to Felice again and again refer back to the question of writing: Kafka "must hold nothing back, since that might disconcert him in the act of writing; he must tell her, in every detail, of the importance, the continuance, and the hesitations of this writing." Two additional essays on Kafka's "Letter to His Father" and the *Letters to Milena* attempt to document the act of writing that these letters embody, which is interwoven as much with Kafka's other writings as with his personal biography. Gerhard Neumann reads the letter to Hermann Kafka as a reflection on, and counterpart to, "The Judgment," developing the notion of writing as an emancipatory act of rebellion against patriarchal authority. My own essay details in the correspondence with Milena Jesenská the same authorial "disappearance" that takes place in the late stories "A Hunger Artist" and "Josephine the Singer"—a disappearance, emblematic of Kafka's desire to efface his relationship to history, which forms the subject of this critical anthology.

The essays in this volume give us a broader and sharper image of Kafka in Prague at the turn of the century. We now know more about the political and social conditions he confronted during his lifetime, more about the milieu in which his own literary talent developed, more about how he wrote his texts and how they were interwoven with his own life. At this point, some readers may object that such historical reconstruction only emphasizes what Kafka sought to omit or obscure in his work. Why fill the canvas with figures and "local color," one might ask, when the author produced an (almost) empty canvas as the appropriate image of the negativity of his age?

The response to this question is twofold. As I suggested above, Kafka's negative relation to history is itself subject to historical analysis—specifically, it developed at a particular phase in the history of West European Judaism. Granted, Kafka's "negativity" is not fully explained by his position in a historical continuum. Many other twentieth-century writers, who were not Jewish and lived in different historical circumstances, have proceeded with a similar "evacuation" of the text, Beckett and the French "New Novelists" being perhaps the most salient examples. There is a necessity to Kafka's negativity which historical reconstruction should not attempt to deny. But nor should one confuse cause and effect by arguing from the vantage point of what Kafka's texts have come to mean for later generations. For Kafka and his contemporaries, negativity had a precise historical content, quite different from that of French Existentialism, Surrealism, the Second World War, or deconstructive theories of language. Negativity does not mean nothing; it exists in relation *to* something, which the present essays attempt to describe.

Secondly, the impulse in Kafka's writings toward the "pure, the true and the immutable" (D 387), toward an ideally unhistorical state of metaphysical truth, should not be confused with this state itself. Even "A Country Doctor," the story which occasioned this diary entry, did not attain this realm of truth. Obviously, Kafka's texts are never totally free of historical matter; relations to a world outside the text exist, if only because his language itself is not entirely pure. He shares it with the world, and it marks a specific moment in the history of the German language and the German literary tradition. This may be one reason why he refused to publish many of his texts, judging that they had not attained a sufficiently pure state. But Max Brod published them and they now belong, *de facto*, to the available corpus of his work. Alongside the formal, allegorical "perfection" of a text like "Before the Law" (which Kafka detached from *The Trial* and published as a fragment), we also have *The Trial* itself, which consists of unfinished chapters, heavily reworked and incomplete segments, and other more or less "raw" material. We also have his letters, diaries, and other writings he did not see fit to publish, but which have all become an essential part of his literary corpus. All these writings are caught up in the circumstances of history; they fall short of "the pure, the true and the immutable"—which is one of the reasons we read them.

The point of these essays is not to limit Kafka's writings to the historical context in which they originated. Kafka undoubtedly understood the effacement of this context as the necessary condition for an "immutable" literature, one that would not be limited to the writer's immediate horizon. But there is a difference between a literature that stands outside history and one that struggles through history toward something else. The poet Paul Celan, whose "negative" relation to German language and history in many respects paralleled Kafka's, put it this way: "The poem is not timeless. Certainly, it raises a claim to infinity, it attempts to grasp its way through time— through it, not over and above it." It is in this sense that the following essays attempt to read Kafka: as a writer who is not timeless but who grasps his way through time, through the suffering and negativity of his own time, toward an immutable, infinite realm beyond.

I.

PRAGUE

PRAGUE AT THE TURN OF THE CENTURY

Klaus Wagenbach

KAFKA FIRST BECAME COGNIZANT of the social, cultural, and political diversity of life in Prague when he began his studies at the German University. He was not to leave Prague—the "damned city" as he had already called it in 1907—for any extended period of time until 1917. Despite his reserved nature, Kafka was never aloof from his native environment—its aggressivity hardly allowed such an attitude. Thus the cultural and literary atmosphere in which he matured left deep, lasting traces on his personality as well as his work. His relation to Prague served as a paradigm for his relation to the world in general. Consequently, only when we take Prague's aggressive environment into account can we see that many of the salient qualities of Kafka's work are, in fact, a forceful response to this environment.

The Moldau (Vltava in Czech) flows through Prague from south to north, dividing the city into two unequal halves (see illustration). To the west are the Kleinseite (Little Quarter) and the Hradschin. East of the Moldau, at the bend in the river, we find the cramped area called the Josefstadt, which was once the Jewish ghetto. Surrounding the Josefstadt in a semicircle is the Altstadt (Old City), with the Neustadt (New City) to the southeast. This urban center was enclosed by an intricate ring of suburbs, a few of which (Wyschehrad,

25

Holeschowitz-Bubna, and Lieben) had already been incorporated into the city by the turn of the century.

Kafka hardly ever left the Altstadt and the Josefstadt, the innermost parts of the city, which in 1900 counted roughly 450,000 inhabitants. "One day," Kafka's Hebrew teacher Friedrich Thieberger recalls,

> we were looking out of the windows onto the Ringplatz. Kafka said to me: "Here was my Gymnasium, over there, facing us, my university, and just a bit further to the left, my office. This small space," he said, drawing a few small circles with his finger, "encloses my entire life." I thought of these words, spoken with a smile of resignation, when, after his death, his fiancée told me that devastating animal story of his about a captive snake that wanders incessantly along the edges of its terrain, never finding its way out.[1]

Only Kafka's office, in the building of the Workmens' Accident Insurance Institute for the Kingdom of Bohemia, at 7 Poric Street, was situated a few steps outside the Altstadt. The Gymnasium was located in the Kinsky Palace (which will later also be the site of Hermann Kafka's shop). The University was in the Klementinum, on the Kreuzherren Square, facing the Moldau and the Charles Bridge. The law school was in the Karolinum, near the German National Theater. Grouped around the Great and Small Rings were the town hall, the Nicholas Church (next to the house where Kafka was born), the "Minuta" house and, a few steps from the Kinsky Palace and the Tein Church, the Oppelt house where Kafka's parents will live later on. East from the Altstädter Ring was the Zeltnergasse, where Kafka lived (at number 3) with his parents at the end of high school and during his university studies. A few steps further to the right (number 12) was his father's first shop. To the north, the Nicholasstrasse led from the Altstädter Ring (passing by the venerable Altneu Synagogue and across the Nicholas Bridge) to the Crown Prince Rudolph Park and the Belvedere, on the other side of the Moldau. At the end of the Nicholasstrasse, in the corner house which looks over the Hradschin and the Belvedere, was the apartment which the Kafkas would occupy after 1907. East of the Nicholas Bridge, the Moldau was crossed by the Franz-Josef Bridge; to the south by the

Kettensteg, the Charles Bridge, the Kaiser-Franz Bridge, and the Pa-
lacky Bridge. The Charles Bridge was by far the oldest, and the sole
one, in fact, until the nineteenth century (rebuilt after its collapse in
1890). It was, incidentally, the only bridge not to levy a toll—a cus-
tom the other bridges clung to until 1918.

Kafka was born early enough to experience the labyrinth of the
former ghetto, the Josefstadt. The house names are indicative of the
ghostly life that reigned in its narrow, tortuous streets until the turn
of the century: "The Mouse Hole," "The Left Glove," "Death," "Gin-
gersnap," and most curious of all, "No Time." The Prague writer Leo
Perutz describes the ghetto thus:

> Decrepit houses piled on top of each other, in the last stages of decay,
> projecting out and up, blocking the narrow streets. Crooked and angu-
> lar streets, in whose confusion one could get hopelessly lost . . . dark
> passages, gloomy courtyards, cracked walls, cavernous vaults. . . . [2]

Although still a child, Kafka would never forget this peculiar world,
as his remarks to Gustav Janouch demonstrate:

> In us all it still lives—the dark corners, the secret alleys, shuttered win-
> dows, squalid courtyards, noisy bars, and sinister inns. We walk through
> the broad streets of the newly built town. But our steps and our glances
> are uncertain. Inside we tremble just as before in the ancient streets of
> our misery. Our heart knows nothing of the *Assanation*, * the slum
> clearance which has been achieved. The unhealthy old Jewish town
> within us is far more real than the new hygenic town around us. With
> our eyes open we walk through a dream: ourselves only a ghost of a
> vanished age. [3] (J 80)

Much of this past survived the "sanitization" of Prague's Josefstadt,
for example in the Hradschin district, which Franz Werfel's novel
Embezzled Heaven brings alive for us:

> A tortuous congeries of dilapidated buildings seems to be waiting for
> the house-wrecker. The city has spread far out into what was once the

---

* "Sanitization" was the official euphemism for the destruction of the ghetto,
which was decreed in 1885 and carried out between 1895 and 1905.—Ed.

countryside, having forgotten this quarter and left it to molder away with its crooked roofs, worm-eaten loggias, squalid little courts, and worn wooden steps. It has the lowest rents in the city, for the houses may be pulled down any day. . . . In the undrained swamps of the past . . . dwell only the lowest ranks of the community, a few feebleminded eccentrics. . . . [4]

Eccentrics such as Kafka, who resided briefly in a room on Alchimistengasse during the war. But the "ghost of a vanished age" continues to linger as well in the apartments of the "sanitized" Altstadt, in the "heavy, enigmatic furniture," described by the young Rilke:

It is the past that is kept alive in the chairs and wardrobes and pictures . . . the tiny rooms, three flights up, are innocent of this strange past, like people whose faces have inherited the name of a feeling from some ancestor and which they cannot wear because of their own weak hearts. [5]

The apartment of Kafka's parents seems to be similarly haunted, according to Max Brod: "The wine cellars are downstairs and a faint cool odor of wine hangs in the stairwell. Cheap plaster angels with chipped black noses decorate the landings."[6] Brod's description of Kafka's own room, however, implies that its austerity may have warded off these ghosts to some extent:

A bed, an armoire, a small, old desk with a few books, many disorderly notebooks. The whole not uninhabitable, but to those used to conventional adornments and luxuries perhaps a little strange. On the bare walls, only two pictures, haphazardly arranged according to the occupant's former taste, not his current: a *Kunstwart* illustration of a farmer plowing a field, and the plaster cast of a small dancing Maenad in veils, brandishing an animal shank.

Nevertheless, he notes that even here "all of the family's unused furniture" would be stored later on.

We would know much less about old Prague if Egon Erwin Kisch, two years younger than Kafka, had not repeatedly portrayed the details of his native city in books such as *Prague Streets and Nights*, *Prague Children*, *Adventure in Prague*, and *Prague Pitaval*. Kisch dedicated a monograph to that unique feature of Prague architecture, the

Durchhäuser or covered passageways that allowed one to avoid the open streets:

> As children setting out on journeys of discovery, we would use the street only to find houses with a second or even third exit. . . . The city always provided them. Even the covered passageways are subject to the law of continuity, one merging with the next, and you can walk through entire areas of Prague without having to use the open street for more than an occasional crossing.[7]

At first sight, Prague might have seemed all too quiet, self-content, a bit sleepy—a provincial capital neglected by Vienna. For instance, another Prague writer describes

> thousands of pensioners, civilian as well as military, [who] lived in pre-war Prague at that time. Particularly in beautiful weather one could see the old, white-haired men taking their dogs for a walk in the public gardens, passing the time in peaceful solitude or lively discussion with their peers about events that had taken place decades ago.[8]

And Kafka's schoolmate Emil Utitz writes: "Something of this sleepiness is symbolic for the German community of that time: a ghostliness which shuts itself off from reality." To be sure, this sleepiness was especially prevalent in the Kleinseite: "Grass still grows there between the cobblestones, and the people sit in front of their doors as though they are living in the country . . . and the old people . . . give this quarter of the city a refined stillness."[9]

Even in the Altstadt the conflict between the two nationalities was repeatedly played down. The Germans in particular needed to minimize the conflict—which they did by pointing out the venerable age and dignity of the Donau monarchy—for obvious reasons: in 1900 only 34,000 of approximately 450,000 inhabitants spoke German. These numbers are deceptive, though. A German historian writing in 1905 noted that "the German population in Prague, as a group, does not correspond to other German cities with a similar population. The large proletariat is missing from the pyramid construction of the social classes. . . . Because of their intelligence and wealth, their cultural and political significance, the Germans of Prague form the upper social class of a genuine German metropolis.[10] Of course, one must add that capital played a large role in their status. Kisch later writes:

> They were almost exclusively members of the upper bourgeoisie, coal mine owners, administrators of the metallurgy industry and the Skoda weapons factory, hops merchants who travelled between Saaz and North America. They moved in the same circles as professors, high-ranking military officers and civil servants. There was hardly a German proletariat. The 25,000 Germans, only five percent of Prague's population, possessed two splendid theaters, a huge concert hall, two universities, five high schools and four vocational schools, two newspapers which appeared morning and evening, large meeting halls and an intense social life.[11]

Miami on the Moldau it certainly was not, but the prominence of the German community exacerbated relations with the Czechs—and the divisions within this community were continually aggravated by Germans flooding to the city from the largely nationalistic provinces. This made for a tense political situation at the German University (more so than in other parts of Prague, which on the whole was rather liberal), so that Kafka's first major political experiences were not exactly happy ones. Yet this additional tension at the University was hardly necessary: the tension between the German aristocracy and upper bourgeoisie, and the socially "lower" positioned Czechs, was by itself explosive. Paul Leppin writes,

> In Prague the Germans live in quicksand. The political tension of the last few decades has made coexistence between the Germans and the Czechs an extremely uncomfortable matter, creating a climate of repressed violence which limits above all the spontaneity of bourgeois life.[12]

This "impossibility of bourgeois life" was felt by many. The German writers in Prague, cut off from a German-speaking people, lived in the stifling atmosphere of a hothouse or looked at the distant world through a telescope, as the Kaiser's peculiar personal physician does in Meyrink's novel *Walpurgis Night*. The Prague linguist Fritz Mauthner was struck by the pervasive cultural indifference of the German upper class, despite its cultural "industriousness." When he first studied the artwork of Prague, he felt that his aesthetic pleasure was "undignified for an educated person," since the people in his social class "never considered such reactions worthy of mention." Literary activities provided one of the few alternatives to this indifference. "In the last years of the Hapsburg monarchy," Mauthner wrote, "it was normal to ask every young Praguer abroad if he had written many books. For one automatically assumed that he had."[13] In fact, the walls of Prague could not contain the abundance of its aspiring writers, talented or otherwise.

Johannes Urzidil, a friend of Kafka, has noted that over the centuries, "Czechs, Germans, Jews, and the supranational Austrian nobles had created a vitally productive world that was always ready to explode."[14] Willy Haas, another friend, devoted a brilliant study to this social conglomeration. After the court decision of 1621, the old Czech palaces were inhabited by

> a crowd of foreigners, *condottieri,* and murderers employed by the Hapsburgs. They spoke a strange idiom composed of the mercenary slang of the homeless, the high German of the Austrian court, fragments of French, Czech and alpine German, which was barely comprehensible to outsiders.[15]

Next, Haas continues, "was the so-called German Prague, concentrated in the Altstadt. There the old rich Jewish families set the tone." Finally, "there were the Czechs, who nevertheless owned everything, the country, the land, the original traditions. . . . But everything was filled with the luxuriant, colorful blossoms of the artificial graft of 1621, when the tree was cut down." At that time the Czechs stood at the beginning of national and cultural emancipation. In a sudden rush they tried passionately, as Hermann Bahr put it,

> to make use of all cultural and intellectual events in Europe and to participate fully in the spiritual fate of Europe. But they are so strongly rooted in their national traditions that they can take hold of nothing without at once appropriating it inwardly, reshaping it in their own way until all foreign traces have been replaced by the particular spirit of this strange, fanatical, narrow-minded, and romantically realistic nation.[16]

Written in 1914, these words indicate only a provisional endpoint. Around 1900 Czech society still seemed "spiritually broken," and Rilke reproached the Czech poets for being "overripe": "They are certainly not of today. They are a childish people, full of unfulfilled wishes, having ripened overnight."[17] To be sure, Kafka (and not only because of his mastery of Czech) was far more insightful than Rilke and Werfel—to cite another example—about the national and social conditions of the Czech people. As the son of a rich glove manufacturer, Werfel encountered Czechs only in the form of his wet-nurses and governesses—and so they appear in his novels *Small Relationships, Barbara,* and *Embezzled Heaven.* Rilke tried to penetrate this world, but never got beyond a superficial, romantic vision:

> Hus the Reformer, a giant,
> rises before us, and though
> we fear his fiery teaching,
> his genius earns our respect.

Alternatively, his representation of the Czechs dissolved into caricature:

> . . . beer-happy musicians strike up
> a song from *The Bartered Bride.*

Kafka's contact with the Czechs was much closer. He attended numerous Czech lectures and political meetings—even those of Czech anarchists. He was on friendly terms with the employees at the Workmen's Accident Insurance Institute, Czech for the most part, and had early contact with his father's Czech employees. As he later wrote to his father: "You called the employees 'paid enemies,' and that was what they were too, but even before they became such you seemed to me to be their 'paying enemy' " (DF 160). As Heinz Politzer notes in a fine essay on Kafka and his Prague environment, Kafka correctly characterized the relation between the two peoples as one of enmity: "He could do this not because he had enthusiastically assimilated to the Czechs, but because he experienced his distance from them as a personal tragedy."[18]

If the position of the Germans in Prague was uncertain, that of the Jews was all the more so. They were by far the largest section of the Prague German community and represented the strongest liberal faction. But their intermediary position had many fateful consequences. As Theodor Herzl, the founder of Zionism, bitterly pointed out:

> What had they done, the little Jews of Prague, the honest merchants of the middle class, the most peaceful of all peaceful citizens? . . . In Prague, people suggested that they weren't Czechs, in Saaz and Eger [the Bohemian provinces], that they weren't Germans. . . . What should they hold on to then? If some wanted to be Germans, the Czechs jumped on them—and the Germans too. . . . If one considers the entirely skewed attitude of the Bohemian Jews, one understands why they are rewarded for their service with physical punishment. Both of the conflicting nationalities found a strange new variant to the old coachman's joke. Two coaches meet each other on a narrow path. Neither of the two coachmen wants to make way and in each car sits a Jew. Each coachman snaps his whip at the other's passenger: "You beat my Jew, and I'll beat yours." But in Bohemia, they add, "And mine, too," so that for one ride the Bohemian Jew receives a double thrashing. One can understand why they tried to keep a low profile in the nationality dispute.[19]

Kafka's father, concerned only with the success of his business, was a typical representative of this group. His attitude is indicated in the "Letter to His Father": "It did sometimes happen that you had no opinion whatsoever about a matter. . . . You were capable, for instance, of running down the Czechs, and then the Germans, and then the Jews, and what is more not only selectively but in every respect . . ." (DF 145).

It was "a peculiar, islandlike seclusion in which a large part of Prague's Jews lived . . . a nature park, whose extent was constantly diminishing. In a way, the Jews lived voluntarily in the ghetto."[20] Pavel Eisner speaks insightfully of the transformation of a religious ghetto into a sociological one. With the progress of emancipation, orthodox faith gave rise to semireligious derivatives, such as cultural or financial industriousness. This development was quite tangible in the generation of Kafka's father, and Kafka explains the "non-

Judaism" transmitted to him by his father thus: "The whole thing is, of course, not an isolated phenomenon. It was much the same with a large section of this transitional generation of Jews, which had migrated from the still comparatively devout countryside to the towns" (DF 174). Kafka's friend Felix Weltsch writes: "The Jewish community itself meant hardly anything to these individuals. Religious belief was practically nonexistent in the younger generation, while in the older generation (Kafka's father, for example) it had ossified into a meaningless form."[21] Weltsch also asserts that "the city of Prague, once among the most devout, has become one of the most irreligious."[22]

This older, predominantly materialistic generation was pleased if their sons received an education; even Kafka's father clung to this "general method of treating sons in the Jewish middle class" (DF 177). But as soon as the sons tried to get "some distance away . . . by [their] own efforts" (DF 176), their efforts were brutally repressed. In this respect Kafka's love-hate relationship with his father caused him to judge his situation much too narrowly, as a personal rather than a general fate, although the social dimensions of the problem were perfectly clear to him. In another passage he noted, "Prague. Religions get lost as people do" (DF 109). Within the larger sociological ghetto of the Jews, who were shunned by the Czechs as "German" and by the Germans as Jews, the isolation of the individual in Prague at that time developed a prototype of modern alienation. Kafka put it quite bluntly: people "lack a sense of community" (D 150). Religious practice, which formerly had united young and old, was irreparably destroyed. Even the bonds of common interest, which might have allowed superficial contact, became increasingly insignificant, particularly in Kafka's case. The resulting estrangement (Fremdheit), surfacing in his personal life as the obsessive conflict with his father, appeared in his works—with the exception of "The Judgment"—in its exact and dangerous proportions.

Clearly, Kafka recognized this situation at an early date: see, for instance, his diary entry of December 25, 1911. Two possibilities offered themselves to the Prague writer. The first was the pathos of "world friendship" (Weltfreundschaft), which Franz Werfel espoused. The second was a romantic obliviousness to the real world, a frenzied mysticism which extended from genuine inspiration to facile mystification and the literary construction of a farcical or bloody micro-cosm. Almost all the young Prague writers—René Rilke, Paul Leppin, Max Brod, Oscar Wiener, Gustav Meyrink—took this latter course. The peculiar, secret world of Prague, the myths and legends of the ghetto, supplied them with an abundance of appropriate material.

A third alternative existed, but it appeared incompatible with literary creation. The original Jewish capacity for insightful, critical analysis (evident in the works of Heine, Marx, LaSalle, and, at the time, Freud and Einstein) was sharpened, in Bohemia, by the Jew's position between nationalities and religions. As Weltsch notes, many Bohemian Jews "became critics and psychologists."[23] Even among the Germans, although from a different perspective, this capacity manifested itself with vigor, the life work of Josef Nadler (begun under August Sauer in Prague) providing the most salient example.

Despite the apparent opposition between critical analysis on the one hand, and literary creation on the other, Kafka chose this third alternative. Extensive passages of his work are dedicated to the question of "judgment," to continual discussions between the characters about themselves and others. Nevertheless, it was hardly possible to maintain a critical distance within such a complex and tenuous sociological situation. This undoubtedly placed a heavy burden on Kafka's work, and may well have been a source of the deep mistrust he felt for his "scribbling." The missing figure of the narrator in his novels and stories is the direct expression of this lack of confidence. In the last years of his life he notes with resignation: "I have seldom, very seldom crossed this borderland between loneliness and fellowship, I have even been settled there longer than in loneliness itself" (D 396). Still, loneliness dominated his early years, even if it was an emotional retreat from the complexity and multiplicity of his social environment as well as from all human relations that required him to "take sides." In 1912 Kafka writes to Max Brod: "How do I live in Prague, after all? This craving for people, which I have and which is transformed into anxiety once it is fulfilled . . ." (L 82). And two years later in his diary: "Leave Prague. Counter the greatest personal injury that has ever befallen me with the strongest antidote at my disposal" (D 263).

To this "greatest personal injury" one must add Kafka's slight or even negative relation to the work of German writers in Prague at that time. Many of the motifs in Kafka's work, especially that of estrangement, can also be found in the writings of other Prague Germans. But in other writers this estrangement expresses itself as a subdued neo-Romanticism (Hugo Salus), as a simple psychological experiment (*Experiments* was also the title of an early prose collection by Brod), or as a wild, erotic ecstasy (Paul Leppin). In his preface to an anthology of German poets in Prague, Oskar Wiener alludes to the dangers of this tendency toward elaborate platitudes: "Here, whoever wanders indoors, disdainful of the path leading to the real world, becomes a salon poet. . . ."[24] In his novel *Prague Atmosphere*, he gives an incisive picture of these *littérateurs*:

> Prague's *jeunesse dorée* screamed with joy . . . The dramatist Whirlwind said that the theater of Pardubitz had rejected his play *Copper Donkey*, and Ottokar Hoff took off his gigantic hat with both hands, threw it in the corner and sighed, "I don't have anything to eat." [. . . .] Mr. Ivory Tower declared: "I'm writing a novel, a murder story with rape, in free verse, of course." "How interesting! Would you read us a chapter?" "Impossible—I've already burned the third canto!" But Theodor the Pale intervened: "Friends of Apollo, would someone else like to recite? No one? Well then, let's go find some women!" . . . and Ottokar Hoff chimed in: "Yes, women! But they have to be ugly; only the ugly ones are truly beautiful!"[25]

The air of this secluded hothouse produced flowers that were suspect both thematically and linguistically. As Josef Mühlberger noted:

> The imagination grew luxuriantly like splendidly poisonous blossoms from a swamp, unbridled sexuality flourished in baroque confusion. [The Prague writers] wanted to discover a new world, but all they did was put powder and makeup on this one or set it on fire and celebrate the conflagration.[26]

Thus, to the social and religious dilemma we must add a literary, and especially a linguistic dilemma, without which Kafka's work and language—as a form of opposition to this excess—would be unthinkable. A brief survey of the literary situation will make this clear.

"The official literary popes at that time were Friedrich Adler and Hugo Salus," writes Emil Utitz.[27] Although their tired, programmatic poetry, which celebrated autumn, the sadness of life, and the freshness of spring, was successful with the public, they were neither recognized nor followed by the younger writers. Even Salus's prose was insipid and worn—take, for example, his story of the unfaithful mermaid Lalanda who, upon revealing her human form, is rejected by her romantic admirer. In a letter to Brod, Kafka noted that an essay of Thomas Mann was indeed "a wonderful broth . . . but because of the quantity of Salus-like hairs floating around in it, one is more inclined to admire than to eat" (L 155). Rilke's early prose conformed completely to this taste, as is evident from a literary sketch written in 1896: "The young blond woman with the large, deep eyes is silent, looks up at the satiny evening sky, and fans herself with a scarf of Brussels lace." Rilke's later work, like the macabre story written in 1903 about a gravedigger obsessed with "corpses, corpses, corpses," was closer to the taste of the Prague avant-garde. Painting and sculpture (as in the work of Richard Teschner, Fritz Hegenbart, and August Brömse), with their peculiar mixture of Jugendstil and late nineteenth-century excess, significantly influenced this taste. The style is also manifest in the early work of Kubin and Orlik—both frequented literary circles—in a subdued manner, but with fantastic, grotesque motifs.

The same tendency reigned in the literary works of the young Prague writers. We find here the curious phenomenon of a *linguistic chaos*, which can be understood neither as the beginning of Expressionist tendencies nor as an opposition to the classicizing Goethe cult of Adler and Salus. A prime example of this chaos is the following passage from Paul Leppin's early novel *Daniel Jesus*:

Suddenly a strident, imperious trumpet resounded somewhere in the room. And Marta-Bianka saw Daniel Jesus and the enormous woman rise from their seats and two mute servants carry a black crown set with jewels that were as deathly pale as tears. And Daniel Jesus took the black band and placed it on his mighty, fantastic head. A wild, pulsating music began playing. In Valentin's eyes a light was torn. . . . The women stopped dancing and looked at her and were amazed. Marta-

Bianka was beautiful. Her amber yellow hair flowed like a stream over
her silvery back, and her body was white like a birch tree. In the sharp
light of the crystal chandeliers, the tips of her small breasts glimmered
with a reddish fire like two wounds, and with wide-open and respectful
eyes she kneeled down at her mother's feet and looked at her. The
countess was frightened. Confused and strangely moved, she sought in
that hour a way to her child. . . . [28]

The hoof noise of this gaudy linguistic stallion with which the poet
parades his talents sounds suspiciously thin. But this passage com-
pares favorably with others in the same novel, whose overwrought
pathos and gaudy sexuality are barely tolerable. Put bluntly, language
is used here to trick the reader; everything is artificial, sweet-
smelling, inflated. For the wealth conjured up by adjectives like
"amber yellow," "silver," and "deathly pale" is false; a lack of taste
dominates vocabulary as well as subject matter. In another passage of
the novel we read: "He came to a birch tree from which the bark hung
down in strips. Red, pulsating blood dripped from the trunk, to which
a child was bound with leather thongs and chains, a silver-white,
tortured, naked body." [29] "Red blood" would have been too flat, so
Leppin added "pulsating." Thongs alone were not enough, so he included chains. And the child's body is also (as it always is in this
novel) "silver-white" or "silvery." In the end it becomes tiresome to
extricate the nouns from a horde of adjectives like "mute," "dull,"
"barren," "confused," "tired," and "dreamy."

This lack of taste and similarly questionable comparisons (patched
together with a ubiquitous "as" or "like") were typical for the entire
Prague school. Take, for example, this excerpt from Meyrink's *The
Violet Death*, which Kafka objected to strenuously in one of his first
conversations with Brod: "Iridescent butterflies, as large as your hand
and with strange patterns, sat on silent flowers, their wings opened
like magic books." Or another passage from an early work of Brod's:
"Like the buds of legendary flowers, the round notes climbed from the
orchestra and unfolded into golden, echoing blossoms. Resplendent
wine glimmers within." [30] Even Rilke had difficulty in freeing himself
from his unholy Prague heritage: his *Malte Laurids Brigge* still contains passages such as, "her watery eyes, which seemed as though a

sick man had spit green phlegm onto her lids," and "the laughter rose from their mouths like pus from open wounds."[31]

Even the most horrific scenes in Kafka's work (the clinical description of the machine and execution procedures in "In the Penal Colony," for example) are narrated in a remarkably unadorned style that struck readers in his own time. But although Kafka's concise, neutral, sparse, logically constructed language was recognized at an early date, its difference from the style of his Prague contemporaries has not yet been noted.

Underlying the stylistic trends was the linguistic situation in Prague, which Fritz Mauthner described quite clearly: "The Germans in the inner parts of Bohemia, surrounded by Czechs, speak a paper German [*papierenes Deutsch*] that lacks the fullness of organic expressions and spoken forms. The melody of the spoken language has also been lost."[32] Heinrich Teweles, editor of *Bohemia,* also complained that "the stream of our language threatens to dry up. . . . In Prague, we have no German people from which the language can be reproduced; we are nothing but cultural Germans."[33] Mauthner was more specific: "The upper Bavarian dialect and a few Alemannic dialects brought me to tears when I first heard them."[34] As a substitute for the missing spoken language, writers used the Viennese dialect—but here too their uncertainty with High German is characteristic. For example, in his first novel *Castle Nornepygge* Brod had one of his characters, a German woman from Stettin who had lived only a few weeks in Prague, say to a horse: "*Ganz abgeschunden schaust aus,*" "You look really bedraggled."[35] The intonation and sentence construction here are instantly recognizable as Prague German. After Brod had recited a selection of Franz Werfel's poems in Berlin, a critic wrote: "It is remarkable how slight an accent this Czech poet has in speaking German."[36] Even Kafka's speech had a distinct Prague coloring. In a letter to Max Brod he described his reception in a sanatorium in Meran:

> After the first few words, it came out that I was from Prague. Both of them—the general, who sat opposite me, and the colonel—were acquainted with Prague. Was I a Czech? No. So now explain to those true German military eyes what you really are. Someone else suggested

"German-Bohemian," someone else "Little Quarter" [Kleinseite]. Then the subject was dropped and people went on eating, but the general, with his sharp ears linguistically schooled in the Austrian army, was not satisfied. After we had eaten, he once more began to wonder about the sound of my German. . . . (L 233)

Czech influenced the pronunciation of Prague German (also called "Little Quarter German"), but even more so its syntax and vocabulary. The most important of these peculiarities fall into three categories:

First: The incorrect use of prepositions, such as *darauf denken* ("think of") and *daran vergessen* ("forget about"), which even Kafka used repeatedly, or phrases like *Auf was brachst Du das?* or *Es steht dafür* (for *es lohnt sich,* "it's worth it"), and so on. These errors—for the most part related to the Czech proposition *na*—give an indication of the uncertainty of Prague German.

Second: The same is true for the incorrect use of reflexive verb forms, such as *sich spielen* ("to play") or *er hat sich das sehr gelobt* ("he praised it highly").

Third: The German vocabulary itself is reduced. Kisch notes:

> For the verbs "put," "sit," "place," "remove," Czech had an equal number of words, but it satisfied itself with the single verb *dati,* "to give." From this, the Germans began to say: *"Gib den Hut herunter"* ("Give the hat down") or *"Gib die Gabel wieder hin"* ("Give the fork back"). Only a native could understand a sentence like this: *"Wenn er geglaubt hat, dass ihm die Frau geben wird, hat er sich schön gegeben,"* which would roughly mean: "If he believes the woman will grant him her favors, he has badly miscalculated."[37]

In his early writings, Kafka also used *geben* ("to give") in this way.

It is not easy to pinpoint individual cases of this linguistic atrophy, but, as Mauthner and others have noted, its influence was significant and expressed itself first of all in the disappearance of infrequent, more arcane words. As Rilke wrote to August Sauer:

> The unhealthy contact of two linguistic bodies . . . in our country has brought about the continual degradation of the marginal areas of these languages. As a result, anyone who was raised in Prague, and was nour-

Map of the Old City in Prague During Kafka's Lifetime

1. Kafka's birth house (1883–1885).
2. Father's shop, 12 Zeltnergasse (from 1882).
3. Residence, 56 Wenzelsplatz (1885).
4. Residence, Geistgasse (1885–1887).
5. Residence, 6 Niklasstrasse (1887–1888).
6. Residence, 2 Zeltnergasse (1888–1889).
7. Residence, 2 Altstädter Ring, "Minuta" House (1889–1896).
8. Kafka's Elementary School, Fleischmarkt (1889–1893).
9. Kafka's Gymnasium, in Kinsky Palace (1893–1901). The father's shop was later located in the same building.
10. Residence, 3 Zeltnergasse (1896–1907).
11. Karolinum. Kafka attended law school here (1901–1906).
12. Building of Assicurazioni Generali, where Kafka worked briefly after receiving his degree (1907–1908).
13. Residence, 36 Niklasstrasse (from 1907).
14. Building of Workmen's Accident Insurance Institute, where Kafka was employed until retirement (from 1908).

41

ished therefore with the rotten refuse of language, later developed an aversion, even a sort of shame, for everything that had been taught to him during his tender childhood.[38]

Rilke's comment confirms in reverse the truth of Hebbel's pronouncement: "What good fortune to be born in such a city. For it is part of your earliest childhood, and with its incredibly vital enigmas and wonders the city will stay with you forever." In his poem "Evening" (1901), Rilke speaks of an "uneasy confusion of words." This confusion allows us to put the above quote from *Malte Laurids Brigge* in a new light: Rilke didn't know the emotional content of the High German word *Eiter* (pus), whereas in Prague one would have said *Materie* (matter). The "refuse of language" criticized by Rilke refers not just to Prague German, but also to one of its variants, *Kuchelböhmish*, a German-Czech pidgin spoken by the two nationalities in their daily intercourse. To give an example: *Stubenmadl pucovala fotrlinku na konku slofrock*, that is, "The maid cleaned the little father's dressing gown in the corridor."

In Jewish families there was the additional influence of *Mauscheldeutsch*, a sort of Germanized Yiddish. Its influence, however, was not necessarily pervasive: as early as 1864 a critical edition of the *Machsor* (prayers for the first day of the Jewish new year) was translated into impeccable High German by the head Rabbi M. I. Landau and published in Prague. *Mauscheldeutsch* survived only in a few colloquial expressions, which Kafka's father used here and there. Nevertheless Hermann Kafka's command of German was—given his childhood in Wohsek, an entirely Czech village—far from perfect. In his "Letter to His Father," Kafka provides several examples: "*Mir gesagt Deine Sorgen*" (I wish I had your worries), or "*Ich hab keinen so geruhten Kopf*" ("The things some people have time to think about" [DF 146]).

Beyond mere incorrect usage, uncertainties such as the reduced vocabulary led to a "confusion of words" with which many Prague writers covered over their own failings. This situation had a strong impact on the young Kafka. In his early letters and stories, a lingering uncertainty in High German usage and vocabulary is undeniable. Thus, at the beginning of 1903 he wrote (in an unpublished letter) to Oscar Pollak about his initial attempts to write after leaving high school: "I was so lost in the frenzy of big words." The language of the *Kunstwart* (which influenced Kafka during his first years at the university) was part of the problem. Doubtless he tried at first—as Rilke did throughout his life—to overcome the barrenness of his mother tongue with brute force. In experimenting with the *Kunstwart* idiom, however, he learned all the more quickly to avoid artificial constructions, and thereby later avoided the stylistic blunders that characterize the work of other Prague writers. Kafka's language became a personalized Prague German, purified of almost all local influence. Rudolf Vasata was the first to point out this connection to Prague German: "a dead language, like Medieval Latin, free from the living terms of language, pure in the sense of sterile . . . it became Kafka's vehicle—correct and sober, but expressive and flexible."[39] This observation went unnoticed for a long time (hardly a surprising fact, given the extraordinary accumulation of secondary literature) or was dismissed too quickly. Only Heinz Politzer, who lived in Prague for years, has seconded this observation about Prague German:

> In its substance, this language was not rich. In intonation and idioms, even in word choice and grammatical flow, Prague German is richly shaded by its Slavic, Czech environment and also by Prague Jewish German. Precisely this particular flavor raises the irony of Kafka's stories above the level of local color. From a material which he only partially mastered, he fashioned his own pure, fully controlled style.[40]

Kafka always clearly recognized the effect of the Prague environment on his language. Not only did he make statements to this effect, but his awareness is evident in his increasingly lucid and sober style. This tendency is already apparent in his first publications, the two "Conversations" of 1909 which appeared in the journal *Hyperion*. Kafka took two passages from "Description of a Struggle," written from 1904 to 1905, and reworked them for publication, simplifying their form to such an extent that the original material is almost completely lost. Two characteristic quotes from the original and the *Hyperion* editions will make this clear:

"Fine," said I, surprised him and seized his right hand. (CS 32)

"Good," I said, holding his right hand tightly. (*Hyperion*)

Yet an hour passed before he stood up, brushed his trousers for such a
long time that I felt like shouting: "Enough, enough. We can all see
that you have trousers on," crossed himself carefully, and with the lumbering gait of a sailor, walked to the holy water font. (CS 29)

Yet an hour passed before he stood up, crossed himself carefully, and
walked in fits and starts to the holy water font. (*Hyperion*)

His aversion to the Prague School's overabundant use of comparisons (feigning wealth to hide poverty) is almost tangible here: "with
the lumbering gait of a sailor" is replaced with the simpler form "in
fits and starts" (*stossweise*). The single word, the single object, is
given more weight; commentary is eliminated. Similarly, the entire
episode with the trousers, which slowed and explained the episode
and was meant as a further insight into the character's "psychology,"
has been deleted. Only the bare event remains.

Franz Blei, the editor of *Hyperion*, noted of Kafka's style: "I'm expressing it somewhat awkwardly when I say that Kafka's prose has a
boyish, self-conscious cleanliness to it."[41] This purism is not only Kafka's response to the linguistic multiplicity and corruption of his environment, but also his defense against the artifice of inflated words,
which his contemporaries pursued in order to compensate for the limited resources of Prague German. Kafka's attitude was expressed in a
singular, if somewhat exaggerated, way by Karl Kraus, whose criticism
bordered on puritanical fanaticism. Kraus, a native of the provincial
Bohemian town of Jicíner, must have had many similar linguistic experiences. Perhaps Kafka was thinking about this when he remarked
to Janouch about Kraus: "Only a converted poacher could be such a
strict gamekeeper" (J 91). This is probably the reason for Kraus's aversion to the poets of the Café Arco (whom he dubbed "the Arco-
nauts") and their leader Franz Werfel—although Kraus judged
Werfel's early works, not surprisingly, with more enthusiasm. Thus,
he failed to notice a passage from the poem "To My Pathos" from
Werfel's first publication, *The World Friend*, which aptly characterizes
the linguistic situation in Prague:

> Therefore I praise complacent dignity,
> My sublime rhetoric, practiced at evening. . . .

> And I'm kept from suicide and evil thoughts
> By decorative, grandiloquent and tragic declamation.[42]

Kafka, however, did not spend his evenings practicing rhetoric, and thus was not immune to "suicide and evil thoughts." When Brod first read to him the "Conversations" that appeared in *Hyperion*, Werfel reiterated this view in a way that accurately reflected the historical situation: "Beyond Tetschen-Bodenbach [a suburb of Prague] no one will understand Kafka." Certainly Kafka was "local" like Yeats, a fact which, apart from his untranslatable stylistic purity, makes translations of his work highly questionable. Werfel later changed his opinion, explaining with characteristic exaggeration: "Franz Kafka was sent by God. He has been chosen, and only the circumstances of his epoch have allowed him to cast his otherworldly knowledge and inexpressible experiences into parables. . . ."[43] Kafka's relationship to Werfel, whom he met through Brod, was quite ambivalent. As he noted on December 18, 1911, in his diary: "Besides, gifted with a sense of music, he has done very good work and easily. He has the happiest life behind him and before him, [whereas] I work with weights I cannot shrug off . . ." (D 141). Another diary entry reads: "All yesterday morning my head was as if filled with mist from Werfel's poems. For a moment I feared the enthusiasm would carry me along straight into madness" (D 145).

Kafka writes about his "enthusiasm" reluctantly, for it was foreign to his nature. He fought against stylistic pathos as well as the impoverished Prague German by imposing an extreme rigor on the verbal material offered to him by his environment. He scrutinized it suspiciously, almost pedantically, because he lacked a native fluency and confidence. Thus even here, in the innermost circle of poetic creation, we find his "uncertainty"—although it derives more from his linguistic environment than from his own idiosyncracies, and consequently he understood it all the more acutely. Brod reports of Kafka's punctiliousness during the editing of his first book, *Meditation*: publication took place "only after much reflection, frequent searches in the *Grimm* dictionary, and uncertainty about punctuation and spelling."[44] This uncertainty is noticeable in the later years as well. As Kafka wrote in 1917 to Felix Weltsch:

In connection with F[elice Bauer] I have a library request. You know
our old dispute over *bis*. It seems I have misunderstood her. She thinks
bis means *until*—and can certainly be used as a conjunction but only in
the meaning of *until*, not in the meaning of *when*. Thus one may not
say, for example: *Bis* you come here, I will give you five hundred kilo-
grams of flour (Hush This is only a grammatical example.) Would you
please decide, on the basis of Grimm (the examples have already slipped
my mind) or other books, whether F. is right. (L 144)

And a few days later he wrote to Brod (who had sent him his translation of the libretto to Janacek's *Jenufa*): "Can one run away from
Schaffen? [creation]. *'Siehst Du, dann soll man Dich lieben?'* ['You see,
one should love you?']. Isn't that the sort of German we have learned
from the lips of our un-German mothers?" (L 152). And he wrote in
a letter to Milena Jesenská, who initially wrote to him in Czech:
"This is something a German doesn't dare to expect from his language, he doesn't dare to write so personally" (M 24). Kafka's view is
distorted—one is tempted to replace "German" with "someone from
Prague"—and it isn't certain whether he recognized that the qualities
he attributes to the German language are, in fact, peculiar to Prague
German. But the consequences he drew from this situation are unmistakable: his constant tendency toward the sharpest forms of self-
criticism played a role in this distortion. Thus, his most significant
remarks about language appear in a somewhat false light in his letter
of June 1921 to Brod (in connection with Kraus's lecture "*Literatur*");
much of what he characterizes as the particularity of the Jewish writer
of German is seen from a Prague perspective:

They [Jewish writers] existed among three impossibilities, which I just
happen to call linguistic impossibilities. It is simplest to call them that.
But they might also be called something entirely different. These are:
The impossibility of not writing, the impossibility of writing German,
the impossibility of writing differently. One might also add a fourth impossibility, the impossibility of writing (since the despair could not be
assuaged by writing, was hostile to both life and writing; writing is only
an expedient, as for someone who is writing his will shortly before he
hangs himself—an expedient that may well last a whole life). Thus
what resulted was a literature impossible in all respects, a gypsy literature which had stolen the German child out of its cradle and in great

haste put it through some kind of training, for someone has to dance on the tightrope. (But it wasn't even a German child, it was nothing; people merely said that somebody was dancing.) (L 289)

How strongly this critical assessment—with its incisive comments about the linguistic situation of Jewish writers—holds true for the special case of Prague is made clear by the harsh criticism of the (non-Jewish) Prague writer Paul Leppin:

In the last few decades the German districts of Prague have completely lacked an organic development of their cultural life. What does exist . . . gives one the impression of prefabricated furniture, bought whole-sale. [It has been] worn out, transplanted and nourished in a foreign climate. . . . [45]

Kafka was perfectly aware of the *sociological* situation of the German community in Prague, which he summed up in a remark to Milena: "I have never lived among a German people . . ." (M 32).

The sense of estrangement that arose from this situation and would have such an impact on Kafka's life and work can be described as a fissure in the rather dark glass of Prague literature. In *The World Friend* Werfel speaks metaphorically of "foreign regions of the self" (*fremdeignen Gegenden*). Leppin wrote, less metaphysically, of one of his characters: "He wasn't the one responsible for his actions. Things themselves gave him their own life, passing through him like an open door. His soul acted, or his hand or a stranger."[46] Leppin even antici-pated the transformation of this estrangement into fear: "She hated her blood and her big body, which she couldn't restrain. She had a dull and greedy fear of her body. She sang. It was like a distress call at sea."[47] Again and again one finds expressions like "mute and aston-ished," "mute and helpless," "foreign and strange." One encounters the autonomous power of things, often in the sense of a helpless suf-fering. Things "gave him their own life" or, as Werfel formulated it in his early poem "The Poet": "I, only I, am like glass. / Through me the world drives its foaming abundance."[48]

The "magic of things" (*Dingmagie*) is particularly evident in Wer-fel's early work: "And do you think that a thing in the universe is without relation to you?" or "They were two very similar days, when a thing in the world held me and guided my thoughts." This was not just a word cult, but even a drug against Prague, "where everything happened unnaturally and in isolation."[49] In certain poems by Werfel, one can already see the danger of this estrangement, for things are imbued with the isolation of the urban landscape:

> And even silent things,
> The bleached-white undergarments,
> Table and books, savory dishes,
> Suit and the colorful hat.
> The pretty place where we fell asleep—
> Even the bed was full of caprices,
> Sheet and wood and glass and iron,
> Nothing was kind or good to me.[50]

The effect of Rilke's isolation from nature on his work hardly needs to be mentioned. Two years after he fled Prague, in response to a question whether he had "always enjoyed such an intimate relationship to nature," even "as a child," he wrote with characteristic reserve: "No, it is quite recent. . . ."[51] For Kafka, the "unnatural isolation" of Prague had serious consequences. In his work the city limits are almost never crossed; nature seldom emerges and then only in a sketchy fashion. In this "lifeless" sphere, the experience of things becomes much more intense and painful; but unlike Werfel and the Prague school it leads him to a linguistic purism.

This tendency grew stronger over the years and is evident in Kafka's increasingly brief, concise diary entries. Immune to synesthetic figures of speech, obscure words, and contorted syntax, Kafka's style was indeed influenced by the impoverished quality of Prague German. But this idiom also served remarkably well his own ascetic tendencies as an instrument for straightforward representation. Kafka's inexhaustible poetic reserves draw from memory, imagination, and especially dreams (which are not subject to any strict determination). Because this determination could only be imperfectly rendered by Prague German, Kafka—due to his particular conception of writing—managed to avoid the danger posed by the poverty of Prague German, which other writers sought to overcome with extravagant and forced images, feigning wealth to cover up poverty.

Moreover, Kafka confronted the estrangement of his environment with more seriousness and honesty than did his contemporaries (for whom it was merely an interesting poetic motif). In Prague, German was a kind of state-subsidized holiday language, which, as Mauthner had already pointed out, was dry and papery, a foreign implant. However, this estrangement permitted a more objective apprehension of individual words, an awareness that is lost in daily use or dialect. Words, particularly unusual ones, are taken literally and reacquire their original meanings. This "literalization" of language is very clear in Kafka's work. To cite only a few examples from "Description of a Struggle": "I couldn't *see through* it. . . . Then I closed my eyes so as to shut out the bad light" (CS 34–35, translation amended). The literal meaning of the verb *durchschauen*, "to see through," which is usually used figuratively, leads to the next image ("I closed my eyes"). Alternatively, such an image can come between phrases: "For you the truth is too *tiring*. . . . The entire length of you is cut out of tissue paper . . . when you walk one ought to hear you rustle . . . *you can't help bending to whatever draft happens to be in the room*" (CS 37). Often one image calls up another: The companion is "wounded," and so immediately the narrator "whistled down a few vultures . . ." (CS 22). The progression of images surrounding the "stealing" of the German language (in the abovementioned letter to Brod) is revealing in this respect: "Gypsies"—"a child stolen from the cradle"—"walking the tightrope." Associations of this kind contribute strongly to the idiomatic nature of many of Kafka's sentences.

Kafka's "key words" have another function, but here too such a process can be identified. Brod has already adduced sound arguments about the effect of Kafka's relationship to Milena on *The Castle*, with which Willy Haas, who knew Milena and her husband Ernst Polak well, agrees. Kafka uses a few traits of Polak in the figure of Klamm. He once punned on the double meaning of Polak's first name Ernst ("serious") in a letter to Milena; thus, the word directly evoked the idea and finally the name Klamm ("clamp," "difficult situation"). Similarly, the name of the Viennese Café "Herrenhof"—where Ernst Polak met with Werfel, Kisch, Blei, Arne Laurin, and Otto Pick— becomes a "Herrenhof" (Gentlemen's Court) in a literal sense.

The idiosyncracy of this process makes it difficult to identify explicit references to the empirical world in Kafka's work. *Words* play the dominant role as the direct source of association for his images. Kafka once said to Janouch, who had asked him whether the protagonist of *Amerika*, Karl Rossmann, "was based on a real person"; Kafka responded, "I did not draw people. I told a story. Those are images, only images."[52] At first, in the early period of "Wedding Preparations in the Country," these images are minutely described, and in this description one can sense Kafka struggling with a meager lexicon to find the most appropriate words for specific subjects. Sentences are joined together with a plethora of "sometime," "often," "from time to time," and particularly "since." In his later work these adverbial particles, which impede the flow of images, are greatly reduced; the images converge, influencing one another and creating chains of associations rather like those in dreams. Their relationship is less causal or inductive than it is metonymic, which means that the "action" in Kafka's work is often reduced to a minimum.

An essential assumption in this discussion has been that Kafka worked against the historical denaturing of language in Prague. From a point of view that allows for distortion (such as the shifting present tense), this may seem like a linguistic Kabbala. In any case, Kafka's intimate relationship to language makes of him a writer, not the prophet that he is often portrayed to be.

The Prague writers, in their pathological search for originality, overlooked the wealth of literary effects that could be achieved through this technique of literalization. "I can write only what I believe to be completely original," says the self-satisfied poet Fulcidus in an early novella by Brod. "My environment was not inconsequential in this regard," Werfel claims, remembering his childhood, in *Embezzled Heaven*: "the snobs who run around as mystics and orthodox believers, only because every tailor, schoolteacher, and journalist has become an atheist who believes in science."[53] The ignorant middle class (the direct cause of this protest snobbery) wasn't entirely wrong when it

reproached the sons of factory owners and merchants for deliberately cultivating an exaggerated metaphysical turgidity. But this criticism didn't apply to Kafka. When his *Meditation* appeared in overlarge typeface, we were surprised to find that, contrary to contemporary taste, the most minimal language prevailed throughout, adjectival embellishments, neologisms, and obscure constructions were nowhere to be found.[54]

The Prague writers' attempts to escape their *linguistic* ghetto remained futile, though diverse: the romantic escape (Hugo Salus, Friedrich Adler, Camill Hoffman, Ernst Lim); the hasty, intoxicated flight into overblown sexuality (Paul Leppin, Franz Blei, Victor Hadwiger, and occasionally Max Brod and Franz Werfel); the desire for an iridescent dreamworld (Leo Perutz, Gustav Meyrink); and finally the complete withdrawal into a cool intellectualism, which looks on impassively as the world passes by. This is Max Brod's strategy in his novel *Castle Nornepygge*:

> I have to agree with everyone. . . . I can't get angry about anything. . . . I'm not a man who stands on principle, I always take all sides equally. . . . I am someone who plays a thousand roles, but I don't have a private life on the side where I play no role and I could be myself . . . a child of our time . . . jaded by too many experiences, too many possibilities, unrestricted, a victim of the cultural free market. . . . [55]

Kafka remained untouched even by this attitude of "indifference," although it was perhaps nearest to his temperament.

This "cultural free market" and excessive receptivity among the Prague writers eventually fill the literary landscape with a horrible waxworks of fantastic figures. At the time of Arthur Schnitzler, Herman Bang, and Stanislaw Przybyszewski—which precedes Expressionism—"extreme types" emerged: eccentrics (Werfel, "Story of the Friend of a Dog"; Paul Kornfeld, "Legend"); murderers (Rilke, "Reflexes"; Brod, "Self-defense"); the ghosts of the Altstadt (Meyrink); the insane (Brod, "Death Is a Passing Weakness"; Paul Adler, "Namely"; Werfel, "Blasphemy of an Insane Man"); and a host of fanatics and wanton, deluded creatures (Brod, "Death to the Dead"; Rilke, "The Laugh of Pan Mraz"; the figures of Charousek in *Golem* and Vondrej in *Walpurgis Night* by Meyrink). Much of this stuffy, oppressive dreamworld left traces in Kafka's work. He stood in astonishment and naïve admiration before the bewildering images of his native city, before the confusion of the petty literary wars, and the peculiar, savage, explosive writings of his Prague contemporaries.

Against this assault he had nothing with which he could defend himself except an unconditional passion for truth, a passion that connects him to a long ancestral line of Jewish prophets and teachers or to his countrymen Jan Hus and Peter von Cheltschizky.

Only with great reserve, with his lucid, frighteningly cool intelligence, did Kafka take in these images, transcribing his own dreams (which "merely reproduce one's daily thoughts in more excited images") in a careful, clean prose that gradually frees itself from its initial awkwardness. His opposition to the Prague environment, his anxious isolation from the outside world, certainly have psychological causes as well. Emancipation from his parents, which Kafka never achieved, was at least won with respect to his surroundings, though at perhaps too high a price. In 1916 Kafka wrote to Felice Bauer:

> I, who for the most part have been a dependent creature, have an infinite yearning for independence and freedom in all things. Rather put on blinkers and go my way to the limit than have the familiar pack mill around me and distract my gaze. . . . Every relationship that I don't create or conquer by myself, even though it be in part to my own detriment, is worthless, hinders my walking. I hate it or am close to hating it. (D 371)

Translated by Warren Habib

KAFKA: JEW, ANTI-SEMITE, ZIONIST

Christoph Stölzl

KAFKA WAS A JEW in an anti-Semitic age, and he suffered for it. Anti-Semitism colored his relations with his profession, his father, his family, Prague, and his contemporaries. Kafka's ambivalence toward his Jewishness offers an extreme example of the problem of "Jewish anti-Semitism," which plagued the assimilated Jewish bourgeoisie at that time. The effect of this problem on Jewish nationalists opposed to assimilation was equally profound. To understand this phenomenon, we must look first at the generation of Kafka's grandfathers, the generation of Jacob Kafka.

Prior to assimilation, European Jews had hardly relied on the Christian society around them for social and moral values, looking instead primarily to Jewish law and traditional wisdom. With their emancipation from the ghetto,* they began to see themselves from a different perspective. Despite anxiety and humiliation from the outside world, the ghetto had been, to use Kafka's words, "my prison cell—my fortress" (DF 380). Now the Jews were offered entry into

---

* Full legal emancipation for Bohemian Jews took place in 1849, when the young Emperor Franz Joseph took the throne. Hermann Kafka was born in 1852.—ED.

bourgeois society by constitutional means. But this initiative came from the state, not society at large; and indeed, as the century wore on, it became increasingly unclear what percentage of the population still favored emancipation. Society reacted to emancipation with a negative stereotype of "the Jew," adopting stereotypes from preindustrial times that were modified to fit the era of bourgeois capitalism. For the Jews the only way out of the spotlight of public prejudice seemed to be assimilation. Thus it happened that the Jews, as a weaker and continually endangered group, themselves accepted anti-Semitic stereotypes in direct proportion to the extent of their own assimilation.

The strong communal nature of the ghetto had been destroyed, but family connections and contacts among Jews continued to play a greater role than any contact with the non-Jewish world. "The Alt-neu Synagogue yesterday," Kafka notes in his diary in 1911: "Kol Nidre. Suppressed murmurs of the stock market" (D 59). To counter the inevitable accusation of divided loyalties, the Jews had only one option: to torment themselves with the same reproaches that the Christian majority used against them. Here we find the root of the radical criticism to which Jews subjected other Jews, a criticism which in the robust figure of Hermann Kafka is expressed somewhat trivially in his tendency to lash out at those around him in mistrust and rage: "Name a single person who was of importance to me in my childhood whom you didn't at least once tear to shreds with your criticism," Kafka asks in the "Letter to His Father" (DF 170). Or, as he writes in a letter to Ottla: "There is hardly any close or very close relation whom Father didn't run down this time. One is a swindler, when the other comes along you have to spit (ugh!), etc." (O 15).

Arthur Schnitzler called this phenomenon the "tragicomedy of contemporary Judaism," a tragicomedy whose eternal truth was

that a Jew never really respected another Jew. Never. As little as prisoners in an enemy country respect each other, especially those who have lost all hope. Envy, hatred, sometimes admiration, and ultimately even love can exist between them, but never respect, for all emotional relations are played out, so to speak, in an atmosphere where respect must suffocate.[1]

In this closed society, members know each other so well that they can inflict far deeper wounds than any outsider could. It is no coincidence, for example, that the Jewish satirist Karl Kraus directed most of his diatribes at other Jews. In a conversation with Gustav Janouch, Kafka explains the reasoning behind Jewish jokes about Jews: "We see each other better than other people, because we are together on a journey" (J 110). It comes as no surprise, then, that Kafka observed the appearance and behavior of his contemporaries primarily in terms of their Jewishness.[2]

Hermann Kafka's generation was still relatively free from this radical form of self-criticism; it had internalized only the contempt for the less assimilated "Galicians" or Eastern European Jews. Hermann Kafka had only "abuse, defamation, and denigration" for his son's Eastern Jewish friend, the actor Yitzhak Löwy, and compared him with "vermin" (DF 146). But their sense of self was preserved, if not by the strict value system of the ghetto, at least by the materialist values of the *Grunderzeit* in the second half of the nineteenth century—values developed during the period in which the Jews "established" themselves economically and socially. "At bottom the faith that ruled your life," Kafka writes to his father, "consisted in your believing in the unconditional rightness of the opinions of a certain class of Jewish society" (DF 174). This was a faith in material things: "If you have food in your jaws you have solved all questions for the time being" (CS 303). At times Kafka seems to take a coldly objective view of this materialism, as when he writes to Milena Jesenská:

> The insecure position of the Jews, insecure within themselves, insecure among people, would make it above all comprehensible that they consider themselves to be allowed to own only what they hold between their teeth, that furthermore only palpable possessions give them the right to live, and that they will never again acquire what they once have lost. . . . (M 50–51)

But such objectivity came late in life. Earlier, he had suffered from his inability to find a solution to his own Jewish question according to the terms of his father's generation. What the one-time itinerant tradesman Hermann Kafka offered as an answer to Jewish suffering—

namely, greater material security and a backward glance to the early years following emancipation when one's very existence was in danger ("Who knows that today? What do children know! No one endured these sufferings! Does a child understand that today?!")—was of no use to a German-Jewish intellectual at the turn of the century.

Kafka laments in his diary, "It is unpleasant to listen to Father talk with incessant insinuations about the good fortune of people today and especially of his children, about the sufferings he had to endure in his youth" (D 154). He became embittered about the impossibility of making his father realize that "these facts, taken together with the further fact that I have not gone through all this, by no means lead to the conclusion that I have been happier than he" (D 199). The highly assimilated Jews of the turn of the century who, like Kafka, had been raised on Goethe in the Austrian Gymnasium, and who, like Kafka, had learned to love Nietzsche and the *Kunstwart*,* now stood to lose their intellectual assets, even their identity as "Germans" or (less frequently) as "Czechs." They suffered most from the anti-Semitic propaganda, focusing it on themselves as if through a magnifying glass, and taking far more notice of it than did the rest of society. Thus, the successful Austrian writer Rudolf Hans Bartsch, whose early novels were particularly anti-Semitic and racially nationalist, could recall with amazement in 1909: "The very people I had attacked and with whom I had feuded, the Jews, were the ones who read my book. They let me know that I had touched them, unsettled them, and that they considered me a poet. My first audience consisted of Jews and Jews alone. . . . My Aryan book was spurned by the Aryans and loved by those it reviled."[3] The weekly newspaper *Selbstwehr* ("Self-Defense"), the official organ of the Prague Zionist movement, reported of German Jews in Western Bohemia: "When you hear how they talk among themselves about their fellow Jews, you would think you were in the best anti-Semitic company."[4]

The character of anti-Semitic accusations had changed together with society itself. In the first decades following emancipation in 1849, critics focused on the notable concentration of Jews in "unproductive" professions like journalism and law, and their unwillingness

---

* "Art Guard"—a nationalistic cultural journal edited by Ferdinand Avenarius. See Wagenbach, "Prague at the Turn of the Century."

to establish themselves as tradesmen, skilled laborers, or farmers—the very occupations that were now open to them. This criticism of Jews was ridiculous: How could an essentially bourgeois, commerce-oriented middle class *avoid* the developing tendencies of the capitalist age? But as liberal capitalism fell into increasing disrepute, successful Jews needed to find an appropriate way to justify their success, and they believed they had found one in the principle of motivating other Jews to take up "productive" trades. Hence the creation of many Jewish organizations for the "promotion of trade and farming among the Israelites" in this period of anti-Semitism. Likewise, the Central Organization for the Fostering of Jewish Affairs, founded in 1884—to which Hermann Kafka (fancy-goods wholesaler) belonged, as did Franz Werfel's father (glove-factory owner) and Max Brod's father (bank director)—felt that as an association for the protection of the Bohemian Jewish bourgeoisie, its primary goal was to groom the next generation of Jews for careers in trade.[5]

But in Kafka's time, the old accusations were supplemented by a new form of hatred born of racially nationalist ideology and social Darwinism. This hatred seemed entirely plausible since—even when not directed against the Jews—it corresponded to general intellectual and cultural concepts such as nation, tradition, and race which were prevalent at the time. Kafka himself had been a Darwinist as a student in the Gymnasium. What then developed might best be explained by the notion of a sociological "osmosis," with individual Jews absorbing the worst of these ideologies in a phenomenon commonly described as "Jewish self-hatred." Kafka writes, "I have vigorously absorbed the negative element of the age in which I live, an age that is, of course, very close to me, which I have no right ever to fight against, but, as it were, a right to represent" (DF 99). One might tentatively describe this shift as a change in the collective patterns of a neurosis in the society at large and which filtered down into smaller groups, families, and individuals, touching even the question of physical and mental illness.

Admittedly, such speculations lead to shaky methodological ground; but supporting evidence does exist. Statistics from the countries represented in the Imperial Council (*Reichsrat*) convey something of what was happening to Jews at that time: within the Jewish population in the Austrian Empire after 1900, mental illnesses accounted for a disproportionately large percentage of all documented illnesses.[6] Hermann Broch once observed, "The aristocrat has a family history, the Jewish bourgeois a neurosis history."[7] In his novel *The Man Without Qualities*, Robert Musil describes the process of a Jewish couple "absorbing" neuroses from society at large. His portrait of this family might also be applied to the relation between Kafka and his father:

> In fact, of course, life is more than half made up not of actions but of harangues, the gist of which one absorbs, and of opinions and corresponding counter-opinions, and of the accumulated non-personality of all one has heard and knows. The destiny of these two spouses to a great extent depended on a dreary, tough, unordered stratification of thoughts that were not even their own but were part of public opinion and had changed with it, without their being able to protect themselves against the process. Compared with this dependence, their personal dependence on each other was only a tiny fraction, a madly overestimated residue. And while they were persuading themselves that they had a private life and were questioning each other's character and will, the desperate difficulty lay in this conflict's unreality, which they covered up with every thinkable kind of irritation.[8]

And if the individual Jew internalized the sum total of anti-Semitic aggression with its political, economic, and even physically defamatory aspects, nothing whatsoever remained that might justify his existence as a human being. For Musil, the Austrian citizen had "at least nine characters":

> a professional one, a national one, a civic one, a class one, a geographical one, a sex one, a conscious, an unconscious and perhaps even too a private one; he combines them all in himself, but they dissolve him, and he is really nothing but a little channel washed out by all these trickling streams, which flow into it and drain out of it again in order to join other little streams filling another channel.[9]

But the fragmented Jewish individual experienced himself as an abstract vessel: either completely empty of meaning, or filled with hatred generated by himself as well as by others. In Kafka's self-interpretation, certain formulations suggest this experience even when Jewishness is not explicitly named, as in the following piece from his collection *Meditation:*

> I stand on the end platform of the tram and am completely unsure of my footing in this world, in this town, in my family. Not even casually could I indicate any claims that I might rightly advance in any direction. I have not even any defense to offer for standing on this platform, holding on to this strap, letting myself be carried along by this tram, nor for the people who give way to the tram or walk quietly along or stand gazing into shopwindows. Nobody asks me to put up a defense, indeed, but that is irrelevant. (CS 388)

Later, Musil would write of the Hapsburg empire in the final years before the war: "In it one was negatively free, constantly aware of the inadequate grounds for one's own existence and lapped by the great fantasy of all that had not happened."[10] Judgments passed by others deprived the individual of a basis for his own existence. As Kafka wrote in a sketch: "He has many judges, they are like a host of birds perching in a tree. Their voices intermingle, questions of precedence and competence cannot be disentangled, and there is also a continual changing of places" (DF 379). In another sketch, a fragment entitled "Advocates," he notes that a legal verdict

> is based on inquiries being made here and there, from relatives and strangers, from friends and enemies, in the family and public life, in town and village—in short, everywhere. Here it is most necessary to have advocates, advocates galore, the best possible advocates, one next to the other, a living wall, for advocates are by nature hard to set in motion; the plaintiffs, however, those sly foxes, those slinking weasels, those little mice, they slip through the tiniest gaps, scuttle through the legs of advocates. So look out! (CS 450)

Hence the necessity of hiding oneself behind an impersonal, collective fate, as one of Kafka's literary protagonists reflects: "so long as you say 'one' instead of 'I,' there's nothing in it and one can easily tell the story; but as soon as you admit to yourself that it is you yourself, you feel as though transfixed and are horrified" (DF 3). The discrepancy between self and world immobilizes Kafka: "Himself he knows, the others he believes, everything is sawn apart for him by this antithesis" (DF 378).

Specifically Jewish fear was the dominant motif in Kafka's life: fear of anti-Semitic threats whose danger was that once they had been uttered, one was compelled to carry them out against oneself. "From the most improbable sides," he writes in a letter to Milena Jesenská, "Jews are threatened with danger, or let us, to be more exact, leave the dangers aside and say they are threatened with threats" (M 51). The threats began the moment the assimilated Jew was asked about his background, a moment that is like "a blow on the chest" (M 52). In a later letter to Milena, Kafka responds to her question "*Jste žid?*" ("Are you Jewish?") with a wonderfully condensed psycholinguistic observation: "Don't you see how in the '*Jste*' the fist is withdrawn to gather muscle-strength? And then in the '*žid*' the cheerful, unfailing, forward-flying blow?" (M 52). Even when there were no threats, it made little difference: "How people do always carry their own enemy, however powerless he is, within themselves" (DF 221).

Only their talent for excessive self-repression enabled the Jews as a whole to avoid living in a state of panic. In "An Introductory Talk on the Yiddish Language" written in 1912 (see Appendix), Kafka ironically sums up the Jews' perceptions of themselves and their surroundings:

> Our Western European conditions, if we glance at them only in a deliberately superficial way, appear so well ordered; everything takes its quiet course. We live in positively cheerful concord, understanding each other whenever necessary, getting along without each other whenever it suits us, and understanding each other even then.

Kafka thought it "the strangest thing" that "anxiety" did not completely dominate all Jews (M 50), yet this offered him no solace. As he tells Milena in 1920, this anxiety overtakes "only isolated ones, but these most poignantly, for instance myself" (M 50). He writes further to his brother-in-law Josef David: "To make me anxious about anything is like carrying coals to Newcastle" (O 79). And in a later diary entry from January 18, 1922, he comments on a remark of Milena's: "fear means unhappiness but it does not follow from this that courage means happiness . . . (there were perhaps only two Jews in my class possessed of courage, and both shot themselves while still at school or shortly after); not courage, then, but fearlessness" (D 400).

Anxiety provided a link with the persecutions in his fathers' and grandfathers' time, a link with the ghetto and the countless traumas of Jewish inner migration and isolation, with the Czech boycott of Jewish stores, and finally with the attempts of many Jews to live in Christian society as assimilated "parasites" from the ghetto. As Kafka remarked to Gustav Janouch, "In us all it still lives—the dark corners, the secret alleys. . . . We walk through the broad streets of the newly built town. But our steps and our glances are uncertain. Inside we tremble just as before in the ancient streets of our misery" (J 80). Kafka's self-accusation in a letter to his sister Ottla voices the same notion of a parasitic self: "It's this way: Once I've attached myself anywhere, I stick like something distinctly repellent" (O 22). Kafka also knew the anti-Jewish poems of the Czech Expressionist Petr Bezruč who, drawing on the traditional anti-Semitism of Czech rustic literature, penned the verses:

> When the Jew comes into town,
> in five years the place is his.
> Once a beggar, now full of strength,
> lusting after virgins newly wed.[11]

Kafka was vividly aware then of social exclusion. In a 1920 fragment he describes the difficulties of entering society:

If you want to be introduced into a strange family, you find someone who is a common acquaintance and ask him to do you the favor. If you cannot find one, you possess yourself in patience and wait for a favorable opportunity.

In the little place where we live there cannot be any lack of such. If the opportunity does not turn up today, it will certainly turn up tomorrow. And if it does not turn up, you will not on that account begin trying to move heaven and earth. If the family can endure having to get on without you, you will find it at least no harder to endure. (DF 266)

The anti-Semitic violence of the Polna era,* when the constitutional state (*Rechtsstaat*) and the "voice of the people" were at extreme odds, can also be heard in Kafka's texts: "Everything, even what is most commonplace, such as being waited on in a restaurant [can be achieved only] with the assistance of the police. This robs life of all comfort" (DF 379).

That the Jews endured such humiliations collectively offered no protection: no solidarity could counteract self-hatred, since the very fact that other Jews *were* Jews transformed them into objects of contempt. Here lies the reason—surprisingly often overlooked—for the "isolation" of the Jews in Prague, which, in fact, did not exist; on the contrary, the Jews in Prague (about 30,000 in 1920) had developed a broad network of social relations. Even the Zionists of the *Selbstwehr* acknowledged that "Prague social life [was] dominated by a unified, self-contained class of Jewish intellectuals,"[12] and that because so many Jews lived in the city together, it had a distinctly "Jewish atmosphere."[13]

"How do I live in Prague, after all?" Kafka wrote in 1912. "This craving for people, which I have and which is transformed into anxiety once it is fulfilled, finds an outlet only during vacations" (L 82–83). And another Prague writer of bourgeois Jewish origins echoed in 1909: "I would like to get to know human beings, not just people."[14] Weren't his Jewish acquaintances and relatives proper human beings? If we listen to Kafka speak about the family milieu to which he felt inextricably bound, it almost seems as if they were not. Thus, we begin to understand why he sought to escape "his" Prague, where if one did not "seem to have any fear of Jewry," it was "something heroic" (M 50). As he writes to his sister Elli, it was a misfortune for a child to have grown up in Prague,

> where prosperous Jews are affected by a particular spirit from which children cannot be shielded. I am not referring to individuals, of course, but to this almost tangible general spirit, which expresses itself somewhat differently in everyone, in each according to his character, which is in you as well as in me—this small, dirty, lukewarm, squinting spirit.

---

* Stölzl is referring here to the "Hilsner Affair" of 1899, when Leopold Hilsner, a Jewish cobbler's apprentice from the town of Polna, was tried for an alleged ritual murder. Kafka was sixteen at the time.—ED.

To be able to save one's own child from that, what good fortune! (L 290–91)

Part of the topography of Kafka's Jewish Prague were the Jewish cafés with their "centenarian Jews." "In our times the cafés are the catacombs of the Jews. Without light and without love" (J 79). Two years after Kafka's death, the Czech Jew Jan Münzer heaped even more scorn on the Jewish coffee houses, the fixed points in Prague's "invisible ghetto." One found there, he writes,

> a ritually vaporous atmosphere in which uncouth, knotted tongues pour forth heartrending jargon, accompanied by wild gesticulations of the entire body. I think of those coffee houses in which fathers calmly discuss business, their sons talk about literature, and where a change in seating from the artists' table to that of the brokers shows social progress. I think of the world of "normalized" thinking, of the countless phrases and sayings prepared for the momentary need but containing no new problems or ideas, no means of solving matters except by asking the one question: How much money can I make? That world where . . . poems are commodities and business a passion, where people speak to each other with a shameless familiarity that turns the issue of a good bowel movement into a matter for public discussion; that world in which the native wallows blissfully, and from which the person unaccustomed to such forays into the human interior takes flight.[15]

For Kafka, Prague compressed itself into his parents, whom he "always looked upon as persecutors." Writing to Felice Bauer in 1912 he charges, "All parents want to do is drag one down to them, back to the old days from which one longs to free oneself and escape" (F 55); consequently,

> for me, they are a hundred times more unclean than they may be in reality, which doesn't really worry me; their foolishness is a hundred times greater, their absurdity a hundred times greater, their coarseness a hundred times greater. On the other hand their good qualities seem a hundred thousand times smaller than they are in reality. . . . So again there is hatred, and almost nothing but hatred. (F 525)

It was his parents who blocked his attempt to escape their control and marry Julie Wohryzek, the daughter of a Czech Jewish shoemaker and custodian for the Prague Vinohrady synagogue, and whose speech was characterized by "an inexhaustible and nonstop store of the brashest Yiddish expressions" (L 213). Kafka's escape attempt was bound to fail, since Hermann Kafka could not bear the disgrace of his son's rejection of the status he had attained, so far from his poor childhood in Wohsek. Prague was the "frenzied family life" (F 525) that would not release its grip on the sons, that tried to frighten them into accommodating themselves, in a typically Jewish fashion, to a society of polemically interlocked nationalities, that pushed them toward mimicry and divided loyalties, naked opportunism, and the exploitation of what Jewish loyalties still existed—at least in remnants—despite assimilation.

"Any relationship not created by myself," Kafka writes to Felice, "even though it be opposed to parts of my own nature, is worthless; it hinders my movements, I hate it, or come near to hating it. The road is long, one's resources few, there is reason in plenty for this hatred" (F 525). Kafka was repelled by the mentality of Jewish businessmen (including his father) "who are German one day, Czech the next" (D 302). Perhaps this was his motivation when, in response to the census of 1910, he was the only family member to rebel against paternal authority and refuse to state falsely that Czech was the language he used colloquially (a claim that helped the reputation of the family's wholesale fancy-goods business).[16] At the same time he detected in himself psychological patterns comparable to the Jews' hypocritical behavior in national politics: "I write differently from what I speak, I speak differently from what I think, I think differently from the way I ought to think, and so all proceeds into deepest darkness" (O 8). To Felice Bauer he admits, "I am a mendacious creature; for me it is the only way to maintain an even keel, my boat is fragile" (F 545). And in two aphorisms from the collection that Max Brod entitled *Reflections on Sin, Suffering, Hope, and the True Way*, he postulates: "Everything is deception. . . . *Can* you know anything other than deception? If ever the deception is annihilated, you must not look in that direction or you will turn into a pillar of salt" (DF 40, 47). Kafka's hatred of Prague, of the Prague *in himself*, culminates in a seldom mentioned and eerily prophetic passage that anticipates the technology of the Holocaust. The passage occurs in a letter to Milena: "Sometimes I'd like to cram them all as Jews (including myself) into the drawer of the laundry chest, then wait, then open the drawer a little, to see whether all have already suffocated, if not, to close the drawer again and go on like this to the end" (M 59).

That human beings define themselves through work has been a commonplace since the time of Hegel. Refusing to take over his father's wholesale business, Kafka instead became an office worker, a private civil servant. Yet all he really wanted to do was write: "My job is unbearable to me because it conflicts with my only desire and my only calling, which is literature. . . . Everything that is not literature bores me and I hate it" (D 230–31). So he found no *modus vivendi* between the office and real life, and experienced his workdays as a hell. Why voluntarily choose this "horrible double life from which there is probably no escape but insanity?" he asks in his diary (D 38). In the "Letter to His Father," he explains that he chose a noncommercial profession solely because of the stultifying atmosphere of the Kafka family business. But is that the whole truth, or is something else hidden behind the "lawyer's tricks" to which Kafka himself admitted in this document?

Social statistics from the period indicate that the majority of offspring from Jewish families in commerce opted for academic professions, and not only because of the threat to Jewish trade posed by the "*Svuj k svému*,"* but in large part also as a rejection of the "typically Jewish" businessman's existence. As Kafka's friend Hugo Bergmann recalled:

> In those days, the situation was such that a Jewish graduate, unless he accepted baptism in order to enter government service, had in fact no other choice but law or medicine, the two professions that offered self-employment. Since these did not interest either Kafka or myself, we looked around for other possibilities and were advised to study chemistry, because there seemed to be employment opportunities for Jews in the chemical industry.[17]

The plan did not last long; shortly after the semester began, Kafka switched from chemistry to law. The move actually might have served

---

* "Each to His Own," a Czech boycott movement of Jewish stores.—ED.

as a springboard into literature, since in old Austria law was "the somewhat indeterminate career-oriented course of study for young men with a general interest in culture."[18] Countless Bohemian Jews who held law degrees worked as editors in the Austrian press, in press offices of Viennese ministries, or in publishing houses. But for Kafka it was impossible to go this route. "In 1906," reports Max Brod,

> when it came to making a living, Franz stipulated that his job should have nothing to do with literature, since that to him seemed a degradation of poetic activity. Earning a living and writing had to remain completely separate enterprises; a mixture of the two such as journalism was impossible for Kafka. He "simply couldn't do it."[19]

Critics often resort to Kafka's definition of "writing as a form of prayer" to explain his attitude. But does that suffice? Was it not that Jewish anti-Semitism made him feel that the door to professional literary activity was closed to Jews?

In Kafka's famous letter to Max Brod about Jewish writers, there are astonishing parallels between his terminology and that of German nationalist writings. For example, the ideological mouthpiece of Bohemian pan-Germans, the *Ostdeutsche Post* of Karl Hermann Wolf (a racist member of parliament), announced in 1901 the "battle of the Aryan artistic spirit against the Semitic and the Un-German." It also proposed "re-Germanizing our literature," demanding that literary works by German-speaking Jews be denied all recognition, despite the attractiveness of "the young boys with curly black hair and dark, friendly eyes who lust after reviews." As one editorial put it, "the most sacred treasure of a people or a race is its language. What sort of nation can it be if it does not find its best, its true essence in its language." Further, it called for an end to the confusion between, on the one hand, the "southern German stock that, in accordance with historically attested rights, calls the East Mark—as a German land—its own" and, on the other, the "Semitic literary enclave in Vienna that, when exposing its true soul, finds itself in the tragic position of having to borrow our language, which it barely knows what to do with."[20]

Similarly, Kafka may have felt that the Jews, as the *Ostdeutsche*

Post again put it, "steal the words of a nation from which they cannot possibly want to free themselves." But he expressed it better in his letter to Brod when he speaks of "a bumptious, tacit, or self-pitying appropriation [by Jewish writers] of [German] property, something not earned, but stolen by means of a relatively casual gesture. Yet it remains someone else's property, even though there is no evidence of a single solecism," because "the whispering voice of conscience confesses the whole crime in a penitent hour" (L 288).

But why should Jewish writers be so irresistibly drawn to this language? Kafka believed that

> there is a relationship between all this and Jewishness, or more precisely between young Jews and their Jewishness, with the frightful inner predicament of these generations. . . . Most young Jews who began to write German wanted to leave Jewishness behind them, and their fathers approved of this, but vaguely (this vagueness was what was outrageous to them). But with their hind legs they were still glued to their father's Jewishness and with their waving front legs they found no new ground. The ensuing despair became their inspiration.

And he continued in a crucial passage:

> An inspiration as honorable as any other, but on closer examination showing certain sad peculiarities. First of all, the product of their despair could not be German literature, though outwardly it seemed to be so. They existed among three impossibilities, which I just happen to call linguistic impossibilities. It is simplest to call them that. But they might also be called something entirely different. These are: The impossibility of not writing, the impossibility of writing German, the impossibility of writing differently. One might also add a fourth impossibility, the impossibility of writing (since the despair could not be assuaged by writing, was hostile to both life and writing, writing is only an expedient, as for someone who is writing his will shortly before he hangs himself—an expedient that may well last a whole life). Thus, what resulted was a literature impossible in all respects, a gypsy literature which had stolen the German child out of its cradle and in great haste put it through some kind of training, for someone has to dance on the tightrope. (L 288–89)

While the *Deutsche Volksbote*, a mouthpiece for the League of Germans in Bohemia, stated broadly that "the Jew learns enough German to do business almost anywhere in Europe and among all peoples, even if he abuses the German language in every syllable,"[21] Kafka himself felt that "in this German-Jewish world hardly anyone can do anything else [but] *mauscheln*—taken in a wider sense, and that is the only way it should be taken" (L 288). Was it still possible to go to Vienna and become a man of letters if, like Kafka, one read Karl Kraus's journal *Die Fackel*, which vituperated against the German-Jewish press and literary industry with monomaniacal obsession, as if this industry were not a marginal phenomenon but the primary cause of contemporary "decay"? Of course, the editor of *Die Fackel* could not see this, since he himself was too deeply, if ironically, rooted in his own self-hating milieu. As Kafka remarked to Janouch: "Only a converted poacher could be such a strict gamekeeper" (J 91). *

During his youth (usually described by critics as his "assimilationist" phase), Kafka may not have spoken in a distinctly anti-Semitic way. But he most definitely *acted* in the spirit of Jewish anti-Semitism by renouncing literature as a means of earning a living. Later, particularly after coming into contact with the Zionists in the *Selbstwehr* circle who preached a "positive Jewish racism," he studied their teaching with almost masochistic satisfaction. Could a Jew be a German writer if he agreed with the *Selbstwehr*, which wrote, "The German language . . . never became completely ours."[22] Could he, if he thought of himself as a "half-German" (O 36), whose Germanness consisted of "deposits of an alien world" (J 69)? Or if he completely denied his world any German character? "The German-speaking Jews in the box seats are, after all, not Germans," Kafka told Janouch about the audience in Prague's German Theater (J 68). Or if he sympathized with the Germans harmed by Jewish assimilation? In a letter to Brod, Kafka claimed:

From early on they [the Jews] have forced upon Germany things that she might have arrived at slowly and in her own way, but which she was opposed to because they stemmed from strangers. What a terribly bar-

---

* Kraus, a Jew by birth, converted to Catholicism.—ED.

ren preoccupation anti-Semitism is, everything that goes with it, and Germany owes that to her Jews. (L 236)

For his part, Max Brod developed a complex ideology of "love from afar" to describe his relation to German culture and to justify his own identity as a Jewish-German author: One is a "friend, but certainly not a member of the German people. . . . A cultural relation is not a blood relation." He too succumbed to the era's biologistic prejudices when he wrote of the distance separating Jews, with their "millennial racial purity," from German culture. Although he might "cherish the profundity of a Kleistian turn of phrase," his reaction still depended on "associations that have been learned within a foreign national tradition, not on something innate." The old slander against the "uncreative," imitative character of Jewish art, all too familiar since the publication of Wagner's pamphlet on Judaism and music, recurs in Brod as well: "Do we need proof that even the best understanding should never be mistaken for one's own feeling of creativity that no longer needs to be checked, and which would be unable to bear it, the self-check learned from a 'foreign' or alien model of existence?" Brod did not shy away from such ridiculous issues as the national content of symphonic music, or which musical "atoms" of Beethoven or Smetana a Jew might legitimately appreciate.[23] Yet despite his Jewish nationalism Brod was able to write in German, and to participate diligently and successfully in the Austrian and German literary market.

By contrast, Kafka found himself in a vicious circle. Although he produced literature, he could grant it no objective value; instead, he had to curse it as "scribbling," and demand in his will that his writings be destroyed. Only in occasional light moments could he see the irony of his situation, as when in a letter to Felice he repeated Brod's description of his stories as "the most typically Jewish documents of our time" (F 517). But he also dismissed the "typically German" quality that others saw in him: "A difficult case. Am I a circus rider on two horses? Alas, I am no rider, but lie prostrate on the ground."

"Legitimate" writing was possible for this generation of Jewish-Germans only if the relation between an author's political and linguistic "homes" was harmonious. Kafka was unable to claim any such harmony for himself, since in his view the "Out with the Jews!" atti-

tude shared by German racial nationalists and Czech chauvinists was
justified. "Language is the music and breath of home. I—but I am
badly asthmatic, since I can speak neither Czech nor Hebrew" (J
138). Thus, he sometimes envied the less problematic status of writers in a "literature of small peoples"* like Yiddish or Czech: in these
languages an author's livelihood was justified by his national-
pedagogical function, and his literary work was supported by the
democratic consensus of his national comrades: "the claim that the
national consciousness of a small people makes on the individual is
such that everyone must always be prepared to know that part of the
literature which has come down to him, to support it, to defend it—
to defend it even if he does not know it and support it" (D 149).

Kafka's literary and sociological analysis of the Czechs and the
Yiddish-speaking Eastern Jews was part of his lifelong reflection on
the possibility of making Jewish life "productive." He wanted to reconstruct the entire social pyramid along racially nationalist lines to
replace what he (together with the anti-Semites as well as the Zionists of the *Selbstwehr*) saw as the "unnatural" professional and social
stratification of the urbanized, industrialized, commercialized, and
overly intellectualized "Western Jews," ostensibly averse to any form
of manual labor. As such formulations show, early Zionism simply
borrowed images from anti-Semitic thinking, and reversed or reflected them as in a mirror. The aims of the staunchest Zionists' ideological writings—the mission to become a militant Jewish nation of
farmers and artisans in the Palestine of biblical times—can be understood as an anticipation of the protofascist myths of *Blut und Boden*
("blood and soil") and of a classless "folk" comradery. Of course,
these myths were already present in Austrian politics, but they had
not yet become state policy, as they later did in fascism. The idea of
Jewish colonization functioned as a stimulus or focal point for the
utopian ideals of the new Jewish individual; any discussion for or
against the idea of a Jewish state remained purely theoretical. Broad-
based geopolitical perspectives were not of prime importance to individual Jews. The psychological urge that drove them to change

---

* The term has also been translated as "minority literature." See the essay by Gilles
Deleuze and Félix Guattari in the present volume.—ED.

professions stemmed from a need to divert their self-directed aggression into physical work; the more completely they adopted the anti-
Semitic stereotype, the stronger the urge.

This motif appears very clearly at one point in Kafka. In 1913 he
yearned "to do some dull, honest, useful, silent, solitary, healthy,
strenuous work" (F 238). He helped in a carpenter's shop and a nursery, and in 1918 again looked for work in a nursery not far from
Prague. He told Janouch in 1920:

> I love to work in woodshops. The smell of wood shavings, the humming
> of saws, the hammer-blows, all enchanted me. . . . There is nothing
> more beautiful than some straightforward, concrete, generally useful
> trade. Apart from carpentry, I have also worked at farming and garden-
> ing. It was all much better and worth more than forced labor in the
> office. There one appears to be something superior, better; but it is only
> appearance. In reality one is only lonelier and therefore unhappier.
> That is all. Intellectual labor tears a man out of human society. A craft,
> on the other hand, leads him towards men. . . . I have dreamed of
> going as a farm laborer or an artisan to Palestine . . . if I could make a
> life that had meaning, stability, and beauty. . . . (J 15–16)

Kafka's dreams present a paraphrased, extreme version of Zionist attitudes toward manual labor that had often been expressed in the
Selbstwehr:

> It is misguided and mistaken ambition on the part of Jewish parents and
> a fallacy to believe that those who are most intelligent will necessarily
> have it better later in life. Aside from time and money, which are often
> lost in pointless wrestling with Aryan competition, the effort is for
> naught! Social prestige—ah, well. At best, it helps one get a rich
> father-in-law, but it does not help one achieve inner satisfaction.[24]

Kafka's artisan-ideology of "hammer-blows" versus "scribbling" displays the inflated vocabulary of petit-bourgeois political parties, such
as the Christian Socialists and the Young Czechs, who had found a
constituency among artisans whose social status had fallen as Central
Europe modernized. Moreover, the opposition between, on the one
hand, "useful" craft, and on the other, "parasitic" Jewish capital,

"Jewish pseudo-intelligence," and so forth, was already a common theme in the demagogic speeches by Georg von Schönerer and Karl Lueger. *

The desire to work the land also informed the bucolic romanticism of Kafka's favorite sister Ottla. Kafka defended Ottla's farmwork against their father's bitter opposition: Hermann Kafka viewed this reversal of the usual Jewish demographic pattern (from the country to the city) as the epitome of "abnormality." In Kafka's view, this return route had to exist, since it offered an escape from the final phase of the misguided urbanization process. As Kafka chastized himself in a letter of 1919: "You are not a peasant whose land feeds his children, you are not even a businessman . . . but (probably a reject of the European professional class) a civil servant" (L 218). Even his earliest writings contain a yearning for rustic life. In the fall of 1902, for example, he wrote to his high-school friend Oskar Pollak, "Have you noticed how rich, heavy soil crumbles under too delicate fingers, how solemnly it crumbles?" (L 5). And in 1916 he believed he had suc-cessfully made the transition to the country: "Over the years I have secretly changed, without realizing it, from a city-dweller into a countryman, or something very like it" (F 527). After the war, while working with Ottla on her brother-in-law Karl Hermann's farm, Kafka even considered becoming a potato farmer. Hermann Kafka had finally, grudgingly, permitted his Zionist daughter to move to the country, the wartime shortages of supplies perhaps having reconciled him to the idea of farming. Ottla had opted for a rural existence because of her yearning, as her brother put it, for the " 'estate' which you have longed to possess for so long, the firm ground, the ancient holding, the clear air, freedom" (O 46). Like many Zionist concep-tions, this one originated in the line of argument used by the pan-German nationalists, whose Country Days, sponsored by the As-sociation of Farmers from the East Mark, drew sustenance in part from a polemic against Jews as "pale children from the big-city air." At these country festivals one could hear pronouncements like the following:

---

* Two prominent anti-Semitic Austrian politicians around the turn of the century: Schönerer was a member of the Austrian Reichstag until 1888, Lueger was mayor of Vienna until his death in 1910.—Ed.

You have to be a farmer yourself if you want to understand the indescrib-
able love of the soil that was worked by our ancestors. . . . The plea-
sures of watching our seeds blossom and flourish, or a tree you have
planted yourself . . . in short, the natural life that for German farmers
like us has in fact become vitally necessary, that makes us forget the
hard labor and the difficulties, and binds us with a thousand ties to our
property. . . . [25]

The purest expression of the Jewish attempt to escape anti-Semitic
stereotypes through work is Kafka's program for "The Brotherhood of
Poor Workers" (1918). It is odd that this text, which is implicitly
based on the model of Jewish-Palestinian kibbutzes ("maximum wage:
bread, water, dates"), has received so little notice.

To get one's living only by working for it. Not to shrink from any work
that one's strength suffices to perform without damaging one's health.
Either to choose the work oneself or, in the event of this not being
possible, to fall in with the arrangements made by the Labor Council,
which is responsible to the Government.
    To work for no wages other than what is necessary to support life (to
be defined in detail according to the various districts) for two days.
    Life to be of the utmost moderation. To eat only what is absolutely
necessary, for instance as a minimum wage, which is in a certain sense
also a maximum wage: bread, water, dates. . . . Each job taken on to
be completed, in all circumstances, except for grave reasons of health.
RIGHTS: . . . Working life as a matter of conscience and a matter of
faith in one's fellow men. (DF 104)

One senses here the importance to Kafka of physical activity—
strenuous physical labor as a cathartic means of changing oneself—
including one's body. Kafka's physical sufferings, his unlimited
mistrust of the body, and his hypochondriacal tendencies are well
known. It seems at least conceivable that they, too, as a kind of
masked neurosis, point toward the syndrome of Jewish self-hatred.
The standard arsenal of racial anti-Semitism included invectives
against "repellent" Jewish physical characteristics, such as bowed legs
and a weak chest. The "humorous" satirical weeklies of the time extracted their dreary jokes from these caricatures of Jews: of Oriental
physiognomies twisted and distorted into European dress. Karl Kraus

writes in his anti-Semitic "Crown for Zion" (1898) about "that vulgar anti-Semitism that raged with even greater force against the hooked nose-bone," noting that "the Jewish type, due to particular physical stigmata, has attracted the ridicule of utterly stupid people."

Another factor should also be kept in mind: at the time, the ideology of physical fitness was closely linked with the concept of nation. Having first emerged in Germany during the nineteenth century, the concept received almost classic expression in the Czech *Risorgimento*. To the surprise of "German Austria," the Czechs had managed within half a century to transform their fragmented, agrarian, petit-bourgeois society into a "nation" (*Volk*), complete with bourgeoisie and intelligentsia, capitalism, socialism, and bureaucracy. Bound together by a sense of national identity, this *Volk* seemed to enjoy great social harmony. Its "unity" was symbolized most clearly by the extremely effective, propagandistic forms of paramilitary mass athletics, which enabled it to present itself in a physically fit, muscular form. Although the Zionist milieu of Prague had excellent opportunities to observe this situation, it resolutely ignored the means by which the Czechs achieved their ostentatious "social harmony": the creation of a mythic archenemy, the legend of eternal conflict between Slav and German. For this reason the newly formed Czech society was no more "natural" than the inherited, ostensibly "unnatural" hybrid creature embodied in the German-speaking, German-Jewish Austrian society.

The Czech gymnastics association Sokol, conceived in the 1860s by the art historian Tyrs, preached an ideology of self-discipline for the sake of community, stressing the link between gymnastics and morality. It assigned each individual gymnast a place in the historical struggle for the future nation, and extolled the vitality of the "top-level achievement" or "deed" (*Spitzentat*). Darwin's theory of natural selection, now politicized, formed the basis of the Sokol ideology, which declared a mythical "totality of the people" as the most sacred authority: "What an entire people does not know, no one knows! What the people could not achieve, no one achieved! What did not occur through [the will of] the people, did not occur at all!"[26]

It is not difficult to recognize a protofascist model in the paramilitary elite troupe of a petit-bourgeois nation. Through the Sokol movement and its impressive mass marches, the Hapsburg monarchy displayed the trappings of political fulfillment, and thereby provided exemplary instances of its promise for the future. The large 1912 Sokol Congress in Prague, attended by groups from all the individual Bohemian lands, deeply impressed the *Selbstwehr* circle, and its echo can be heard even in some of Kafka's texts, such as the following excerpt from "The Great Wall of China":

> The desire once more to labor on the wall of the nation became irresistible. They set off earlier than they needed; half the village accompanied them for long distances. Groups of people with banners and streamers waving were on all the roads; never before had they seen how great and rich and beautiful and worthy of love their country was. Every fellow countryman was a brother for whom one was building a wall of protection, and who would return lifelong thanks for it with all he had and did. Unity! Unity! Shoulder to shoulder, a ring of brothers, a current of blood no longer confined within the narrow circulation of one body, but sweetly rolling and yet ever returning. . . . (CS 238)

One can hardly think of a better allegory for the ideology of nationalism with its quintessential belief that "true" life is possible only for the individual who is fully integrated into the mediating circle of the larger community. Late in his life Kafka would admire an example of the "folk" individual up close, Ottla's gentile husband, a proud Sokol gymnast, of whom Kafka wrote: "He takes pleasure in his vocation; he lives among his own people, is cheerful and healthy, essentially (the incidentals do not matter) is rightly content with himself, content with his large circle, rightly (there is no other word for it, just the way a tree rightly stands upon its own ground)" (O 45). Earlier, in 1913, Kafka had reflected on the "tremendous advantage of the Christians who always have and enjoy such feelings of closeness in general intercourse, for instance a Christian Czech among Christian Czechs" (D 222).

Community, intimacy, athletics: for these things one needed a body other than the "typically Jewish" one. In 1911 Kafka described his body as "a major obstacle to my progress. . . . Nothing can be accomplished with such a body" (D 124). In a literary sketch of 1920, a figure appears who feels excluded from an outdoor community event, in part because of his poor physique:

He contemplated the gala, which was not really a gala at all, but still, one could call it so. He naturally had a great desire to join in, indeed he longed to do so, but he could not conceal from himself that he was excluded from it, it was impossible for him to fit in there, it would have required such a great deal of preparation that not only this Sunday, but many years and he himself would have passed away in making it, and even if time could have come to a standstill here, it still would have been impossible to arrive at any other result: his whole origin, upbringing, and physique would have had to be different. (DF 380)

Kafka passionately sought to compensate for his physique in many ways. From 1908 on, following a bodybuilding program developed by the Danish gymnastics teacher J. P. Müller, he did calisthenics in front of an open window, and also recommended this "Müller-ing" to Felice. Long before the outbreak of his illness, he visited homeopathic sanatoriums in Germany and Switzerland where people played ball, sang, and did gymnastics in the nude. In addition to working as a gardener in the spring of 1913, he swam, rode horseback, and rowed—out of a desire "to cure my neurasthenia through my work" (D 219). And shortly before his death he wrote to Ottla from Berlin: "If there is a moving men's school where everybody can be turned into a mover, I would enter it with passionate eagerness" (O 82).

Another link in the chain of programs to liberate himself through work, athletics, and a physically improved body is Kafka's vegetarianism, which he learned about from an obscure German-Bohemian natural health practitioner. Consistent with his radicalism in all aspects of life, Kafka for a time elevated vegetarianism to the level of an artistic ritual built upon an edifice of morality and guilt.[27] In doing so, he was fully aware that his homeopathy rested on a problematic psychological foundation. As he wrote to Ottla: "It is a highly sensitive and reliable feeling to sense in vegetarianism . . . something isolating, something akin to madness. Only, with frightful superficiality, people forget that vegetarianism is a wholly innocent phenomenon, a minor concomitant produced by deeper reasons" (O 44–45).

Had he been more naïve, he would have found a niche in one of the Jewish nationalist gymnastics clubs formed after 1900 with heroic names such as *Makkabi*, where the racist jargon of the *Turnwarte*

(Gymnast Guards) was translated into a Zionist appeal: We must, they said,

> get rid of our heavy stress on intellectual achievements . . . and our
> excessive nervousness, a heritage of the ghetto. . . . In our own inter-
> ests and those of our people, we need harmoniously balanced personal-
> ities. We spend all too much time debating, and not nearly enough in
> play and gymnastics. . . . What makes a man a man is not his mouth,
> nor his mind, nor yet his morals, but discipline . . . what we need is
> manliness.[28]

But Kafka was not the kind of Zionist the Jewish nationalist ideo-
logues wanted, not even at the time of the First World War, which
some biographers have characterized as his "Zionist phase."[29] What
linked him with the movement—his pessimistic interpretation of the
fate of Jewish assimilation, his understanding of Jewish urbanization
as a process of alienation—were but starting-points of his self-
criticism. The *Selbstwehr* sadly proclaimed the demise of a "magnificent, robust, simple, diligent agrarian Jewishness."[30] Kafka too saw
Judaism "buried under the noise of the city and the business world,
under the jumbled pile of conversations and ideas that have besieged
one over the course of many years."[31] He adopted the Zionist attitude
of political masochism—"Around us anti-Semitism increases, but
that is all to the good"—and distrusted social democracy, which, as
Karl Kraus said, "made everything—even noses—equal." To Janouch
Kafka remarked, "I believe that anti-Semitism will also seize hold of
the masses" (J 174). More radically than any Zionist he insisted on
the relationship between Jewish collectivity and familial, individual
neurosis:

> Yesterday it occurred to me that I did not always love my mother as she
> deserved and as I could, only because the German language prevented
> it. The Jewish mother is no "Mutter," to call her "Mutter" makes her a
> little comic. . . . We give a Jewish woman the name of a German
> mother, but forget the contradiction that sinks into the emotions so
> much the more heavily, "Mutter" is peculiarly German for the Jew, it
> unconsciously contains, together with the Christian splendor Christian
> coldness also, the Jewish woman who is called "Mutter" therefore be-

comes not only comic but strange. . . . I believe that it is only the
memories of the ghetto that still preserve the Jewish family, for the word
"Vater" too is far from meaning the Jewish father. (D 88)

And yet, unlike his friends Felix Weltsch, Max Brod, and Hugo
Bergmann, who believed they had found what they were seeking in a
Jewish national state, he achieved no leap into a "new life." During
the war Robert Weltsch noted that

young Jews, brothers and sisters, extend a hand to one another. A new,
strong spiritual community is visible on the horizon, a community that
was forged in the shadow of a larger-than-life idea, and sealed with an
oath of loyalty. Jewish youth is once again demanding a genuine, unified, pure life.[32]

Although Kafka admired the Zionist plan, he also felt "nauseated by
it" (F 423). Did it nauseate him because, as "a completely antisocial
man" (F 423), he disliked having to take part in the nationalist and
racial discussions of narrow-minded Zionist coteries? "I [am] as if
made of wood, a clothesrack pushed into the middle of the room," he
wrote of himself at a Zionist gathering (D 332). He was a Zionist
insofar as he felt a strong bond, even a blood brotherhood, with Eastern European Jewry; and according to reports of his later life, this
feeling of kinship became increasingly evident over time. But unlike
his friend Max Brod, Kafka was unable to draw nationalist conclusions from this feeling. On the occasion of his sister Ottla's mixed
marriage, he invoked the racially nationalist principle of ethnocul-
tural identity, and lamented "a loss of Jewishness and . . . your losing
Jewishness for yourself and the future" (O 38). Yet at the same time,
he was pleased by any successful escape from Jewish neurosis, and
therefore legitimized even Ottla's conscious Czech assimilation:

if you never forget the responsibility of such a difficult action, if you
remain aware that you are stepping out of line as confidently, as, say,
David [Ottla's fiancé] out of the army, and if in spite of this awareness
you keep believing that you have the strength to carry the thing to a
good end, then you will have done more than if—to end with a poor
joke—if you had married ten Jews. (O 37)

For Kafka there was no such good end. About his attempts to liberate himself, he noted in 1922 that he "despaired boundlessly" (D 406), that his life up until then had been "merely marking time," and that his chosen escape methods—including "the study of German literature, anti-Zionism, Zionism, Hebrew, gardening, carpentering, writing"—had been of no use (D 404). In the end, the genius of metaphor experienced his fatal physical illness as "a mental illness overflowing its banks." What remained behind were the traces of his efforts to free himself through "literature," the status and mesmerizing quality of which resist every deterministic form of sociological and sociohistorical analysis—including the present essay.

Translated by Elizabeth Bredeck

WHAT IS A MINOR LITERATURE?*

Gilles Deleuze and Félix Guattari

INTRODUCTORY NOTE

THE PROBLEM OF EXPRESSION is staked out by Kafka not in an abstract and universal fashion but in relation to those literatures that are considered minor, for example, the Jewish literature of Warsaw and Prague. A minor literature doesn't come from a minor language; it is rather that which a minority constructs within a major language. But the first characteristic of minor literature in any case is that in it language is affected with a high coefficient of deterritorialization.† In

---

* The following essay, taken from Deleuze and Guattari's book *Kafka: Toward a Minor Literature*, is based on Kafka's diary entry for December 25, 1911, which concerns "small," or "minor," literatures. The background for Kafka's reflections is the Yiddish theater troupe of Yitzhak Löwy, whose performances in Prague coffee-houses had led him to question the difference between "minor" literatures in Yiddish and Czech and a "major" literary tradition such as in German. Because of the centrality of this diary entry for their discussion, which Deleuze and Guattari cite only in passing, the full passage has been provided in the Appendix. (See also the essay by Giuliano Baioni in this volume.)—ED.
†A key term in Deleuze and Guattari's notion of a minor literature, "deterritorialization" refers to the movement of desire away from fixed categories of perception, representation, and meaning. Opposed to Freud's definition of Oedipal desire, it is described as "wandering," "nomadic," subversive of traditional authority, etc.—ED.

this sense, Kafka marks the impasse that bars access to writing for the Jews of Prague and turns their literature into something impossible—the impossibility of not writing, the impossibility of writing in German, the impossibility of writing otherwise.[1] The impossibility of not writing because national consciousness, uncertain or oppressed, necessarily exists by means of literature ("The literary struggle has its real justification at the highest possible levels"). The impossibility of writing other than in German is for the Prague Jews the feeling of an irreducible distance from their primitive Czech territoriality. And the impossibility of writing in German is the deterritorialization of the German population itself, an oppressive minority that speaks a language cut off from the masses, like a "paper language" or an artificial language; this is all the more true for the Jews who are simultaneously a part of this minority and excluded from it, like "gypsies who have stolen a German child from its crib." In short, Prague German is a deterritorialized language, appropriate for strange and minor uses. (This can be compared in another context to what blacks in America today are able to do with the English language.)

The second characteristic of minor literatures is that everything in them is political. In major literatures, by contrast, the individual concern (familial, marital, and so on) joins with other no less individual concerns, the social milieu serving as a mere environment or a background; this is so much the case that none of these Oedipal intrigues are specifically indispensable or absolutely necessary but all become as one in a large space. Minor literature is completely different; its cramped space forces each individual intrigue to connect immediately to politics. The individual concern thus becomes all the more necessary, indispensable, magnified, because a whole other story is vibrating within it. In this way, the family triangle connects to other triangles—commercial, economic, bureaucratic, juridical—that determine its values. When Kafka indicates that one of the goals of a minor literature is the "purification of the conflict that opposes father and son and the possibility of discussing that conflict," it isn't a question of an Oedipal phantasm but of a political program. "Even though something is often thought through calmly, one still does not reach the boundary where it connects up with similar things, one reaches the boundary soonest in politics, indeed, one even strives to see it before it is there, and often sees this limiting boundary everywhere. . . . What in great literature goes on down below, constituting a not indispensable cellar of the structure, here takes place in the full light of day, what is there a matter of passing interest for a few, here absorbs everyone no less than as a matter of life and death" (D 150).

The third characteristic of minor literature is that in it everything takes on a collective value. Indeed, precisely because talent isn't abundant in a minor literature, there are no possibilities for an individuated enunciation that would belong to this or that "master" and that could be separated from a collective enunciation. Indeed, scarcity of talent is in fact beneficial and allows the conception of something other than a literature of masters; what each author says individually already constitutes a common action, and what he or she says or does is necessarily political, even if others aren't in agreement. The political domain has contaminated every statement (énoncé). But above all else, because collective or national consciousness is "often inactive in external life and always in the process of breakdown," literature finds itself positively charged with the role and function of collective, and even revolutionary, enunciation. It is literature that produces an active solidarity in spite of skepticism; and if the writer is in the margins or completely outside his or her fragile community, this situation allows the writer all the more the possibility to express another possible community and to forge the means for another consciousness and another sensibility; just as the dog of "Investigations of a Dog" calls out in his solitude to *another science*. The literary machine thus becomes the relay for a revolutionary machine-to-come, not at all for ideological reasons but because the literary machine alone is determined to fill the conditions of a collective enunciation that is lacking elsewhere in this milieu: *literature is the people's concern.*[2] It is certainly in these terms that Kafka sees the problem. The message doesn't refer back to an enunciating subject who would be its cause, no more than to a subject of the statement (*sujet d'énoncé*) who would be its effect. Undoubtedly, for a while, Kafka thought according to these traditional categories of the two subjects, the author and the hero, the narrator and the character, the dreamer and the one dreamed of.[3] But he will quickly reject the role of the narrator, just as he will refuse an author's or master's literature, despite his admiration for Goethe. Josephine the mouse renounces

the individual act of singing in order to melt into the collective enunciation of "the immense crowd of the heros of [her] people." A movement from the individuated animal to the pack or to a collective
multiplicity—seven canine musicians. In "Investigations of a Dog,"
the expressions of the solitary researcher tend toward the assemblage
(*agencement*) of a collective enunciation of the canine species even if
this collectivity is no longer or not yet given. There isn't a subject;
there are only collective assemblages of enunciation, and literature expresses these acts insofar as they're not imposed from without and
insofar as they exist only as diabolical powers to come or revolutionary forces to be constructed. Kafka's solitude opens him up to everything going on in history today. The letter K no longer designates a
narrator or a character but an assemblage that becomes all the more
machinelike, an agent that becomes all the more collective because
an individual is locked into it in his or her solitude (it is only in
connection to a subject that something individual would be separable
from the collective and would lead its own life).

The three characteristics of minor literature are the deterritorialization of language, the connection of the individual to a political
immediacy, and the collective assemblage of enunciation. We might
as well say that *minor* no longer designates specific literatures but the
revolutionary conditions for every literature within the heart of what
is called great (or established) literature. Even he who has the misfortune of being born in the country of a great literature must write in
its language, just as a Czech Jew writes in German, or an Uzbek writes
in Russian. Writing like a dog digging a hole, a rat digging its burrow.
And to do that, finding his own point of underdevelopment, his own
patois, his own third world, his own desert. There has been much
discussion of the questions "What is a marginal literature?" and
"What is a popular literature, a proletarian literature?" The criteria
are obviously difficult to establish if one doesn't start with a more
objective concept—that of minor literature. Only the possibility of
setting up a minor practice of major language from within allows one
to define popular literature, marginal literature, and so on.[4] Only in
this way can literature really become a collective machine of expression and really be able to treat and develop its contents. Kafka emphatically declares that a minor literature is much more able to work
over its material.[5] Why this machine of expression, and what is it?

We know that it exists in a relation of multiple deterritorializations
with language; it is the situation of the Jews who have dropped the
Czech language at the same time as the rural environment, but it is
also the situation of the German language as a "paper language."
Well, one can go even farther; one can push this movement of deterritorialization of expression even farther. But there are only two ways
to do this. One way is to artificially enrich this German, to swell it
up through all the resources of symbolism, of oneirism, of esoteric
sense, of a hidden signifier. This is the approach of the Prague school,
Gustav Meyrink and many others, including Max Brod.[6] But this attempt implies a desperate attempt at symbolic reterritorialization,
based in archetypes, Kabbala, and alchemy, that accentuates its break
from the people and will find its political result only in Zionism and
such things as the "dream of Zion." Kafka will quickly choose the
other way, or, rather, he will invent another way. He will opt for the
German language of Prague as it is and in its very poverty, always go
farther in the direction of deterritorialization, to the point of sobriety. Since the language is arid, make it vibrate with a new intensity.
Oppose a purely intensive usage of language to all symbolic or even
significant or simply signifying usages of it. Arrive at a perfect and
unformed expression, a materially intense expression. (For these two
possible paths, couldn't we find the same alternatives, under other
conditions, in Joyce and Beckett? As Irishmen, both of them live
within the genial conditions of a minor literature. That is the glory
of this sort of minor literature—to be the revolutionary force for all
literature. The utilization of English and of every language in Joyce.
The utilization of English and French in Beckett. But the former
never stops operating by exhilaration and overdetermination and
brings about all sorts of worldwide reterritorializations. The other
proceeds by dryness and sobriety, a willed poverty, pushing deterritorialization to such an extreme that nothing remains but intensities.)

How many people today live in a language that is not their own?
Or no longer, or not yet, even know their own and know poorly the
major language that they are forced to serve? This is the problem of
immigrants, and especially of their children, the problem of minori-
ties, the problem of a minor literature, but also a problem for all of
us: how to tear a minor literature away from its own language, allowing it to challenge the language and making it follow a sober revolu-

tionary path? How to become a nomad and an immigrant and a gypsy in relation to one's own language? Kafka answers: Steal the baby from its crib, walk the tightrope.

Rich or poor, each language always implies a deterritorialization of the mouth, the tongue, and the teeth. The mouth, tongue, and teeth find their primitive territoriality in food. In giving themselves over to the articulation of sounds, the mouth, tongue, and teeth deterritorialize. Thus, there is a certain disjunction between eating and speaking, and even more, despite all appearances, between eating and writing. Undoubtedly, one can write while eating more easily than one can speak while eating, but writing goes further in transforming words into things capable of competing with food. Disjunction between content and expression. To speak, and above all to write, is to fast. Kafka manifests a permanent obsession with food, and with that form of food par excellence, in other words, the animal or meat—an obsession with the mouth and with teeth and with large, unhealthy, or gold-capped teeth.[7] This is one of Kafka's main problems with Felice. Fasting is also a constant theme in Kafka's writings. His writings are a long history of fasts. The Hunger Artist, surveyed by butchers, ends his career next to beasts who eat their meat raw, placing the visitors before an irritating alternative. The dogs try to take over the mouth of the investigating hound by filling it with food so that he'll stop asking questions, and there too there is an irritating alternative: "They would have done better to drive me away and refuse to listen to my questions. No, they did not want to do that; they did not indeed want to listen to my questions, but it was because I asked these questions that they did not want to drive me away." The investigating hound oscillates between two sciences, that of food—a science of the Earth and of the bent head ("Whence does the Earth procure this food?")—and that of music which is a science of the air and of the straightened head, as the seven musical dogs of the beginning and the singing dog of the end well demonstrate. But between the two there is something in common, since food can come from high up and the science of food can only develop through fasting, just as the music is strangely silent.

Ordinarily, in fact, language compensates for its deterritorialization by a reterritorialization in sense. Ceasing to be the organ of one of the senses, it becomes an instrument of Sense. And it is sense, as a correct sense, that presides over the designation of sounds (the thing or the state of things that the word designates) and, as figurative sense, over the affectation of images and metaphors (those other things that words designate under certain situations or conditions). Thus, there is not only a spiritual reterritorialization of sense, but also a physical one. Similarly, language exists only through the distinction and the complementarity of a subject of enunciation, who is in connection with sense, and a subject of the statement, who is in connection, directly or metaphorically, with the designated thing. This sort of ordinary use of language can be called extensive or representative—the reterritorializing function of language (thus, the singing dog at the end of the "Investigations" forces the hero to abandon his fast, a sort of re-Oedipalization).

Now something happens: the situation of the German language in Czechoslovakia, as a fluid language intermixed with Czech and Yiddish, will allow Kafka the possibility of invention. Since things are as they are ("it is as it is, it is as it is," a formula dear to Kafka, marker of a state of facts), he will abandon sense, render it no more than implicit; he will retain only the skeleton of sense, or a paper cutout.

Since articulated sound was a deterritorialized noise but one that will be reterritorialized in sense, it is now sound itself that will be deterritorialized irrevocably, absolutely. The sound or the word that traverses this new deterritorialization no longer belongs to a language of sense, even though it derives from it, nor is it an organized music or song, even though it might appear to be. We noted Gregor's warbling and the ways it blurred words, the whistling of the mouse, the cough of the ape, the pianist who doesn't play, the singer who doesn't sing and gives birth to her song out of her nonsinging, the musical dogs who are musicians in the very depths of their bodies since they don't emit any music. Everywhere, organized music is traversed by a line of abolition—just as a language of sense is traversed by a line of escape—in order to liberate a living and expressive material that speaks for itself and has no need of being put into a form.[8] This language torn from sense, conquering sense, bringing about an active neutralization of sense, no longer finds its value in anything but an accenting of the word, an inflection: "I live only here or there in a small word in whose vowel. . . . I lose my useless head for a moment. The first and last letters are the beginning and end of my fishlike emotion (D 51). Children are well skilled in the exercise of repeating a word, the sense of which is only vaguely felt, in order to make it vibrate around itself (at the beginning of *The Castle*, the schoolchildren are speaking so fast that one cannot understand what they are saying). Kafka tells how, as a child, he repeated one of his father's expressions in order to make it take flight on a line of non-sense: "end of the month, end of the month."[9] The proper name, which has no sense in itself, is particularly propitious for this sort of exercise. *Milena*, with an accent on the *i*, begins by evoking "a Greek or a Roman gone astray in Bohemia, violated by Czech, cheated of its accent," and then, by a more delicate approximation, it evokes "a woman whom one carries in one's arms out of the world, out of the fire," the accent marking here an always possible fall or, on the contrary, "the lucky leap which you yourself make with your burden" (M 58).[10]

It seems to us that there is a certain difference, even if relative and highly nuanced, between the two evocations of the name Milena: one still attaches itself to an extensive, figurative scene of the phantasmic sort; the second is already much more intensive, marking a fall or a leap as a threshold of intensity contained within the name itself. In fact, we have here what happens when sense is actively neutralized. As Wagenbach says, "The word is master; it directly gives birth to the image." But how can we define this procedure? Of sense there remains only enough to direct the lines of escape. There is no longer a designation of something by means of a proper name, nor an assignation of metaphors by means of a figurative sense. But *like* images, the thing no longer forms anything but a sequence of intensive states, a ladder or a circuit for intensities that one can make race around in one sense or another, from high to low, or from low to high. The image is this very race itself; it has become becoming—the becoming-dog of the man and the becoming-man of the dog, the becoming-ape or the becoming-beetle of the man and vice versa. We are no longer in the situation of an ordinary, rich language where the word *dog*, for example, would directly designate an animal and would apply metaphorically to other things (so that one could say "like a dog").[11] *Diaries*, 1921: "Metaphors are one among many things which make me despair of writing" (D 398). Kafka deliberately kills all metaphor, all symbolism, all signification, no less than all designation. Metamorphosis is the contrary of metaphor. There is no longer any proper sense or figurative sense, but only a distribution of states that is part of the range of the word. The thing and other things are no longer anything but intensities overrun by deterritorialized sound or words that are following their line of escape. It is no longer a question of a resemblance between the comportment of an animal and that of a man; it is even less a question of a simple wordplay. There is no longer man or animal, since each deterritorializes the other, in a conjunction of flux, in a continuum of reversible intensities. Instead, it is now a question of a becoming that includes the maximum of difference as a difference of intensity, the crossing of a barrier, a rising or a falling, a bending or an erecting, an accent on the word. The animal does not speak "like" a man but pulls from the language tonalities lacking in signification; the words themselves are not "like" the animals but in their own way climb about, bark, and roam around, being properly linguistic dogs, insects, or mice.[12] To make the sequences vibrate, to open the word onto unexpected internal intensities—in short, an asignifying *intensive utilization* of language. Furthermore, there is no longer a subject of the enunciation, nor a subject of the statement. It is no longer the subject of the statement who is a dog, with the subject of the enunciation remaining "like" a man; it is no longer the subject of enunciation who is "like" a beetle, the subject of the statement remaining a man. Rather, there is a circuit of states that forms a mutual becoming, in the heart of a necessarily multiple or collective assemblage.

How does the situation of the German language in Prague—a withered vocabulary, an incorrect syntax—contribute to such a utilization? Generally, we might call the linguistic elements, however varied they may be, that express the "internal tensions of a language" *intensives* or *tensors*. It is in this sense that the linguist Vidal Sephiha terms intensive "any linguistic tool that allows a move toward the limit of a notion or a surpassing of it," marking a movement of language toward its extremes, toward a reversible beyond or before.[13] Sephiha shows well the variety of such elements which can be all sorts of master-words, verbs, or prepositions that assume all sorts of senses; prenominal or purely intensive verbs as in Hebrew; conjunctions, exclamations, adverbs; and *terms that connote pain.*[14] One could equally cite the accents that are interior to words, their discordant function. And it would seem that the language of a minor literature particularly develops these tensors or these intensives. In the lovely pages where he analyzes the Prague German that was influenced by Czech, Wagenbach cites as the characteristics of this form of German the incorrect use of prepositions; the abuse of the pronominal; the employment of malleable verbs (such as *geben,* which is used for the series "put," "sit," "place," "take away" and which thereby becomes intensive); the multiplication and succession of adverbs; the use of pain-filled connotations; the importance of the accent as a tension internal to the word; and the distribution of consonants and vowels as part of an internal discordance. Wagenbach insists on this point: all these marks of the poverty of a language show up in Kafka but have been taken over by a creative utilization for the purposes of a new sobriety, a new expressivity, a new flexibility, a new intensity.[15] "Almost every word I write jars up against the next, I hear the consonants rub leadenly against each other and the vowels sing an accompaniment like Negroes in a minstrel show" (D 29). *Language stops being representative in order to now move toward its extremities or its limits.* The connotation of pain accompanies this metamorphosis, as in the words that become a painful warbling with Gregor, or in Franz's cry "single and irrevocable." Think about the utilization of French as a spoken language in the films of Godard. There too is an accumulation of stereotypical adverbs and conjunctions that form the base of all the phrases—a strange poverty that makes French a minor language within French; a creative process that directly links the word to the image; a technique that surges up at the end of sequences in connection with the intensity of the limit "that's enough, enough, he's had enough," and a generalized intensification, coinciding with a panning shot where the camera pivots and sweeps around without leaving the spot, making the image vibrate.

Perhaps the comparative study of images would be less interesting than the study of the functions of language that can work in the same group across different languages—bilingualism or even multilingualism. Because the study of the functions in distinct languages alone can account for social factors, relations of force, diverse centers of power, it escapes from the "informational" myth in order to evaluate the hierarchic and imperative system of language as a transmission of orders, an exercise of power or of resistance to this exercise. Using the research of Ferguson and Gumperz, Henri Gobard has proposed a tetralinguistic model: vernacular, maternal, or territorial language, used in rural communities or rural in its origins; a vehicular, urban, governmental, even worldwide language, a language of businesses, commercial exchange, bureaucratic transmission, and so on, a language of the first sort of deterritorialization; referential language, language of sense and of culture, entailing a cultural reterritorialization; mythic language, on the horizon of cultures, caught up in a spiritual or religious reterritorialization. The spatiotemporal categories of these languages differ sharply: vernacular language is *here*; vehicular language is *everywhere*; referential language is *over there*; mythic language is *beyond*. But above all else, the distribution of these languages varies from one group to the next and, in a single group, from one epoch to the next (for a long time in Europe, Latin was a vehicular language before becoming referential, then mythic; English has become the worldwide vehicular language for today's world).[16] What can be said in one language cannot be said in another, and the totality of what can and can't be said varies necessarily with each language and with the connections between these languages.[17] Moreover, all these factors can have ambiguous edges, changing borders, that differ for this or that material. One language can fill a certain function for one material and another function for another material. Each function of a language divides up in turn and carries with it multiple centers of power. A blur of languages, and not at all a system of languages. We can understand the indignation of integrationists who cry when Mass is said in French, since Latin is being robbed of its mythic function. But the classicists are even more behind the times and cry because Latin has even been robbed of its referential cultural function. They express regret in this way for the religious or educational forms of powers that this language exercised and that have now been replaced by other forms. There are even more serious examples that cross over between groups. The revival of regionalisms, with a reterritorialization through dialect or patois, a vernacular language— how does that serve a worldwide or transnational technocracy? How can that contribute to revolutionary movements, since they are also filled with archaisms that they are trying to impart a contemporary sense to? From Servan-Schreiber to the Breton bard to the Canadian singer. And that's not really how the borders divide up, since the Canadian singer can also bring about the most reactionary, the most

Oedipal of reterritorializations, oh mama, oh my native land, my cabin, olé, olé. We would call this a blur, a mixed-up history, a political situation, but linguists don't know about this, don't want to know about this, since, as linguists, they are "apolitical," pure scientists. Even Chomsky compensated for his scientific apoliticism only by his courageous struggle against the war in Vietnam.

Let's return to the situation in the Hapsburg empire. The breakdown and fall of the empire increases the crisis, accentuates everywhere movements of deterritorialization, and invites all sorts of complex reterritorializations—archaic, mythic, or symbolist. At random, we can cite the following among Kafka's contemporaries: Einstein and his deterritorialization of the representation of the universe (Einstein teaches in Prague, and the physicist Philipp Frank gives conferences there with Kafka in attendance); the Austrian dodecaphonists and their deterritorialization of musical representation (the cry that is Marie's death in *Wozzeck*, or Lulu's, or the echoed *si* that seems to us to follow a musical path similar in certain ways to what Kafka is doing); the expressionist cinema and its double movement of deterritorialization and reterritorialization of the image (Robert Wiener, who has Czech background; Fritz Lang, born in Vienna; Paul Wegener and his utilization of Prague themes). Of course, we should mention Viennese psychoanalysis and Prague School linguistics.[18] What is the specific situation of the Prague Jews in relation to the "four languages"? The vernacular language for these Jews who have come from a rural milieu is Czech, but the Czech language tends to be forgotten and repressed; as for Yiddish, it is often disdained or viewed with suspicion—it *frightens*, as Kafka tells us. German is the vehicular language of the towns, a bureaucratic language of the state, a commercial language of exchange (but English has already started to become indispensable for this purpose). The German language— but this time, Goethe's German—has a cultural and referential function (as does French to a lesser degree). As a mythic language, Hebrew is connected with the start of Zionism and still possesses the quality of an active dream. For each of these languages, we need to evaluate the degrees of territoriality, deterritorialization, and reterritorialization. Kafka's own situation: He is one of the few Jewish writers in Prague to understand and speak Czech (and this language will have a great importance in his relationship with Milena). German plays precisely the double role of vehicular and cultural language, with Goethe always on the horizon (Kafka also knows French, Italian, and probably a bit of English). He will not learn Hebrew until later. What is complicated is Kafka's relation to Yiddish; he sees it less as a sort of linguistic territoriality for the Jews than as a nomadic movement of deterritorialization that reworks the German language. What fascinates him in Yiddish is less a language of a religious community than that of a popular theater (he will become patron and impresario for the traveling theater of Yitzhak Löwy).[19] The manner in which Kafka, in a public meeting, presented Yiddish to a rather hostile Jewish bourgeois audience is completely remarkable: Yiddish is a language that frightens more than it invites disdain, "dread mingled with a certain fundamental distaste"; it is a language that is lacking a grammar, filled with vocables that are fleeting, mobilized, emigrating, and turned into nomads that interiorize "relations of force." It is a language that is grafted onto Middle-High German and that so reworks the German language from within that one cannot translate it into German without destroying it; one can understand Yiddish only by "feeling it" in the heart. In short, it is a language where minor utilizations will carry you away: "Then you will come to feel the true unity of Yiddish and so strongly that it will frighten you, yet it will no longer be fear of Yiddish but of yourselves. Enjoy this self-confidence as much as you can!"

Kafka does not opt for a reterritorialization through the Czech language. Nor toward a hypercultural usage of German with all sorts of oneiric or symbolic or mythic flights (even Hebrewifying ones), as was the case with the Prague School. Nor toward an oral, popular Yiddish. Instead, using the path that Yiddish opens up to him, he takes it in such a way as to convert it into a unique and solitary form of writing. Since Prague German is deterritorialized to several degrees, he will always take it farther, to a greater degree of intensity, but in the direction of a new sobriety, a new and unexpected modification, a pitiless rectification, a straightening of the head. Schizo politeness, a drunkenness caused by water.[20] He will make the German language take flight on a line of escape. He will feed himself on abstinence; he will tear out of Prague German all the qualities of underdevelopment that it has tried to hide; he will make it cry with an extremely sober and rigorous cry. He will pull from it the barking of the dog, the cough of the ape, and the bustling of the beetle. He will turn syntax into a cry that will embrace the rigid syntax of this dried-up German. He will push it toward a deterritorialization that will no longer be saved by culture or by myth, that will be an absolute deterritorialization, even if it is slow, sticky, coagulated. To bring language slowly and progressively to the desert. To use syntax in order to cry, to give a syntax to the cry.

There is nothing that is major or revolutionary except the minor. To hate all languages of masters. Kafka's fascination for servants and employees (the same thing in Proust in relation to servants, to their language). What interests him even more is the possibility of making of his own language—assuming that it is unique, that it is a major language or has been—a minor utilization. To be a sort of stranger *within* his own language; this is the situation of Kafka's Great Swimmer.[21] Even when it is unique, a language remains a mixture, a schizophrenic mélange, a Harlequin costume in which very different functions of language and distinct centers of power are played out, blurring what can be said and what can't be said; one function will be played off against the other, all the degrees of territoriality and relative deterritorialization will be played out. Even when major, a language is open to an intensive utilization that makes it take flight along creative lines of escape which, no matter how slowly, no matter how cautiously, can now form an absolute deterritorialization. All this inventiveness, not only lexically, since the lexical matters little, but sober syntactic invention, simply to write like a dog (but a dog can't write—exactly, exactly). It's what Artaud did with French—cries, gasps; what Céline did with French, following another line, one that was exclamatory to the highest degree. Céline's syntactic evolution went from *Journey to the End of the Night* to *Death on the Installment Plan*, then from *Death on the Installment Plan* to *Guignol's Band*. (After that, Céline had nothing more to talk about except his own misfortunes; in other words, he had no longer any desire to write, only the need to make money. And it always ends like that, language's lines of escape: silence, the interrupted, the interminable, or even worse. But until that point, what a crazy creation, what a writing machine! Céline was so applauded for *Journey* that he went even further in *Death on the Installment Plan* and then in the prodigious *Guignol's Band* where language is nothing more than intensities. He spoke with a kind of "minor music." Kafka, too, is a minor music, a different one, but always made up of deterritorialized sounds, a language that moves head over heels and away.) These are the true minor authors. An escape for language, for music, for writing. What we call pop—pop music, pop philosophy, pop writing—*Wörterflucht*. To make use of the polylingualism of one's own language, to make a minor or intensive use of it, to oppose the oppressed quality of this language to its oppressive quality, to find points of nonculture or underdevelopment, linguistic Third World zones by which a language can escape, an animal enters into things, an assemblage comes into play. How many styles or genres or literary movements, even very small ones, have only one single dream: to assume a major function in language, to offer themselves as a sort of state language, an official language (for example, psychoanalysis today, which would like to be a master of the signifier, of metaphor, of wordplay). Create the opposite dream: know how to create a becoming-minor. (Is there a hope for philosophy, which for a long time has been an official, referential genre? Let us profit from this moment in which antiphilosophy is trying to be a language of power.)

Translated by Dana Polan

ZIONISM, LITERATURE, AND THE YIDDISH THEATER

Giuliano Baioni

THE FIRST DOCUMENT revealing Kafka's interest in Judaism is the draft of a review he wrote of Max Brod's novel *The Jewesses* (1911). This short sketch, written in his diary on March 26 (D 45), would not seem important in itself if it did not reveal the extent of Kafka's disagreement with the Zionist position. An article by Leo Herrmann, published in May in the *Selbstwehr*, had reproached Brod for having represented the problem of assimilation only from a Jewish perspective. Since the novel lacked a portrayal of the Christian world, Herrmann maintained, the reader could not understand the reasons for the conflict between Christians and Jews that would justify the birth of Zionism.[1]

Kafka's judgment was quite different. Among the novel's weaknesses he does indicate the absence of an opposing character, but this is not so much a criticism of Brod as it is an anticipation of the objection that the reader can recognize the Jewish world only when it is opposed to Christianity.[2] In this sketch we find the first articulation of the stance that Kafka will maintain in his own writing all his life. For obvious reasons, the Zionists are interest in pointing out the contrast between Jews and Christians. But in his literary texts, Kafka depicts Judaism from within, as a completely autonomous world

95

which, precisely because of this autonomy, is in itself a paradigm for a universal human condition.

This totalizing vision of "the Jewish problem," as it was commonly referred to, is confirmed moreover by a passage from Kafka's first diary entries about the Lemberg actors, who from October 1911 to January 1912 gave a cycle of Yiddish theatrical performances in a café in the center of old Prague. This short but exceedingly important passage reveals the violent emotion he felt at his first encounter with a group of Eastern Jews on the evening of October 4, during a performance by the Lemberg actors.[3] The actors' unusual costumes and the surprising gestures accompanying their songs strike him, of course. But he is most astonished by the greeting of an actress who turns to the audience with a mother's affectionate warmth: "Some songs, the expression '*yiddishe kinderlach*,' some of this woman's acting (who on stage, because she is a Jew, draws us listeners to her because we are Jews, without any longing for or curiosity about Christians) made my cheeks tremble" (D 65).

It would be difficult to find a more revealing document of Kafka's state of mind in his encounter with the Eastern Jews. For the first time in his life he understands that being Jewish can be a perfectly natural fact. The violent and intense attraction he feels for this company of impoverished actors, forced to perform in a rather tawdry nightclub, despised and insulted not only by the waiters but also by the doorman (a brothel-owner and notorious pimp) for their frequent acting lapses and amateurishness on stage, can perhaps best be understood in conjunction with his unfinished review of Brod's novel. The actors represent for him the unbelievable, moving wonder of a Judaism whose identity does not depend on Christianity.

Before discussing Kafka's relation to the Yiddish theater, we must first consider how the Eastern Jews were viewed in Prague at the turn of the century. The official Zionist stance toward Eastern Judaism had been set for some years by Max Nordau, who, at the Fifth Zionist Congress in Basel, lectured on the "Problems of Jewish Physical, Spiritual, and Economic Advancement," in which he called for "precise anthropological, biological, economic, and intellectual statistics on the Jewish people"; this he thought to be a prerequisite for the work of rebuilding the nation.[4] The Western Jews, Nordau argued, had attained relative prosperity, improving their health and physical vigor to the point where they had even produced athletic champions. The Eastern Jews, however, debilitated by unspeakable poverty and the crude education inculcated from an early age by teachers of the Talmud, could present only miserable physical specimens—small, pale, emaciated—visible examples of the physical decadence of the race.[5]

It is important not to underestimate the influence of this viewpoint, which at the time was quite common in the Zionist press. It sparked numerous programs for Jewish physical regeneration, led to the founding of Jewish athletic associations and a youth movement,[6] and certainly stimulated Kafka's passion for rowing, swimming, and gymnastics.[7] The essential point, however, is that Nordau failed to consider the cultural tradition of the Eastern Jews. He presented them as a sorry mass of *luftmentshen,* people without any practical abilities who lived in the clouds, barely surviving from one day to the next.[8] Obviously this view, shared by the overwhelming majority of Western Jews, could not lead to an understanding of Yiddish folk culture. Even the intellectuals of the Jewish Enlightenment (*Haskalah*), who used the *Jargon** to spread the ideals of emancipation among the people, considered Yiddish to be a crude dialect devoid of literary dignity. Like numerous other languages, large segments of the Jewish population had adopted it as their primary language—to the exclusion of Hebrew, the language in which the sacred traditions of Israel are recorded. Moreover, it bore the marks of the many languages composing it, and thus, in their view, it was a humiliating reminder of misery in the exile (*galut*) and of ghetto obscurantism.

If the official Zionist position in 1901 equated the defense of Yiddish with the continuation of Jewish oppression, Martin Buber's cultural Zionism would soon profoundly recast these policies. However, the credit for the reevaluation of Yiddish does not go to Buber, who always supported Hebrew as the Jewish national language, although he did recognize in the flourishing Yiddish folk literature a sure sign of the *jüdische Renaissance.*[9] The true initiator of this reevaluation was Nathan Birnbaum, who with Buber exercised a significant influence on the Bar Kokhba, the Zionist student association in Prague.

---

*The term *Jargon* ("dialect") was often used pejoratively to refer to Yiddish. Kafka used the term, although without any overt negative connotations.—ED.

He also influenced Kafka, who, barely a month before writing his
own "Introductory Talk on the Yiddish Language" (see Appendix),
heard Birnbaum speak in Prague at a Zionist meeting.[10]

Known under the pen name of Mathias Archer, Birnbaum, who
coined the term "Zionism" and conceived of a Jewish state in Israel
before Herzl, had given up his career as a scholar of Judaism and become a passionate advocate of Eastern Jewry.[11] As early as 1897 he
had maintained that only the Ostjuden possessed a truly Jewish culture; the Jews of Western Europe, he believed, lacked all cultural
identity and were forced to ape the culture of the goyim.[12] Birnbaum
thus established a major distinction between the two strains of Judaism and, before Buber, attributed the evident lack of Jewish creativity
to the separation from nature brought about by life in the ghetto.[13]
However, his most original contribution to cultural Zionism, and to
Jewish culture in general, is certainly his defense of Yiddish folk literature. Martin Buber, it is true, had made Hasidism known in the
West, basing on it his mystical conception of a new developing Jewish
culture that would culminate in the future unity of Zion and Israel.
While remaining faithful to the idea of a Jewish Palestine, Birnbaum
reminded Buber and his disciples that this new Jewish culture—
which they projected into the future in the form of a utopian spiritual
revolution—already existed in Eastern Europe.[14]

According to Birnbaum, the first step of the Zionist cultural program was the acknowledgement of Jewish culture as it existed at that
time. He opposed Buber's celebration of the Maccabean heroes and
his invocation of an intellectual avant-garde's cultural revolution
(which, in any case, was ideologically compromised by the reactionary and racist views of the Jena publisher Eugen Diderich).[15] Instead,
he asserted, the Western Zionists should recognize the superior culture of the Ostjuden and revitalize their own Jewishness through direct contact with the millions of Eastern European Jews. In the
millennary history of the Diaspora, only they had managed to create,
with unparalleled energy and enthusiasm, a community based not on
religious dogma but on national folk values.[16] This extraordinary
unity was not the result of Hebrew, a language of the educated classes
which was only read and written, but of the reviled Yiddish dialect
which was alive with the exuberant vitality of the Jewish folk soul.
"Only under the aegis of this despised dialect of the galut," Birnbaum

concluded, "can the Jewish people develop its full autonomy and acquire that second, higher emancipation which is national emancipation."[17]

This new conception of Eastern Judaism—very close, as we shall see, to Kafka's—not only conflicted with Nordau's negative portrayal; it also proposed an interpretation of the Yiddish-speaking world that differed radically from those of Achad Haam and Martin Buber. Achad Haam rejected Yiddish on principle, believing that, as a product of the *galut*, it was foreign to the essential Jewish spirit. Martin Buber, though, drew on the mysticism of Hasidism for a messianic project in which Jewish culture would redeem the world. Yet both ignored the reality of a folk culture which, as Birnbaum pointed out, unified some four-fifths of all Jewry, linking together the Jews of Lemberg and New York, Odessa and London, Chicago and Czernowitz.[18] Admittedly, Yiddish was a non-Semitic language; even if it had been adopted during the *galut*, it nevertheless was a language spoken only by Jews and, more importantly, it constituted a homogeneous, autonomous form of Jewish life unknown to Western Jews. For the first time since the Diaspora, a great number of Jews speaking this language were present in the same geographical area, and were, moreover, united by rituals, customs, and practices that were undeniably Jewish.[19]

This new vision of the *Ostjudentum* so impressed Kafka that he would remain faithful to it for the rest of his life. The reason for his adherence to Birnbaum's ideas—and it matters little if one can speak of a direct influence—was twofold: on the one hand, Birnbaum's rejection of Buber's utopian spiritual revolution, and on the other, his matter-of-fact embrace of an existing, simple, everyday Judaism.

In a lucid article published on February 18, 1910, in *Die Welt* (the official organ of the world Zionist movement) and summarized in its entirety by the *Selbstwehr* on March 4,[20] Franz Oppenheimer affirmed Birnbaum's distinction between the two Judaisms and expanded the argument substantially. The Western Jew, Oppenheimer argued, was only a *Stammesjude*, a racial Jew: he was conscious of the origins that distinguished him from the gentiles around him, but this did not suffice to make him a *Kulturjude*, a cultural Jew, because he had assimilated into one of the European cultures. His Jewish identity, oriented as it was toward the past, was no more than the memory or an awareness of his origins. His racial consciousness (*Stammesbewusstsein*) consisted of little more than the presumption that he possessed a culture incomparably superior to the one his medieval forefathers had known in the ghetto. The Eastern Jew, though, and only the Eastern Jew, was Jewish in the full sense of the term. He possessed in fact an authentic *Nationalbewusstsein*, that is, a true national consciousness based on both the unity of the Yiddish language and a set of folk values expressing an integral Jewish culture untouched by assimilation. His identity as a Jew was not an artifact of memory: it was not based on a rejected, repressed, or forgotten past, but on an existing Judaism so vital that even the most ancient religious traditions became a spontaneous act of everyday life.[21]

The *Selbstwehr*, which published a summary of Oppenheimer's thesis, reacted rather critically to it for two specific reasons. First, by suggesting that Western Jews had no national consciousness, Oppenheimer undermined the political foundations of the Prague Zionist movement—which, in the very first issue of its weekly newspaper, demanded the recognition of a Jewish nationality within the multinational Hapsburg monarchy.[22] And second, by maintaining the cultural superiority of the Eastern Jews, Oppenheimer questioned the legitimacy of an avant-garde movement, which had called on the German-speaking Zionist youth to synthesize the two Judaisms (presuming, of course, that the Western brand was superior). Still, reaction to Oppenheimer's arguments was not completely negative; the Bar Kokhba, remembering the lectures Buber had given in Prague in 1909 and 1910, realized immediately that the folk culture of the *Ostjuden* could serve to refute anti-Semites who declared Jews to be inherently incapable of producing an autonomous national culture.[23] Familiarity with the Yiddish world could thus go hand in hand with Buber's Zionist militancy. As Birnbaum had maintained for some time, the Eastern Jews were not at all a mass of rejected and miserable inhabitants of the *shtetlekh*, but an extraordinarily healthy and vital people that had created a joyful, earthly pantheism of Hasidic mysticism. One could simply reject Oppenheimer's theoretical assumptions while nevertheless retaining their practical corollaries, in an effort to reaffirm the guiding role of the Western avant-garde which, thanks to its German culture, would consolidate the literary and religious treasures of Eastern Jewry for the future Jewish community.[24]

The problem with this strategy was that Oppenheimer's distinction between the two Judaisms was more significant than that between "national" and "racial" consciousness. Infinitely richer in its cultural implications—and much more disturbing for Kafka—was the opposition he suggested between a Judaism of presence and a Judaism of memory. Beyond the homogeneity of Eastern Judaism's folk culture, its essential element was the temporal continuity of tradition, thanks to which (and one should recall here Kafka's letters to Milena, in which he declares himself the most Western of the Western Jews*) past and future merged in a sort of absolute present of the grand Jewish family. This understanding of a "Judaism of presence" would have immeasurable consequences for Kafka, as we shall see. The Western assimilated Jew—in Oppenheimer's view, an individualist without roots, with a censored and repressed past—had to place the origin of his own culture in the historical moment when the technical and bureaucratic organization of European societies began to supersede national cultures. In only a few decades the assimilated Jew had gone from the medieval ghetto to modern industrial society, and the consequent disorientation made him the paradigm of a crisis in European consciousness. He, more than any other, was condemned to a laborious search for his cultural memory and the meaning of his superseded historical tradition—in other words, to reestablish the continuity between national culture and bureaucratic modernity.

As a European writer, Kafka was rooted in the culture of the Hapsburg empire, a culture that was confronting—in radical and inventive ways—the fundamental modern problem of the disintegration of the self and the temporality of tradition. Kafka experienced his encounter with Eastern Judaism as a crisis of the self: he was a "Jew of memory" who had to reacquire, day by day, a history that could no longer be reconstructed or deciphered. Without giving in to Buber's ideological and neo-Romantic mysticism, Kafka would transform his suffering as a Jew without history into the anxiety of the modern self without history or tradition. In this way he experienced his Judaism with unparalleled inventiveness, making it the metaphoric vehicle for

---

* See Kafka's letter to Milena Jesenská (M 218–19) on his perception of himself as "the most typical Western Jew" of his circle. —Ed.

an absolute literary expressivity. Unlike his friend Max Brod, who put his literary talents in the service of Zionism, Kafka conceived of himself first of all as a writer, and his literature drew on the energies of the Jewish revival in a blatantly parasitic way.

Eastern Jewry eventually becomes for Kafka a fetishized construct in which, as Oppenheimer had asserted, the miraculous "Judaism of presence" is manifest. Later, as his consciousness of himself as a writer grows stronger, the Eastern Jews become precisely what he is not and thus serve as the reminder of his guilt as a Western Jew who is "contaminated" by the vice of literature.[25] Max Brod, who first introduced him to the Yiddish theater, would always see Eastern Jewry through Buber's eyes, as the absolute substance of Judaism; later, however, he cites Birnbaum along with Buber as the decisive figures in his conversion to Zionism.[26] By contrast, Kafka was wary of Buber's national mysticism while nevertheless receptive of Birnbaum's ideas; he would see in Eastern Jewry a legendary and fabulous world in which, as a parable, the great contradiction of modern Judaism was being consummated.

If one reads carefully Kafka's diary entry for October 5, 1911, in which he describes the Yiddish actors' first performance in Prague (D 64–66), the significance of this experience—which permanently marked his sensibility as a writer and determined the fantastic manner in which he portrayed the Eastern-Jewish world in his writings—gradually becomes clear. Kafka is not particularly impressed by the plays and operettas themselves, whose plots he notes perfunctorily. Rather, he is fascinated by the play's staging, specifically the groupings of the actors and the movement of their bodies in time with the singing. He especially notes a couple in caftans: he doesn't know who they are but thinks they are meant to be "sextons, employees of the temple, notorious lazybones with whom the community has come to terms, privileged shnorrers for some religious reason, people who, precisely as a result of their being set apart, are very close to the center of the community's life, know many songs as a result of their useless wandering about and spying." For Kafka, these two represent "people who are Jews in an especially pure form because they live only in the religion, but live in it without effort, understanding, or distress." Thus, they can laugh when a good Jew kills himself or dance when a bad Jew dies.* But when they do this—rising on the tips of their toes and throwing their legs up or spreading their arms wide, moving them in time with the melody—they do so because they "haven't the slightest specific gravity." They sink to the ground under the slightest pressure, then bounce back up, throwing out their legs and snapping their fingers while behind them the baptized Jew kills himself in the name of the God of Israel.[27]

It is clear from his diary entry that Kafka was intrigued by the two actors' exaggerated pantomime. (His description of them bears striking similarity to that of the judges in *The Trial*, who often move their hands in a mocking gesture, or flap them up and down as if they were wings.) More importantly, he is fascinated by the fact that the dramatic action so easily sustains their grotesque gestures, which are accompanied by traditional folk songs. Before most German Expressionists, Kafka had already made use of gestures in his early text "Description of a Struggle" to portray the explosive inner desires and neuroses of his protagonists. In the movements of these two figures in caftans (who, as Max Brod observed, are also the first incarnation of the land surveyor's assistants in *The Castle*), he no doubt found a parallel to the protagonists' wild gestures in his own first story. But the actors had nothing of the hysterical, forced movement of Kafka's figures; their gestures arose—and here is probably the source of his enthusiasm for the Yiddish theater—from an "unquenchable fire" of imagination (F 264), from a joyful vitality that could express itself freely without disrupting the play's dramatic seriousness.

The drama, in other words, became a spectacle and an absolute drama. Words were accompanied by music and music by gestures in a sort of choral hymn representing an autonomous human world in which joy and suffering could coexist simultaneously. The actors performed in the same manner in which the Hasidim prayed in the synagogue, accompanying the movement of their arms and body with religious chants. The importance of this discovery of a new type of gesture is confirmed by Kafka's diary notes for November 29, 1911, in which he describes Hasidim who discuss Talmudic questions from morning to night. If their discussion, which is normally lively and

---

* The author is following Kafka's summary of the play *Der Meshumed* by Joseph Lateiner.—ED.

happy, is interrupted, or if one of them remains silent, the Hasidim begin to sing a song or invent a new melody on the spot; they then call their women and children so that they can learn it and repeat it with them (D 129).

Song, accompanied by gesture, thus signifies for Eastern Jews the joyous sense of existence and community. This is why the actors' movement transmits itself to the audience so irresistibly. "At times," the diary for October 10 reads, "we did not interfere in the plot because we were too moved, not because we were mere spectators" (D 73). Kafka describes an old man in the audience who holds his arm up "in order better to enjoy the melody that his fingertips follow" (D 66).

> The melodies are made to catch hold of every person who jumps up and they can, without breaking down, encompass all his excitement. . . . The two in caftans are particularly in a hurry to meet the singing, as though it were stretching their body according to its most essential needs, and the clapping of hands during the singing is an obvious sign of the good health of the man in the actor. (D 66)

There can be little doubt that this interpretation of the Eastern Jews, derided by the Zionist press as "deformed" and "sickly," reveals an attitude quite similar to that which Nathan Birnbaum displayed toward Yiddish-speaking Judaism. The Eastern Jew's love of life stemmed from his happiness at being part of a large family, and this was precisely what the actors communicated to the audience through song: with a gesture they invited the audience to participate in a community where actors and spectators were simply Jews together, unconcerned about the world of the goyim. These vital actors revealed to Kafka an entirely new understanding of Judaism—and they did so despite the extreme limitations of their performances, which Kafka describes in detail. They argued with one another on stage, made the curtain collapse, and were literally kicked out by the headwaiter (as a result of which the association of Jewish office workers, the Zukunft, canceled the play scheduled for the following day). The Zionists in attendance were ashamed of these miserable comedians, who make such a sad spectacle of themselves, disappoint the Zionist ambition to show the world that Jews are at least as respectable as Christians.

Kafka, however, appreciates the actors precisely for this reason. If Yitzhak Löwy dies on stage, singing, while the two actors holding him up hide their heads behind his shoulders in order to laugh without—they think—the audience seeing them, Kafka too cannot help from laughing the next day when he remembers the scene—unlike his Zionist friends.

"What I said about the Yiddish theater was certainly not meant to be ironical," Kafka writes to Felice Bauer on November 6, 1912 (F 29). "I may have laughed at it, but that is part of loving." Certainly, he quickly discovers that among the *Ostjuden* the sense for community existed side by side with the authoritarianism of the *tsaddikim*, or "devout ones," the religious leaders of Eastern Europe. Already opposed to the militant rhetoric of Zionism, Kafka could not help but be attracted by the childlike and joyous Judaism of the *Ostjuden*, which struck him as authentic precisely because of its innocently comical nature. Löwy, who committed the worst gaffes on stage, became a quick favorite: Kafka wanted to see him daily and admired him in an unreserved, almost servile manner. Despite the fact that he was a terrible actor, Löwy had an extremely direct stage manner, an authenticity similar to that of Frau Tschissik, who speaks as if "independent of the play and of us" (D 85). Kafka writes that she directs the production "like the mother of a family" (D 107).

If Kafka loves the Yiddish actors, as he claims several times in his diary, it is because he believes them to be Jews without an identity problem. If they argue with one another in endless discussion in cafés, divided into two parties gathered at separate tables, this is only to decide who is the best Yiddish author, Edelstadt or Rosenfeld, Peretz or Gordin (D 86). Kafka responds with profound wonder to their unrestrained behavior; he is enchanted by these flesh-and-blood Jews whose identity *as such* is not contingent on Christianity. The very amateurishness that shocked his Zionist friends was, for Kafka, the most convincing proof of the actors' authenticity: an "immediate Jewishness that is always being improvised" shines through their crude performances and tattered costumes. The "clamor of this Jewishness" is lawless and comic, often involuntarily, but for this reason magnanimous, direct, vital (D 88).

Although the troupe's repertory has left significant traces in his work,[28] Kafka was attracted neither by the literary quality of the plays

nor by their dramatization of the conflict between Jews and Christians—nor, for that matter, by their depiction of a Judaism that he
sympathizes with. "When I saw the first plays," he writes in his diary
on January 6, 1912,

> it was possible for me to think that I had come upon a Judaism on which
> the beginnings of my own rested, a Judaism that was developing in my
> direction and so would enlighten and carry me farther along in my own
> clumsy Judaism. Instead, it moves farther away from me the more I hear
> of it. The people remain, of course, and I hold fast to them. (D 167)

The attraction he feels toward the actors' humanity leads him to believe that he is in love with the hefty Frau Tschissik and to form a
close friendship with Löwy, whose volubility he greatly admires.
"Löwy, given his way, is a man of continuous enthusiasm, known in
Eastern Europe as a 'hot Jew,'" he will write to Felice Bauer (F 29).
Often depressed, Kafka was drawn to the irresistible fire Löwy transmitted in telling stories. Martin Buber spoke of mysticism, of the
Jewish soul's creative nature, of biblical myths and archetypes that
had been preserved through the ages in the parables of the *tsaddikim*—about which Kafka cares not in the least. His curiosity is directed at the quotidian life of a Jewish world whose improbable,
miraculous originality never ceases to amaze him.

Thus, he is fascinated by Löwy's description of his grandfather, a
righteous Jew whose death the entire village gathered to witness. Or
he notes the circumcision rites in the *shtetl*, so different in their combination of chants, magical formulas, and kabbalistic signs from the
boring and arid ceremony of his nephew's circumcision, which seems
to him a historical atavism, "nothing but an imitation fairy tale" (L
116). Or he is amused by the story of how the Warsaw Jews managed
to have the telephone and telegraph wires put up around the city in a
complete circle which, in accordance with the Talmud, made the city
"a bounded area, a courtyard, as it were, so that on Saturday it is
possible even for the most pious person to move about, carry trifles
(like handkerchiefs) on his person, within this circle" (D 129). And
when Löwy mentions to him the few days he spent in the famous
Yeshiva of Ostro after running away from home, Kafka does not forget

to record the smell, the dirt, the petty and sinister aspects of these schools—especially the fact that these centers of orthodoxy were by then cauldrons of assimilation, training centers for Western thinking from which the most progressive and revolutionary intellectuals would emerge.

Kafka does not idealize the Yiddish world; if he turns it into a myth, he does so by fetishizing its daily life, exalting the aspects which most disgusted him. The unspeakable filth in which the Yeshiva students lived—they don't undress for bed, never wash and are full of fleas—is already the fundamental characteristic of the court in *The Trial*. But the disgust and fascination he feels for the students' filth and corruption in listening to Löwy's stories is akin to the humble and self-deprecating love he feels for the actors, with their amateurism and argumentative fervor. These are, as it were, the natural secretions of human beings who live as a *community*, eating, sleeping, studying, and talking together in close quarters and who, as Kafka writes, are "bound to each other by their Jewishness in a degree unknown to us" (D 170).

Ten years later, in a series of letters to his sister Elli, Kafka will describe the family in the same terms of physical union, calling it "merely an animal connection," or "a single bloodstream": indeed, the "animal family" (L 294), with its biological torpor, suffocates his rational desire for individual identity. There is no doubt that the Eastern Jews suggested this image of an animal family in which he sees the most elementary form of a court judging him (as assimilated Jew). His lavish descriptions of the filth of this world are not meant to erase but to celebrate it. The Zionists champion cleanliness because the Jew must wash himself of the filth of the *galut*. Kafka sees in this dirt the organic totality of an autonomous world. Many unforgettable scenes in *The Trial*, set in closed, narrow, airless spaces, derive from Kafka's keen sensitivity to the confined, "dirty" spaces inhabited by the Eastern Jews. For the first time he doesn't see individual Jews obsessed with the bourgeois values of cleanliness, but Jews living together, Jews who compose a single family and as he writes in his diary, "flee to one another, so to speak," seizing every opportunity to be together, whether for ritual, prayer, or discussion (D 152).

Kafka's conception of Judaism as an extended family, and thus as a "bloodstream," an "organism," or "animal connection," also informs the most salient document of his encounter with the Eastern Jews— his "Introductory Talk on the Yiddish Language," which he delivered on February 18, 1912, at the Jewish Town Hall to introduce a performance by Yitzhak Löwy. The *Selbstwehr* announced the lecture, recalling the popularity that Yiddish literature had enjoyed in Prague in recent times.[29] But Kafka had probably imposed Löwy's performance on the members of the Bar Kokhba, who must have been reluctant to hire such a poor actor (infamous for his blunders in the Café Savoy) to perform before prestigious members of the Jewish community. In fact, Kafka had to arrange all the practical details: he personally drew up the evening's program, took care of numbering the seats, selling tickets, advertising, obtaining police and rabbinical permission, and so on. He based his speech on Meyer Isser Pines's *Histoire de la littérature judéo-allemande,* which he had read in January, as well as on his direct impressions of Löwy's reading of Yiddish texts. The talk was Kafka's most committed public cultural appearance in his native city.

As he notes in his diary, Kafka spoke in a state of "proud, unearthly consciousness" (D 181). A brief notice which appeared in the *Selbstwehr* a few days later described the speech as "refined and brief,"[30] two unusual adjectives which certainly reflect the " coolness in the presence of the audience" that Kafka mentions in his summary of the evening in his diary of February 25. Although he had intended it to be engaging and urbane, it was in fact hostile, ironic, aggressive, and provocative. Written the day before the performance, at a time when he was fighting with his father over his friendship with Löwy, this short speech reveals Kafka's intention to try himself and the assimilated bourgeoisie of Prague before the court of the Eastern Jews, represented by Löwy. He began by declaring that he was not speaking to those who looked down on Yiddish, but to those whose fear of the language was so great that he "could read it in their faces." Although the political debate about Yiddish originated in the Zionist circles of the Bar Kokhba, Kafka wasn't speaking as a Zionist to fellow Zionists for whom Yiddish signified in an abstract way the misery of the Diaspora; rather, his audience consisted of the assimilated Jews of his parents' generation (although his own parents failed to attend, as he notes in his diary), who felt not only fear but also disgust for a very vivid world they had abandoned only a few decades earlier.

This mixture of attraction and disgust, which Kafka too felt toward the actors, is perhaps the key to understanding his speech. Yiddish, he tells his audience, is full of contradictions: it is certainly a dialect but at the same time a language; it is a kind of medieval German and yet, because of this linguistic affinity, is more distant from contemporary German than any other language; and it is, above all, as Kafka notes in a revealing phrase, a mixture of "law and arbitrariness." In this paradoxical combination of law and arbitrariness, which again recalls the court in *The Trial*, the most disturbing element is certainly the second. Yiddish is something so immediately alive, palpitating with such an unpredictable organic vitality, that it cannot fail to terrify an audience accustomed to the clear, logical separations of bourgeois rationalism.

Thus Kafka's first concern is to liberate the spectators from their visible fear of Yiddish. He attempts to rationalize this fear by declaring it to be understandable in an audience of Western Jews living, as he says with evident irony, "in almost thoughtless harmony." The peace and order of bourgeois life allow them to understand each other when necessary but also to ignore each other when convenient—the paradox of bourgeois society that consists in a mutual understanding based on indifference. Kafka is evidently alluding here to the atomism of Western societies which are governed by stable, predictable rules guaranteeing the individual's privacy. A person accustomed to the clean, rational order of Western social relations cannot fail to be terrified by the exuberant chaos of the Yiddish-speaking population. "Who, looking at it from this order of things," Kafka asks, "could understand this confused, intricate dialect and who would even want to?" A very young language, he continues, composed of foreign words gathered during the wanderings of the Diaspora—of which it preserves all the instability and anxiousness, intensifying them with its variety of dialects—Yiddish can neither be described by any syntactic or grammatical systems, nor can it be ordered by rules and norms. "The people won't leave it in the hands of grammarians," he claims. The dialect never rests, its recognizable linguistic rules and vestiges of dead languages are in continual movement: that is, it is a mixture of law and arbitrariness, of neologisms and archaic words, all of them in a state of such flux "that one would need tremendous strength to hold together all these German, Jewish, French, English, Slavic, Dutch, Rumanian, and even Latin words."

If Yiddish reveals its folk character in the vitality of its disorder, Kafka continues, only the vitality of a large family is capable of unifying it without resorting to the predictable categories of rationalism. The explanations given in the program will be useless, Kafka warns the spectators, if they are not willing to listen with their hearts rather than their intellects: they must rely on that "knot of Jewish strength" they still possess. Only by giving themselves over to Yiddish will they not feel excluded:

> As soon as Yiddish has taken hold of you—and the dialect is every-thing, word, Hasidic melody and the very nature of this Eastern Jewish actor—you will no longer recognize your former tranquility. You will then have to feel the true unity of the dialect and feel it so intensely you will be afraid, though not of the dialect, but of yourselves.

Kafka is clearly inviting this audience of Prague Jews to give up the individualism of assimilation. At the beginning of his speech he had announced his desire to exorcise their fear by making it comprehensible. Now he confronts them with the terror they must feel at having betrayed the great family. No one, he warns, can tolerate this fear without the confidence that Yiddish inspires, the confidence of no longer being alone or excluded. Here Kafka seems to be anticipating a sort of happy end to *The Trial* (in which Joseph K. would enter the realm of the Law rather than be excluded, through his execution, from it). And if he concludes his speech by assuring the spectators that he does not want to punish them by having a poor Yiddish actor perform in the center of their community, he does so with the threatening irony of a judge who speaks with the authority of a court of law. In the name of this court he invites them to respond to its call, confidently entering the door of the Law.

Whoever has read the parable "Before the Law" will know that the presentation of the Law in *The Trial* is very different from that in the "Introductory Talk on the Yiddish Language." Between the two texts lies the long and tortuous path that Kafka followed, never once falling into Romantic Zionism of Martin Buber. He does feel tempted to give himself over to the family represented by Eastern Jewry, shedding the tears he speaks of in the "Letter to His Father," when he recalls the few times his father showed affection for his son. But his desire to take refuge in the love of family joined together in an affectionate community always conflicts with his fierce determination to defend his identity as a writer against every other identification, particularly those of institution and family.

This determination is demonstrated by his diaries in the winter of 1911 to 1912, which contain, along with frequent discussions of Judaism, numerous passages relating to the problem of writing and literary production. If the former are almost always objective summaries, memory aids, bizarre but apt sketches of a world that has surprised him with its novelty, the latter are dramatic and often desperate expressions of a man who knows of his own great talent but has not yet settled for the literary facility of a Max Brod or a Franz Werfel. Kafka was twenty-eight years old when he was first introduced by Hugo Bergmann to the Zionism of the Bar Kokhba and by Max Brod to the Yiddish theater. He had written only a few, fragmentary prose pieces, and thus was plagued by doubts about the nature of his disturbing inspiration and—given his disorderly and unmethodical work habits—about his future as a writer. Above all, he was in open conflict with his family for the first time: in the fall of 1911 he had been forced by his father to become the co-owner, with his brother-in-law Karl Herrmann, of a small asbestos factory with quite modern machinery and some twenty workers. Hermann Kafka was concerned about the future of his only son—whose employment was barely respectable and whose literary ambitions he considered dubious—and had given him the money for this reluctant venture, and now evidently expected from him the same economic success that characterized the prestigious Jewish bourgeoisie in Prague. Kafka had given in passively to his father's wishes and taken on the responsibility of overseeing production quality; in truth it was a rather minor activity but, when added to his work in the office, it robbed him of precious time for writing.[31]

Kafka reacted to this paternal imposition by intensifying his friendships with Max Brod—whom his father called, using a Yiddish expression, a "*meschuggene ritoch,*" an insolent hot-head—and with

Yitzhak Löwy, whom his father with sneering irony compared to fleas, bedbugs, and various other vermin. It is in this state of open war with his father that Kafka began to concern himself explicitly with Jewish questions.[32] In fact, almost the day after having expressed his hatred for his father in his diary for the first time—Hermann Kafka had called him a bad son because of his unseemly friendships—he begins reading, "greedily and happily," Heinrich Graetz's *History of the Jews* (D 98). One must not underestimate the context of this reading, in November 1911, which extends to other Jewish subjects in the succeeding months. Kafka's interest in Judaism and its history begins the moment his father condemns two possible models for his filial revolt: the Zionist Max Brod, who already supported the Bar Kokhba and was quite aggressive in his confrontations with the assimilated bourgeoisie (typically represented by Hermann Kafka); and the Yiddish actor Löwy, a member of a troupe that above all rejects conversion and assimilation. These are the two forms of Kafka's own revolt which, if it masks itself in terms of the Bar Kokhba debate about Zionism and Eastern Jewry, in fact issued from his need to define himself as a writer.

Kafka's contact with the Lemberg actors—an affront to his father's bourgeois ambitions—represents the only "bohemian" gesture of a man who was otherwise reserved and incapable of provocative behavior. But if Kafka openly provoked his father by frequenting the Café Savoy, inviting Löwy several times to his house and even speaking publicly at his friend's final performance, it was not only because Löwy was an Eastern Jew. Rather, Löwy was also the example of a son who had followed his own artistic vocation against the express wishes of his wealthy and devout father, risking a life of hunger and physical deprivation. Moreover, until the age of twenty Löwy had had no qualms about letting his father support him, thus imitating George Bernard Shaw who, as Kafka notes in his diary, had had the courage to exploit his parents mercilessly in order to realize his literary vocation.

Confronted with these "miraculous" examples of open defiance of paternal authority, Kafka cannot help but feel that he has betrayed himself, the self that would like to identify with Löwy, his admired model in these months. This conflict, exacerbated by the catalyzing encounter with Felice Bauer, will be given surreal expression in his story "The Judgment." There Kafka takes on the role of the judging father, allied with the Russian friend, and punishes himself with a sentence of suicide for having betrayed his own ideal self, represented by the figure of the distant friend, who was quite probably based on Löwy. Kafka feels guilty on two counts: toward his father who wanted him to go into business, whereas he wanted only to write; and toward himself because, having accepted the job in the factory, he failed his duty to literature. His desperation can be seen in the repeated suicide plans confided to his diary from November 1911 to March 1912.

His obsession in these months is, therefore, not just Judaism but also, and above all, literature. Kafka's birth as a writer does *not* take place in his encounter with Felice Bauer, who brings to the surface the Oedipal complex in "The Judgment" and *The Metamorphosis;* rather, it occurs in his encounter with the Judaism of the Yiddish actors who reveal to him, *through literature,* his own most Western and assimilated characteristics. Never do we find in his diary as many descriptions of his troubled attempts to write as we do during the period of his friendship with the Lemberg actors. And never, as in these months, does writing appear to him so ecstatic and destructive, allowing him not only the incomparable pleasure of creation but also the equally incomparable pleasuring of punishing himself through literature. The impossibility for him of reconciling his Jewish consciousness with his consciousness as a writer, which he knows is tied to the solitude of aesthetic existence, provokes in him a humiliating envy of those who, like Brod, effortlessly combine their literary and religious vocations. And yet he also envies those who are not plagued by the anxiety of assimilation and experience literature in a vital, joyful manner. In addition to the Kafka who, in Brod's company, meets with the actors on a daily basis during the winter of 1911 to 1912, there is also the Kafka who appears with unusual regularity in assimilated literary milieux such as the Café Arco, where Franz Werfel holds forth before Prague's most brilliant young writers— among them, Willy Haas, Rudolf Fuchs, Otto Pick, and Ernst Polak, Milena Jesenká's future husband.[33]

That Kafka would frequent an assimilated literary circle reveals his attraction to writers with an apparently natural, spontaneous relation to literary creativity. As ever, he admires Max Brod's fertility as poet, novelist, essayist, philosopher, literary and music critic, and even pianist and composer; and he envies the literary success of Oskar Baum (with Brod and Felix Weltsch his best friend) to the point of experiencing "stomach pains." But the overwhelming personality of Franz Werfel, the poet he envies more than any other and who was viewed in Germany as the leader of the new literary generation, seriously torments him. "I hate Werfel, not because I envy him, but I envy him too," he notes in his diary on December 18, 1911:

> He is healthy, young, and rich, everything that I am not. Besides, gifted with a sense of music, he has done very good work early and easily, he has the happiest life behind him and before him, I work with weights I cannot get rid of, and I am entirely shut off from music. (D 141)

And on December 23, 1911, he writes again: "All yesterday morning my head was as if filled with mist from Werfel's poems. For a moment I feared the enthusiasm would carry me along straight into madness" (D 145). Werfel, who knows his poems by heart and recites them to his friends at the Café Arco with an exalted pathos, seems to him incontestable proof that to "live literature" one needs a healthy body, the natural instrument for a literary vocation.

This theme of his body's inadequacy—constantly repeated in his letters and diary—is only one part of a complex metaphoric grouping that includes the problems of writing, Eastern Judaism, and even marriage, which was without doubt the most violent trauma of his existence. In addition to the themes of Eastern Judaism and writing, one also finds in Kafka's diary entries for the winter of 1911 to 1912 references to his melancholy and despair about his bachelor existence, most notably expressed in the entry for November 14, 1911, and the prose piece "Bachelor's Ill Luck." For Kafka this theme too derives from writing and Judaism, since the inadequacy of his body not only prevents him from being a productive writer but cuts off the alternative to literature: marriage, family, and an active role in the Jewish community. The bachelor, Kafka notes in his diary on December 3, can consume only himself and his own strengths, whereas the married man participates in the strength and energy of the community, which supports and nourishes him with its inexhaustible vitality (D 130–31). However, this parasitic vocation (which, as he will suggest in *The Metamorphosis*, is also the expression of his monstrous voracity as a writer) is immediately frustrated by Kafka's perception of his own physical inadequacy. As he writes in his diary after the performance of a play by Jacob Gordin, his body seems to have emerged from a lumber room or an attic and should thus be thrown out, an empty shell useless not only for literature but also for community life. If the actors seem to embody the prodigious energy of the grand Jewish family, Kafka, frustrated in the solitude of an impotent writer, can only transcribe in his diary a saying from the Talmud he has just heard in Gordin's play: "A man without a wife is not a human being."

Translated by Mark Anderson

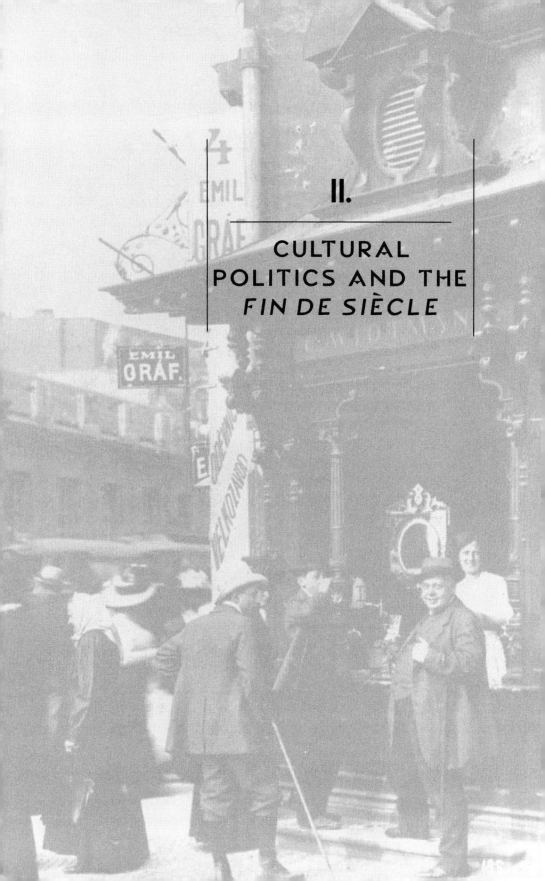

II.

CULTURAL
POLITICS AND THE
FIN DE SIÈCLE

LIBERTARIAN ANARCHISM IN AMERIKA

Michael Löwy

IN A CONVERSATION with Gustav Janouch, commenting on Plato's exclusion of the poets from the state, Kafka observed: "The poets . . . are politically dangerous elements, because they want to make a change. For the state, and all its devoted servants, want only one thing, to persist" (J 140). It is no accident that Kafka's own work has also been labeled as "dangerous" by all authoritarian states of the twentieth century.

To a large extent, Kafka shares in the neoromantic critique of modern (capitalist) *Zivilisation* which was developed by his friends in the cultural Zionist circle *Bar Kokhba*.[*][1] This influence shows up powerfully in his novel *Amerika*, especially in the descriptions of mechanized labor. The employees of Karl Rossmann's uncle, who owns an enormous commercial enterprise, pass their days enclosed in telephone booths, indifferent to everything, their heads "bound in a steel band" which presses the receivers against their ears: only their fingers move, twitching with "inhuman regularity and speed" (A 47). The work of the Hotel Occidental elevator operators is similarly corrosive, exhausting, and monotonous. They confine themselves to

---

[*] See the essays in this volume by Stölzl and Baioni.—ED.

pushing buttons, and ignore anything that might have to do with the functioning of the machines. In the offices and the streets, the din is invasive: deafening alarms, honking cars, a whirlwind of noise which is like "some strange element quite unconnected with humanity" (A 53). One could cite numerous other examples, but it is the entire atmosphere in Kafka's novel which reveals the unease and distress of human beings exposed to a pitiless world, to a technological civilization that eludes them. As Wilhelm Emrich aptly observes, *Amerika* is "among the most lucid critiques of modern industrial society known to modern literature. This society's secret economic and psychological mechanism and its satanic consequences are unveiled without concessions."[2] It is a world dominated by the monotonous and circular return of the same, by the purely quantitative temporality of the clock. Kafka's novel presents America, furthermore, as a *Zivilisation* without *Kultur*: art and the mind no longer seem to play any role, and the only book mentioned is, not surprisingly, a book on commercial correspondence.

We know that one of the principal sources for the novel was the book by the Jewish socialist Arthur Holitscher, *Amerika heute und morgen* (America Today and Tomorrow), published in 1912, which contains a detailed description of the "hell" of modern American civilization and a mordant critique of assembly-line work: "The specialization of labor, resulting in mass production, reduces the worker further and further, until he is on the same level as an inanimate piece of the machine, a cog or a lever, functioning precisely and automatically."[3] Kafka's correspondence during this period reveals his own sense of anguish before a mechanized world. In a letter to Felice Bauer of 1913, he refers to a dictation machine as an example of the machines that exercise "a greater, more cruel compulsion on one's capacities than any human being" (F 149). Several years later, in a conversation with Janouch, he gives free reign to this "repugnance" for assembly-line work, resorting to a language of biblical resonance: "Such a violent outrage can only end in enslavement to evil. It is inevitable. Time, the noblest and most essential element in all creative work, is conscripted into the net of corrupt business interests. Thereby not only creative work, but man himself, who is its essential part, is polluted and humiliated. A Taylorized life is a terrible curse which will give rise only to hunger and misery instead of the intended wealth and profit" (J 115).

This moral and religious hostility to industrial, capitalist "progress" is accompanied, in Kafka, by a nostalgia for traditional community, for organic *Gemeinschaft*, which draws him to the Yiddish culture and language of the Eastern Jews, to his sister Ottla's plans for a rural life in Palestine, as well as (more ambiguously) to the romantic cultural Zionism of his Prague friends. The Czech peasant community, living in peace and harmony with nature, arouses his awed admiration: "General impression given one by peasants: noblemen who have escaped into agriculture, where they have arranged their work so wisely and humbly that it fits perfectly into everything and they are protected against all insecurity and worry until their blissful death. True dwellers on this earth" (D 388). It is striking to compare this idyllic and peaceful tableau with his description of the pathological fever of New York harbor in the first chapter of *Amerika*: "A movement without end, a restlessness transmitted from the restless element to helpless human beings and their works!" (A 17).

Almost the only passage in Kafka's novels that could be interpreted as a positive allegory of messianic redemption is the famous last chapter of *Amerika* with its Nature Theater of Oklahoma, in which "everyone has a place," even the young Karl Rossmann, the hero and victim of the novel. This interpretation appears even more plausible in light of a conversation reported by Max Brod, during which Kafka let it be understood, "smiling and with a few enigmatic words," that the novel would probably end with young Karl's rediscovery of happiness, in an atmosphere of "heavenly magic."[4] Unfortunately, in Kafka's diary there is an entry which envisions an altogether different conclusion for the book: "Rossmann and K., the innocent and the guilty, both executed without distinction in the end, the guilty one with a gentler hand, more pushed aside than struck down" (D 343–44). In Alfred Wirkner's view, the Oklahoma Theater is nothing but a great trick for exploiting the naïveté of the immigrants. The final chapter, then, is in harmony with the rest of the book: it shows Karl Rossmann's fall into his last and worst servitude, from which he is freed only by death. Wirkner also puts forth the hypothesis that the pseudonym Karl chooses upon joining the Theater—"Negro"—refers to an image in Holitscher's book of a black man being lynched, labeled "Idyll in Oklahama." We know that Kafka was aware of this image because the manuscript of *Amerika* duplicates Holitscher's typographic error in the spelling of "Oklahama." It is possible, then, that Kafka meant Karl Rossmann to end up like the black man in the image.[5] If one were to take into account the diary's more benign formulation—Karl will be executed, but "more pushed aside than struck down"—it is also possible to imagine a conclusion that would correspond to the expectations raised by the first chapter: moved by his sense of justice to take up the defense of a black man menaced by mob law (just as he tried to defend the stoker in the opening chapter), Karl Rossmann would be "pushed aside" by the lynchers.

Kafka's *theologia negativa,* his negative messianism, has a corollary in the political realm: a *utopia negativa,* a negative anarchism. Heinz Politzer speaks of Kafka as a "metaphysical anarchist."[6] It seems to me in fact that his central works formulate a critique of bureaucratic reification and hierarchical state authority (juridical or administrative) that is clearly inspired by anarchism. This political interpretation is obviously only part of the solution: Kafka's universe is too rich and varied to be reduced to a single formula. But such an interpretation is in no way incompatible with a religious or theological reading: rather, there is a striking structural analogy between the two. The absence of redemption, the index of a damned era, corresponds to the absence of liberty in the stifling universe of arbitrary bureaucracy. It is only by contrast, through their negation, that messianic and utopian hope stand out, as the radically *other.* Anarchism is thus imbued with a religious spirituality and takes on a "metaphysical" dimension.

A number of biographical facts offer confirmation of Kafka's interest in the anarchist movement and its ideas. At about the same time that he began to work at the Workmen's Accident Insurance Institute, Kafka started to attend various anarchist meetings in Prague. According to information furnished by Michal Kacha (one of the founders of the anarchist movement in Prague) and Michal Mares (then a young Czech anarchist), Kafka was present at the gatherings of the *Klub Mladych* (Youth Group) of the workers' political association *Vilem Körber,* and of the Czech Movement, with its anarchist, syndicalist orientation. Both of their accounts agree that Kafka observed and listened at these meetings with the greatest interest, with-

out, however, participating in the discussions. Kacha called him
Klidas, "the silent giant."[7]

Michal Mares relates that at his invitation, Kafka went to several
anarchist lectures and meetings. The first, in 1909, was a demonstration against the execution of the Spanish anarchist teacher and
thinker Francisco Ferrer, who was later released by the police. Kafka
attended other meetings, Mares writes, for instance those dedicated
to free love (1910), the anniversary of the Paris Commune (1911),
and the antiwar effort (also in 1911). Finally, in 1912, Kafka took
part in a demonstration against the execution of the anarchist Lia-
beuf in Paris, a demonstration violently suppressed by the police, who
arrested many of the demonstrators, among them Franz Kafka. At
the police station he was given the choice between a one-gulden fine
and twenty-four hours in prison. Kafka chose to pay the fine.[8]

According to Mares, Kafka read with great interest and sympathy
the works of anarchist writers and leaders such as the Reclus brothers,
Domela Niewenhuis, Vera Figner, Bakunin, Jean Grave, Kropotkin,
Emma Goldman, and others.[9] In fact, several of these authors are
mentioned in Kafka's diary (D 233, 333); and Janouch too reports a
conversation in which Kafka showed interest in Ravachol and in the
work and life of Godwin, Proudhon, Stirner, Bakunin, Kropotkin,
Tolstoy, Erich Mühsam, and Rudolf Grossmann.

It is well known that Kafka had a profound hatred for his job at the
Workmen's Accident Insurance Institute (which he described to Janouch as an "oppressive nest of bureaucrats") and that he was indig-
nant over the lot of the disabled workers and the poor widows who
found themselves trapped in the legal and administrative labyrinths
of the institute. One of Kafka's comments, reported by Max Brod, is
an ironic, terse, and violent expression of his "anarchist" feelings
about such institutions: "How humble these people are. . . . They
come here to plead. Instead of attacking and sacking the Institute,
they come to plead."[10] It is not unlikely that Kafka's feeling about his
bureaucratic employment was at least one of the sources of the libertarian aspect of his writings.

Was this tendency only a "youthful episode" in his life, limited to
the years 1909–1912? Kafka did stop participating in Czech anarchist
activities after 1912, becoming more involved in Jewish Zionist
circles in Prague. But his conversations with Gustav Janouch around

1920 show that his early inclinations endured. Not only did he characterize the Prague anarchists as men who were "nice, jolly people," "so nice and friendly that one has to believe every word they say" (J 86); he also continued to formulate political and social ideas that had a close affinity with anarchism.

For example, his definition of capitalism as "a system of relationships" in which "everything is relative, everything is in chains" (J 152) is typically anarchist in its emphasis on the oppressive and authoritarian character of the existing regime (rather than on economic exploitation, as in Marxist analysis). Even his skepticism for the organized labor movement seems inspired by a libertarian mistrust of political parties and institutions. Referring to a workers' demonstration parading past with banners and flags unfurled, he observed: "These people are so self-possessed, so self-confident and good-humored. They rule the streets, and therefore think they rule the world. In fact, they are mistaken. Behind them already are the secretaries, officials, professional politicians, all the modern satraps for whom they are preparing the way to power. . . . The Revolution evaporates, and leaves behind only the slime of a new bureaucracy. The chains of tormented mankind are made out of red tape" (J 119–20).

Janouch's testimony suggests, then, that Kafka stayed close to anarchist ideas throughout his life. This was not, of course, a matter of militant political conviction, but rather of spiritual affinity, of a profound sympathy for the anti-authoritarian philosophy of Bakunin, Kropotkin, and their Czech disciples. Libertarian utopia is not the object of any kind of "demonstration" in Kafka's novel.[11] It can only be seen in the profoundly critical way in which Kafka presents the obsessive and omnipresent face of nonfreedom: *authority*.

An antiauthoritarian spirit (originating in libertarianism) infuses all of Kafka's narrative works in an increasingly universal and abstract manner, developing from a critique of paternal and personal authority toward one of administrative and impersonal authority. From the outset, Kafka perceived a connection between the despotic authority of his father and political or social authority. In the "Letter to His Father, " he recalls: "For me you took on the enigmatic quality that all tyrants have whose rights are based on their person and not on reason" (DF 143). Commenting on his father's brutal, unjust, and arbitrary treatment of his employees, he writes: "[This] made the business insufferable to me, reminding me far too much of my relations with you. . . . That was why I could not but side with the staff" (DF 162). It is possible to see here one of the intimate and personal sources of his sympathy for the Prague anarchists—and also, more directly, of his interest in Otto Gross. Imprisoned at his father's order in a psychiatric hospital in 1913, the Freudian anarchist Otto Gross owed his liberation to a newspaper campaign led by the Expressionist writers. Inspired by Nietzsche, Freud, and Max Stirner, Gross had, in his writings, attacked the will to power and patriarchal authority, and the principle of authority, both in the family and in society. Kafka made his acquaintance on a train trip in July of 1917, and later, during a meeting in Prague, Gross suggested to Werfel and Kafka that they publish a journal called *Combat Writings Against the Will to Power* (*Blätter zur Bekämpfung des Machtwillens*). In a letter to Brod in November 1917, Kafka voices his enthusiasm for this project. Everything suggests that Gross personified, in his eyes, the convergence of the revolt against paternal tyranny and (anarchist) resistance to institutional authority. [12]

In his first major work, "The Judgment" (1912), Kafka focuses on paternal authority alone. This is also one of the rare works in which the protagonist seems to submit entirely and without resistance to the father's authoritarian death sentence (he drowns himself in the river). Comparing "The Judgment" with *The Trial*, Milan Kundera observes: "The resemblance between the accusations, guilty verdicts, and executions in the two works reveals the continuity that ties the intimate familial totalitarianism to that of Kafka's great visions." [13] This continuity is essential to understanding the atmosphere of the novels; but they contain another element missing in "The Judgment": the increasingly anonymous, hierarchized, opaque, and remote nature of power.

Amerika, Kafka's first novel (1912–1914), is in this respect a transitional work. The characters who represent power are the paternal figures (Karl Rossmann's father and Uncle Jakob), the marginal characters (Delamarche), and the high-level administrators (the headwaiter and the head porter in the Hotel Occidental). These figures have in common the unbearable authoritarianism whose characteristics will show up in the narrative work of the following years: 1) they adopt an utterly arbitrary attitude, without any moral, rational, or human justification; 2) they make inordinate and absurd demands on the hero/victim; 3) they mistakenly and unjustly consider the hero's guilt to be self-evident, indubitable; 4) they propose a punishment completely disproportionate to the hero's "crime" (nonexistent or trivial). Anyone who obeys them invariably winds up becoming "a dog": when you are always treated like a dog, says Robinson, "you begin to think you actually are one" (A 231). The young Karl Rossmann thinks, however, that this is the case only for those who let themselves be abused. He obeys only the paternal characters and tries, even physically, to resist the others. The most despicable characters are without question the heads of the administrative hierarchy in the Hotel Occidental, who incarnate the principle of authority. Refusing the conciliatory gestures of the Manageress, the headwaiter exclaims: "It's a matter of authority, there's too much at stake, a boy like that might corrupt the whole lot of [the employees]" (A 178). Their authority combines bureaucratic coldness with an individual despotism bordering on sadism, especially in the head porter, who derives a sinister pleasure from brutalizing Rossmann.

The symbol of this punitive authoritarianism appears on the first page of the novel. In a significant modification, Kafka depicts the Statue of Liberty at the entrance to New York harbor as holding a sword rather than the traditional torch. In a world with neither justice nor liberty, naked force (or arbitrary power) reigns without rival. The hero's sympathies are with the victims of this society: for instance, the stoker in the first chapter, an example of the suffering "poor man" who must submit to his superiors; or Theresa's mother, pushed to the point of suicide by hunger and misery. He finds his friends and allies among the poor: Theresa, the student, the people in the lower-class neighborhood who refuse to turn him in to the police, because, writes Kafka, "the workers had no liking for the authorities" (A 219).

Characteristic details show the extent to which certain bureaucrats in *Amerika* can, again, be linked to personal or paternal models of authority. In one of the hotel offices, the porters throw down objects that the exhausted messengers must then pick up and put away. In the "Letter to His Father," Kafka describes his father's behavior toward the employees: "You would push goods you did not want to have mixed up with others, knocking them off the counter . . . and the assistant had to pick them up" (DF 161).

The authoritarian side of American civilization is much less evident in Holitscher's book. It is Kafka who stresses the omnipresence of *domination* in social relations. This difference is particularly striking if one looks at the chapter of Holitscher's book entitled "Hotel Atheneum, Chautauqua." In this big, modern hotel there is an elevator boy who is a high-school student—just like Karl Rossmann in the Hotel Occidental. Unlike the hero of *Amerika*, however, this young "elevator boy," far from being oppressed by a hierarchic and merciless bureaucracy, chats with a rich guest about Latin grammar, and Holitscher concludes that the difference between the social classes must be less accentuated in America than in Europe.[14]

Libertarian utopia does not appear, as such, in *Amerika*. It exists only *by its absence*, as a critique of a world entirely devoid of liberty, subjected to the absurd and arbitrary logic of an all-powerful "apparatus." Kafka reveals an anarchist point of view through his critique of the existing state of things. The structural resemblance that exists between this negative, absent utopia and a *theologia negativa* is striking. In both cases, the positive "beyond" of this world (libertarian utopia or messianic redemption) is *radically absent,* and it is precisely this absence that defines human life as demeaned, damned, or devoid of sense.

Translated by Julie Stone Peters

NIETZSCHE, FREUD, AND KAFKA

Gerhard Kurz

THE ARCHAEOLOGICAL IMPULSE, the search for the "city beneath the cities," unites Nietzsche, Freud, and Kafka in a single configuration as modern excavators of the human psyche (DF 342). Kafka struggled to come to terms with Nietzsche and Freud, and thus a discussion of their importance for him will help to illuminate his literary intentions and themes.

Freud acknowledged late in life that he had avoided reading Nietzsche's remarks on psychology (remarks that coincide with his own theories in the most astonishing way) in order to maintain his own objectivity. He feared the possibility of encountering his double, as he did also in his relation to Arthur Schnitzler.[1] References to Nietzsche appear frequently in his work, as, for example, his note that the term "id" (*es*, literally "it") derives from Nietzsche, who employed it to stand for the "irreconcilable and, so to speak, natural necessities in our being." Freud's debt is also clear in the ease with which he speaks of the "transvaluation of all psychic values," without additional reference, in *The Interpretation of Dreams*. "Transvaluation" of all traditional values was of course Nietzsche's answer to the question: "What happens down below?" However, the similarity of their methodological starting points is more enlightening than the correspondence of particular intellectual terms, and it certainly has more relevance for Kafka. Both undertake an archaeology of the mind,[2] of life itself, at the risk of disturbing deeply repressed emotions; and both envision a psychology that probes the mind's depth in order to enter an inner world which they regard as constitutive of human nature, and to explore "fundamental problems." Both attempt to answer the question "What is it [es] actually?" by asking, "Where does it come from?" and both discover deep in the human psyche the expressive force of the body.

Nietzsche and Freud understand their respective archaeological projects as a subversive, ideologically skeptical investigation of meaning and intention. The principal subjects of their interrogations are the role of the body in the formation of thoughts and expressions, the individual's existential needs, and the unconscious. Moreover, each understands the path into psychic depth as a kind of therapy, for an individual or for an entire culture. Freud's "healing" consists of solving the puzzle of an illness's origins and of the analysand's "acceptance" of this solution—a view that already presupposes Nietzsche's central insight that thoughts and words are inseparably bound to passions and affects. Otherwise the "talking cure" could not be effective.

As students of Schopenhauer, Freud and Nietzsche pursue the archaeology of life forms as a natural history of human suffering. Methodologically their archaeologies proceed as a "critical symptomatology." Human phenomena are interpreted as *symptoms* whose meaning is to be sought in the psychic energies that produced them. The symptoms are examined in terms of their value to the individual and explained in terms of his or her needs. But because they are symptoms, they always signify something other than themselves, especially because the individual subject, at a deep level, is never what he believes himself to be. This critical symptomatology led to a universal subversion of knowledge, to a "transvaluation of all values," whose provocative force is difficult to imagine today. Stefan Zweig called Freud the "second great destroyer" after Nietzsche. His greatest transvaluation was the dethronement of the self: the self is no longer "Master in his own house." At first Freud set the word "Ego" in quotation marks. Nietzsche, too, scorned the "so-called Ego" as a fiction, an invention: "It [Es] thinks: but that this 'It' is precisely that famous, old 'Self' [Ich] is, to put it mildly, merely an assumption." In truth, the subject is a confused "multiplicity," a plurality of voices, and even the body is a "social construction of many souls."

The disintegration of the unified subject was the basis for Kafka's creative experiences of the self. Such terms as "swarm," "army," "cry of jackdaws," "orchestra," "noise," "we," "nomadic people" are all metaphoric figures Kafka used to describe the dissolution of the subject into an inner plurality. The "self" is a misleading term for a complex scene of conflicting "voices," an incomprehensible and confused plurality of selves. Kafka depicts "different subjects in the same person"; the physical organism as a "people," the self as a "folk leader of this organism." But the leader, too, is not master of his people; he is only partially conscious of what is happening—consciousness of the whole being "unimaginable." What is foreign is not the other person, but one's own self. As Kafka notes in aphoristic verse about a man drowning, "in strife with the elements":

> I do not know the contents,
> I have not the key,
> I do not believe the rumors
> all as a matter of course,
> for it is myself. (DF 77)

One's own self is depicted as a world unknown to the Ego. Take, for example, his surreal sketch from the eighth octavo notebook: "I am in the habit of relying on my coachman in everything. When we came past a high white wall, slowly bulging at the sides and at the top, and ceased to drive ahead, driving along the wall, touching it, the coachman finally said: 'It is a forehead' " (DF 128).

Admittedly, prior to Nietzsche a literary tradition of psychological analysis, above all in German Romanticism, had already exposed the individual subject as a fiction. To Novalis, for example, it was clear that "pluralism is our innermost essence."[3] And in his philosophical essay *The Vocation of Man* (1800), Fichte had dissolved the self into a flight of "images that drift by." Since the end of the eighteenth century, psychological literature has considered, as the true problem of subjectivity, not the ego per se, but the ego's lack of self-identity, its instability and estrangement, the confused plurality of voices inside it, its disintegration, and, finally, its own astonishment that it can nevertheless say "I." Hugo von Hofmannsthal's notion of the self as a mere "metaphor," as nothing more than a "busy pigeon coop," is remarkably close to Kafka's use of bird metaphors; it too derives from Nietzsche.

Such instances refer back to a cultural syndrome dating from the *fin de siècle:* an intense experience of the alienation and dissociation of the self, a crisis of identity. In 1904 Hermann Bahr titled a chapter of one of his books "The Unsalvageable Self." And Georg Lukács wrote in *The Theory of the Novel* (1914–1915): "As the objective world breaks down, so the subject, too, becomes a fragment; only the self [*"Ich"*] continues to exist, but its existence is then lost in the insubstantiality of its self-created world of ruins."[4] The "self" is only one voice in a crowd of other, whispering voices, an unclear trace in a contradictory conglomeration of diverse attitudes, instances, and demands. This syndrome crystallized in particular in *fin-de-siècle* Vienna, in the culture of Ernst Mach,[5] Sigmund Freud, Arthur Schnitzler, Robert Musil, Hermann Broch, Hugo von Hofmannsthal, Karl Kraus, Gustav Mahler, and many others.[6] Hofmannsthal's "A Tale of the Cavalry" (1905) and "The Mines at Falun" (1899), Rilke's *The Book of Pictures* (1899–1903) and *The Notebooks of Malte Laurids Brigge* (1910), and Musil's *The Confusions of Young Törless* (1906) are exemplary literary articulations of this experience. In his 1908 essay "The Relation of the Poet to Daydreaming" Freud noted the tendency of modern writers "to split up their ego by self-observation into component-egos, and in this way to personify the conflicting trends in their own mental life in many heroes."[7]

The experience of the self's disintegration and pluralization is one of the fundamental thematics of German literary Expressionism. The pathos of the Expressionist poets' cry for a new self, a new humanity, can only be understood as a response to a deep social crisis of identity. One can interpret the disintegration of the self merely as the internalization of a pathological disintegration of society; but in doing so one should not overlook the insights that writers gained in diagnosing and exploring this "unknown world" of the self—namely, that the self is a fragile synthesis of conflicting demands and forces, a plurality of voices.

The technique of splitting the self into multiple selves, essential to Freud, is basic to literary archaeology. It manifests itself above all in the motif of "the double," which runs through nineteenth-century literature in the works of Jean Paul, E. T. A. Hoffmann, Storm, Droste-Hülshoff, Raimund, Nestroy, Dostoyevsky, Heine, Maupassant, Musset, Nerval, Poe, Dickens, Stevenson, Oscar Wilde, and others. In the double, several figures coalesce into an entity, internally as contradictory as it is complementary. One can interpret this doubling technique as the literary translation of a consciousness that has experienced its own immanent plurality and estrangement, though this consciousness is not the same as the author's and should thus not be taken as a symptom of "hysteria," as some of Freud's followers assumed. This technique is also a dramatic portrayal of the self's destruction, or its healing. The fundamental subversion of the identity and self-transparency of the self emerges in the complex communicative structure of the modern literary text itself. The psychoanalyst's question "Who is speaking?" or "Who is saying 'I'?" in an analysand's dreams is no different from the reader's question of who is speaking in the literary text—the author, the narrator, the person asking the question, or an omniscient consciousness. Yet behind each of these speakers in the text there seems to hide an unknown *soufleur*, an "it" that speaks. [8]

This literary manifestation of the plurality of consciousness can be traced through the middle of the twentieth century. In Beckett's *Murphy* the characters remark of themselves: "Our central axes, or whatever they're called, converge in Murphy. Outside of us." In Kafka's work, even more than in Beckett's, the experience of transience in the self and the world of phenomena becomes the impulse behind the writing. Nothing is certain any longer, neither the self, nor external reality. In *Description of a Struggle* (1904–1905), the narrator's "new acquaintance" asks him: "And I hope to learn from you how things really are, why it is that around me things sink away like fallen snow, whereas for other people even a little liqueur glass stands on the table steady as a statue" (CS 34). Kafka's articulation of the narrator's lost confidence in reality, even in everyday objects and routines, has become part of the present-day theoretical discussion of the crisis of the self and its world. His story begins with an indirect suggestion of the first-person narrator's instability and isolation:

I sat at a tiny table—it had three curved, thin legs—sipping my third glass of benedictine, and while I drank I surveyed my little store of pastry which I myself had picked out and arranged in a pile.

Then I saw my new acquaintance, somewhat disheveled and out of shape, appear at the doorpost of an adjoining room; but I tried to look away for it was no concern of mine. (CS 9)

What "appears" as the narrator's "acquaintance" and then asks him a series of questions, is in fact the narrator's own unconscious, the hidden, distant center of the self, his double. Later, this secret identity is unveiled: "We sat close together in spite of not liking one another at all, but we couldn't move apart because the walls were firmly and definitely drawn" (CS 50). Through character-doubling, "Description of a Struggle" demonstrates that both the self and the world of phenomena have lost their "beautiful contours," the unity and the boundaries of the self have blurred, the self has lost self-control. "And I followed him," we read for example, "without noticing it." The narrator is split from himself and his body; his movements recall those of a marionette. In the course of this intricately constructed story, other figures evolve out of the first-person narrator, figures of other selves. Their common traits unite them in a single configuration: the narrator and the Supplicant are both marked by their puppetlike awkwardness; the Companion and the Fat Man are both grotesquely overweight; the Fat Man is carried around like the narrator, who "rides" his rival; the Companion and the Supplicant both seek an audience.

Kafka employs the technique of doubling in his very first story, the complicated "tale of Shamefaced Lanky and Impure of Heart" (L 6), where two characters form a single configuration. Though still rather crudely executed, the doubling in this tale becomes the basis for Kafka's entire oeuvre, reaching its most developed expression in "The Judgment" (1912). Kafka's heroes are all split figures, split into a self and others, *his* others. Kafka himself was a split figure—a fastidious office worker who took his duties seriously, and someone else for whom "nothing else" existed but literature. To Felice he confided: "As you know, there are two combatants at war within me" (F 544).

Constructed character configurations, a widespread technique in German Expressionist prose, was developed in opposition to the lit-

erary tradition of psychological causality. Carl Einstein wrote his
novel *Bebuquin, or the Dilettantes of Miracle* (1912) as an "obituary
of the self," which dissolves the fiction of substantive personal identity. The main character Bebuquin functions as the synthetic center
of the other characters. The boundaries between the separate figures
begin to blur and often one cannot be sure who is speaking. Remarkable resemblances can be found to Kafka's *Description of a Struggle* in
the motifs of narcissism, the marionette, the Fat Man, and finally of
death.

Nietzsche and Freud display an affinity to such literary models of
the self by developing their respective archaeologies and symptamol-
ogies of the human psyche as a kind of textual exegesis. Both conscious and unconscious life constitute languages to be translated and
texts to be interpreted. Nietzsche sets out to read spoken language as
a symptom of what has been covered over in silence, and thus can
call his enterprise a "semiotics" of life. Similarly, psychoanalysis is an
exegesis of those discourses operating beneath the surface of what the
subject "intends" to say publicly, in the mind's depth, in dreams and
fantasies, and in bodily symptoms. Psychoanalysis interprets human
emotions and memories as ancient texts whose wording—additionally obscured by continual emendations, distortions, and interpola-
tions—must be deciphered. Such methods and assumptions clearly
indicate the influence of a model of textual interpretation that
emerged with Thomas de Quincey and Heinrich Heine in the nineteenth century, more specifically, a model for deciphering palimp-
sests. The obvious difference, though, is that Freud and Nietzsche
never locate an original text; rather, in the beginning there is not *the*
primal scene, but the *possibility* of many such scenes, of scenes within
scenes. Beneath each interior absence lies yet another more profound
absence, a "groundless abyss beneath each ground," as Nietzsche
writes. And for Freud the languages of consciousness and of the body
are constantly circumscribed by other languages, which, in turn, are
"circumscriptions" of other circumscriptions. Consequently, any interpretation is an interpretation of other interpretations. In his
tetralogy *Joseph and His Brothers*, Thomas Mann, who was well acquainted with Freud and Nietzsche, objects to the division between
dream and interpretation: "our dreams arise from interpretations."
Interpretation precedes the interpreter.

For Nietzsche and Freud this archaeology of accumulated interpretations leads to the discovery of archaic situations and patterns, the "primal scenes of mankind's beginnings." The history of mankind remains its "primal" prehistory.[9] Nietzsche maintained that the past streams on in us, in hundreds of waves. This attentiveness to the persistence of archaic history is characteristic of the modern period. In a discussion of Baudelaire, Walter Benjamin notes that the modern period repeatedly cites its archaic past.[10] In Kafka's time the centrality of primal prehistory in consciousness becomes even more prevalent. The turn to the archaic past coincides with an expansion of available aesthetic forms and the development of a literary aesthetic based on primal fears; but it also signifies a growing need for diagnosis, for a critique of modern culture and, thus, a solution to its problems. An observation by Nietzsche exemplifies this moment of aesthetic and cultural critique: "How wonderful and new and yet how terrible and ironic I feel facing the whole of existence with my knowledge! I've discovered for myself that all mankind and the animal kingdom, the entire primordial past and the history of all sensory existence continue to create, to love, and to hate in me."[11] The First World War confirmed this discovery to contemporaries. It put an end to any idea of cultural progress.

Walter Benjamin has rightly characterized the prehistoric world as Kafka's secret present; thus, an interpretation of Kafka must therefore keep in mind that his work leads into the dark womb of the mind's depth. In Kafka, an awareness of the continuing presence of primal ages is allied to motifs of Jewish theological history. Gustav Janouch reports his observation about the "unhealthy, old Jewish city within us," that is more real than the new, "sanitized" one. He once asked Milena Jesenská to consider that a "38-year journey" lay behind him: "and since I'm a Jew an even much longer one" (M 47). Dora Dymant recalls that "Kafka's entire world demands another, more ancient language; a primitive consciousness remains in him, ancient things and ancient fears."[12] He demanded of his writing that it be rooted in ancient centuries. His stories ask to be read as ancient histories—histories of a self that is imagined as a monstrous "tenement house" built on "indestructible medieval ruins" (DF 56–57). Of the ancient Christian martyrs he wrote that they do not "underrate the body," but simply put it on the cross. "In this they are at one with their antagonists" (DF 37). This aphorism, which might seem to come from Nietzsche, displays Kafka's use of a critical symptomatology similar to that found in *Beyond Good and Evil*: there, ascetic priests are said to represent Christianity as a whole. This allegedly life-negating ideal is for Nietzsche a contradiction in terms, and he unmasks it as one of the great forces that preserves and affirms life: through his or her asceticism, the individual reveals himself to be one who desires—especially when, *faute de mieux*, there is nothing to desire. It is in this sense that the martyr, according to Kafka's aphorism, is at one with his antagonists.

This contradictory nature of the ascetic ideal is the subject of Kafka's story "Investigations of a Dog," in which a scholarly hound examines the question of the meaning of life. Fasting signifies for him the "last and strongest means" for his investigations: "The way goes through fasting; the highest, if it is attainable, is attainable only by the highest effort, and the highest effort among us is voluntary fasting" (CS 309). As presented by the dog, fasting is the path of a metaphysical quest, the quest for "sustenance from above." He fasts, he maintains, "to achieve truth and escape from this world of falsehood, where there is no one from whom you can learn truth, not even from me, born as I am a citizen of falsehood" (CS 312).

Similarly, Nietzsche had written that, for the ascetic, life figures as a "bridge" to another existence, much as the dog had sought mastery over life itself. The "experiment" of fasting fails: it is "impossible," says the dog, attributing his failure to his survival instinct. But his explanation that individual "freedom" is powerless against one's animal instincts is still not the complete truth; it seems rather to be an excuse. Later the dog confesses the actual motives behind his rigorous efforts, thereby providing a satirical, symptomatological analysis of all science. His investigations and his fasting are simply attempts to find a meaning to life, to console and placate himself in the face of life's puzzling, unbearable facticity:

> Recently I have taken more and more to casting up my life, looking for the decisive, the fundamental error that I must surely have made; and I cannot find it. And yet I must have made it, for if I had not made it and yet were unable by the diligent labor of a long life to achieve my desire,

that would prove that my desire is impossible, and complete hopelessness must follow. (CS 292)

The dog's rationale for assuming a mistake in his life betrays him: he
wants to have made a mistake because the alternative he must otherwise acknowledge, the hopelessness of existence, is unbearable. To
do so would mean having to forsake life in order to "cross over" into
the realm of truth, as Kafka phrases it in "On Parables" (CS 457).
However, to assume he is mistaken—as he does—suggests that an
explanation of existence still lies within the individual's grasp: there
are reasons enough, the dog confesses, to "protect oneself against
troubling questions." At this point, asking whether he actually wants
to pass from this life of falsehood into truth amounts to just such a
troubling question: "Reasons give solace," Nietzsche notes: thus, the
ascetic ideal reveals the attempt to give meaning to, and justify, suffering as a fact of life, that is, to credit the subject with dominion
over life. The search for a mistake, then, is an attempt to explain and
justify one's life when all other justifications have failed. In Kafka's
story the dog's mistake preserves the possibility of hope and betrays
his will to live; the scholarly dog demonstrates the contradiction inherent in asceticism, which affirms life by claiming to negate it.

Apparently, Kafka knew Nietzsche's work in detail, which is not
surprising. It would be odd if he hadn't, given Nietzsche's ubiquitous
influence at the turn of the century. As Samuel Lublinski observed in
1909, Nietzsche dominates the period "almost to an excessive degree."[13] His thinking—correctly interpreted or otherwise—forms the
background to the period's widely divergent movements and theories.
Only recently have we learned to see how much even German Expressionism owes to Nietzsche its notion of vitalism and social criticism.
The young Walter Benjamin celebrated Nietzsche alongside Tolstoy
and Strindberg as a prophet of the New Man and as a critic of the
primitive hypocrisy of cerebral mankind. Nietzsche figures in this period as a liberator, and specifically a liberator of possibilities for a new
poetic language. The "Dionysian-Dithyrambs" and Thus Spake Zarathustra employ a poetic language that Nietzsche calls "mythic"; it has
its base in no single thought, but represents the act of thinking itself
in its "rhythmic diversity," its "corporeality of expression," its se-

quence of action and suffering. In this "mythic" means of expression one recognizes the main features of Expressionist poetry.

The study of Kafka's relation to Nietzsche was long obstructed by Max Brod's denial of such an influence.[14] The relation first came to light in 1954, when Erich Heller named Nietzsche as Kafka's "intellectual predecessor." Having discovered him while in Gymnasium, Kafka remained faithful to Nietzsche's thinking until his death.[15] For example, in a letter to Brod written on August 7, 1920, he writes that the Greeks created their "whole pantheon" as a means of keeping certain elemental, determining forces "at a distance from man's physical being, so that human lungs could have air" (L 242). This view of Greek religion corresponds quite closely to Nietzsche's analysis in *The Birth of Tragedy* of the roots of the "Olympian magic mountain": "The Greeks were keenly aware of the terrors and horrors of existence; in order to be able to live at all they had to place before them the shining fantasy of the Olympians."[16]

The gesture of transcendence Kafka expresses in his scholarly dog's wish to "achieve truth" exemplifies his affinity with Nietzsche. His brief story "On Parables" (CS 457) similarly deals with the wise men's command to "Go over" to a metaphysically different realm, against which the "many" protest with practical, everyday reasons. The parable presents the possibility of transforming existence, if one would only follow the parables of the wise, including their paradoxical command to "go over"—an echo, it appears, of Nietzsche's Zarathustra, who invokes the "desire that surpasses mankind," who loves those who go "gladly across the bridge," and who is himself "a crossing and a downfall." "I love the downfallen," he says, "with all my love: because they go over." In Kafka's parable, as in *Thus Spake Zarathustra*, the invocation of death combines with an aesthetic view of life. It is difficult to conceive of the notion of life as parable other than in terms of artistic creation, which, said Nietzsche, lightens the burden of life.

Of course, there is also a radical difference between Kafka and Nietzsche. The connection between a desire for death and an aestheticized life, forcefully illustrated in the Jugendstil movement, is by no means a mechanical relation; when viewed as such, it can easily lead to a rigid, forced heroism. Although Kafka's parable "Go over" resembles Nietzsche's on a thematic level, the meaning of death in their respective works marks a point at which the two diverge entirely. Nietzsche's invocation of defeat stands in the service of his phantasmagoria of an overpowering, exuberant life. His mock heroic, aestheticizing attitude, which prefers defeat to mediocrity, turns danger into a "profession"; he fixes his fatal, non-nostalgic gaze at the future, but finally ends in disaster. Kafka, on the other hand, invokes death to regain his failed, guilty existence. His work is a thanatology, a metaphysics of dying. In this respect, Schopenhauer is his dominant predecessor.

In this context a further similarity between Nietzsche and Kafka should be pointed out. Kafka's reflections, observations, and aphorisms are based on a technique and logic of argumentation that corresponds closely to Nietzsche's method of "skeptical questioning." Nietzsche himself was given over to aphorism, both in his own work and in the work of those whom he respected. Aphoristic thinking is characteristically open-ended, pursuing a single train of thought which is antithetical to system, synthesis, and resolution; rather, it relies on—very often deriving from—conflict between the general and the particular, paradox and ambivalence. When effective, it criticizes ideology and takes nothing, not even the safest assumptions, for granted. The aphorism appeals to the reader's own reflections about himself and his experiences, and thus has traditionally served the purposes of moral didacticism.

Kafka's collection of aphorisms "He" stands in this tradition. The personal pronoun "he," the subject of these aphoristic notes, expresses both self-referentiality and distance from the self, the "borderland between loneliness and fellowship" (D 396). At the core of these texts is a mode of skeptical questioning that, as with Nietzsche, leads to the "reversal of customary views and values." Kafka formulates this reversal into startling paradoxes, for example, "A cage went in search of a bird" (DF 36). Similarly, he reverses the accepted view of modern freedom and individuality: "who searches, will not find, but who doesn't search, will be found." The surprising point of this aphorism emerges through the parallel construction and oppositional conjunction that lead the reader to expect the words "will find" in the latter clause: instead one reads "is found." With this turn the aphorism also poses the possibility of salvation. Kafka reinterprets the "saving" of Robinson Crusoe in a similar manner:

> If Robinson had never left the highest, or more correctly, the most vis-
> ible point of the island, he would've soon met his demise; however,
> since he began to explore the island and to enjoy it, without paying
> further attention to the ships and their weak telescopes, he kept himself
> alive and, in what stands to reason as a necessary consequence, he was
> finally found.

The ships' "weak" telescopes are able to find Crusoe only because he
begins to live without regard for being found, for his "Salvation" (*Ret-
tung*).

These aphoristic notes suggest that truth is achieved by asking
questions based on the logic of symptoms. By treating any common
expression as the symptom of a misunderstanding, such questioning
discovers the expression's true meaning. Of course, this is the form of
all critiques of ideology, which in turn raises the difficult question of
the dogmatic basis of ideology. This mode of questioning is based on
the constant suspicion that all phenomena are masks that have to be
stripped away to show the true face of things.

As discussed, Nietzsche analyzes the ascetic ideal of "life against
life" as a "provisional expression" that in truth signifies its opposite,
the preservation of life. His skeptical philosophy claims to accurately
reconstruct the hidden meanings of an expression. The provisional
expression, he says, is not a lie but its real value is *as a symptom*. In
his exegesis of the doorkeeper parable in *The Trial*, the priest explains
to Joseph K. that one can make a true statement even though he or
she is confused about its meaning: "The commentators note in this
connection: 'The right perception of any matter and a misunderstanding of the same matter do not wholly exclude each other' " (T
216). Kafka's phrase "constructive destruction" (DF 103) might serve
as a caption to this logic of skeptical questioning. He reduces the
symptomatic meaning of an expression to its true meaning: "Self-
forgetfulness and self-canceling-out of art: what is an escape is
pretended to be a stroll or even an attack" (DF 81). Art's self-under-
standing is unmasked as self-forgetting and self-negation. In fact, art
is an escape: insofar as it sees itself simply as a diverting activity, as a
"stroll," it forgets what it actually is. In seeing itself as an attack, art
negates itself:

Abraham is laboring under the following delusion: he cannot endure the monotony of this world. Now the fact is that this world is notoriously and uncommonly manifold, which can be put to the test at any moment if one just takes up a handful of World and looks at it a little more closely. Naturally, Abraham knows this too. And so his complaint about the monotony of the world is actually a complaint about an insufficiently profound mingling with the manifold nature of the world. And so it is actually a springboard into the world. (DF 103)

The logic of this analysis is based on the opposition of self-deception—the acceptance of a symptom as the truth—and the knowledge of what "is." The lament about the monotony of the world is thus only the provisional, ideological expression of its opposite, the truth—namely, the need to merge with the world.

Kafka's analysis in the passage "Know Thyself" provides an especially poignant example of his "constructive destruction":

"Know Thyself" does not mean "Observe Thyself." "Observe Thyself" is what the Serpent says. It means: "Make yourself master of your actions." But you are so already, you are the master of your actions. So that saying means: "Misjudge yourself! Destroy yourself!" which is something evil—and only if one bends down very far indeed does one also hear the good in it, which is: "In order to make yourself what you are." (DF 72)

The injunction "Know Thyself" is subjected to a series of questions in order to dispel its apparent meaning. It does not mean "Observe Thyself"; rather, it amounts to "Make yourself master of your actions." This, however, undermines itself: it assumes that the self already *is* master of its actions. Thus, because the imperative "Know Thyself" presupposes a condition of selfhood that does not yet exist, it cannot then demand that conditions change in order to create what is assumed to be the case. Therefore, the command must be directed *against* the present condition, that is, against mastery of one's actions and against the authority of the subject. The expression signifies its opposite: "Destroy Thyself!" Thus, it means something evil, in whose depths one nevertheless hears something good, namely, the challenge to "become" what one actually "is" inside.[17] In fact, the subject has no mastery over itself and its actions, and *this* is the "good" of which one should be fully conscious, as the challenge indicates. The injunction obliquely retracts the subject's claim to live as master of its own actions and instead promotes an attitude of humility or belief whose meaning is identical with "Being." "Believing means liberating the indestructible element in oneself, or, more accurately, liberating oneself, or, more accurately, being indestructible, or, more accurately, being" (DF 78).

This type of interrogation—that the truth is always other than it appears and other than we think it is—is also at work in Kafka's stories and novels. Unrelentingly, his works reverse our accustomed views and values in order to reveal the "truth" hidden in their depths. His narrative structures reverse, reduce, and negate complacent verities. This narrative method is subversive, a technique of suspicion, drawing commonplace formulations into a vortex of skeptical questioning in order to make visible the truth concealed within them.

Nietzschean themes also seem to provide the context for Kafka's reception of psychoanalysis. The cultural revolution between 1890 and 1920 is not least a result of the growing influence of psychoanalysis, which in turn was part of this cultural revolution. The discovery of the impotence of consciousness and the power of the unconscious certainly contributed to the undermining of traditional social and political hierarchies. Freud's teachings about the pathogenic effects of the family on the individual, about the individual as an unfortunate family animal, and about the struggle between fathers and sons as an anthropological constant (cf. *Totem and Taboo*, 1912) correspond remarkably to themes of Expressionist literature—though one cannot in every case speak of a Freudian influence. After Strindberg's *The Father* (1887) the murderous conflict between a son and his father becomes an increasingly common theme. Walter Hasenclever's drama *The Son* (1913), Sorge's *The Beggar* (1912), Johst's *The Young Man* (1916), Bronnen's *Patricide* (1915), Werfel's *Not the Murderer, the Victim Is Guilty* (1920) all treat this theme, often simply as a gesture of rebellion. Moreover, Kafka considered publishing "The Judgment" (1912), "The Stoker," and *The Metamorphosis* in a single volume entitled *The Sons*, since there exists between the stories "an obvious connection among the three and, even more important, a secret one" (L 96). In 1919 Paul Federn interpreted the revolutionary character of the period as a repetition of primal rebellion against the father. Kafka's "Letter to His Father," which vacillates between revolt and admiration, also belongs in this context, for it formulates a fundamental critique of the "spell of our upbringing" (DF 165), of education as a parental conspiracy, and imagines a utopia where children are raised apart from their parents. In the letter he analyzes the "terrible trial" (DF 168) between himself and his father as both unique and archetypal, particular and primal. Finally, the letter also reflects the contemporary notions of genetic determinacy that had accompanied presentations of generational conflict since Strindberg's *The Father.*

One important promulgator of Freud's ideas was Otto Gross— himself a contemporary *cause célèbre* of the father-son conflict. In 1913 his father had him committed to a psychiatric clinic because of his drug addiction and anarchist writings.[18] In the April 2 issue of the journal *Aktion,* Gross had published an essay entitled "On Overcoming the Cultural Crisis" in which he treats Freud as the successor to Nietzsche, and both as witnesses to the coming revolution against patriarchal authority, which would result in matriarchal social structures. In 1917 Kafka met with Franz Werfel, Max Brod, and Gross to discuss plans for a journal that would promote the cause of psychoanalysis. This project seemed to him for a long while "tempting enough" (L 167). His comment after completing "The Judgment"— "thoughts on Freud, of course"—also testifies to his familiarity with psychoanalysis. He seemed to himself "obsessed" by the "realm of damnedly psychological theory" (L 159).

During this time, however, Kafka had also become critical of the methods of psychoanalysis. For him, a psychic "illness" was only a "provisional" name for something else entirely. As he wrote to Milena Jesenská and later noted in his diary:

> You say you do not understand it. Try to understand it by calling it illness. It is one of the many manifestations of illness that psychoanalysis believes it has revealed. I do not call it illness, and I regard the therapeutic claims of psychoanalysis as an impotent error. All these so-called illnesses, however sad they may look, are facts of belief, the distressed

human being's anchorages in some maternal ground or other; thus, it is not surprising that psychoanalysis finds the primal ground of all religions to be precisely the same thing as what causes the individual's 'illnesses.' . . . Such anchorages, which do grip real ground, are, however, not an individual possession of each man's; they are something that is pre-established in man's nature and which afterwards goes on transforming his nature (and his body too) in the same direction. And does anybody really think this is a subject for treatment? (DF 300–301)

Kafka's criticism here is in the spirit of Nietzsche, who interpreted illness as the necessary expression of a vital need. Of course this interpretation of the function of illness is not far from Freud's, since the founder of psychoanalysis also saw illnesses as the first attempts to cure oneself. Kafka, too, insists that his lung "wound" was part of his nature and that if his illness were "disentangled," he would "fall apart." "In any case my attitude toward the tuberculosis today resembles that of a child clinging to the pleats of its mother's skirt" (L 138). In a similar vein he describes his need to write as being anchored in him like "delusions in a madman." Criticizing psychoanalysis for not going far enough, he interprets his tuberculosis as "a germ of death itself, intensified, though to what degree we cannot at the time being determine" (L 151). Psychoanalysis fails in its therapeutic task because it evades the fact of death, because it fails to recognize, as Heidegger would put it shortly thereafter in 1927, that being is a "Being unto death." Kafka interpreted his own illness as a symptom of his body's intention to die.

Kafka's objection to psychoanalysis derives from his interpretation of existence as an inscrutable, inexplicable Being unto death, an interpretation that becomes clear in his allegorical denial of all notions of progress or enlightenment. In a literary sketch he uses the metaphor of a mine deep below the Earth: a worker on the night shift urges the director of the mine to improve the "construction and filling of our lamps." The progressively minded director answers:

But here is something for you to tell your workmates downstairs: we here shall not rest until we have made a drawing-room of your shaft, and if you do not all finally go to your doom in patent-leather shoes, then you shall not go at all. And with this I wish you a very good day! (DF 113)

His words become ludicrous, since even in patent-leather shoes one will still die the same death, and the untiring ambition to transform a mineshaft into a drawing room will also end with an old-fashioned burial.

Kafka's contemporary Italo Svevo criticized psychoanalysis in a similar fashion. In *The Confessions of Zeno* (1923), Zeno Cosini protests against psychoanalysis "because life is always fatal. It suffers no cures." Svevo and Kafka criticize psychoanalysis as an impossible attempt to cure life itself, as a means of repressing the fact of death. However, it is important to note that Freud shows surprising affinities to Kafka in his *Beyond the Pleasure Principle* (1920), where he introduces the metapsychological notion of life as a conflict between a death drive and a life drive, a conflict reaffirmed in his subsequent work. Similarly, Kafka places his protagonists in an ambivalent position between these two drives, in the end giving the death drive preeminence over the life drive. Freud's metapsychological opposition between Eros and Thanatos actually disrupts the methodology of psychoanalysis and has therefore remained controversial. Interestingly, Freud too turns to Schopenhauer. We cannot deny, he writes, that "we have entered the port of Schopenhauer's philosophy, in which death is 'the real result' of life, and thus its purpose." [19]

Aside from his pronounced reservations, Kafka attributes significant value to psychoanalysis as being itself a symptom of the period, a symptom of the suffering of his generation. As he remarks about Franz Werfel's treatment of psychoanalysis in his drama *Schweiger:*

> This I consider a debasing of the sufferings of a whole generation. Anyone who has no more to say about this than psychoanalysis has ought not to meddle with the subject. There is no pleasure in spending any time on psychoanalysis, and I keep as aloof from it as I possibly can, but it does at least exist every bit as much as this generation does. Jewry has always produced its sufferings and joys almost simultaneously with the appropriate Rashi commentary, and thus it is in this case too. (DF 247–48)

For Kafka, psychoanalysis is a chapter of Jewish history, which has eternally been forced to comment upon itself, to question and interpret itself. This view does not do justice to psychoanalysis as a whole, but it does provide it with a profound justification. Psychoanalysis is a commentary upon the "terrible inner condition" of the contemporary generation of Jews, particularly writers. Their sufferings, in this insightful analysis, cannot be explained by the model of a father complex because they are less concerned with the father than with the father's Judaism. Freud himself acknowledged that it was perhaps no coincidence that the founder of psychoanalysis was Jewish. To identify oneself with psychoanalysis, Freud wrote, "required a considerable willingness to adopt the fate of isolated opposition, a fate more familiar to Jews than to others." For Freud the slain father was not a legendary Greek king, but Jacob Freud, a Jew who came to the West from a tiny Galician town. Of course, Freud's tendency to equate Western and Jewish cultures belies a fair bit of rationalization—that is, his attempt to deny his father's Judaism as well as his own.

The complexity of Kafka's attitude toward psychoanalysis prevents us from viewing him simply as the translator of Freud's ideas into literature. It is more correct to say that he treats psychoanalysis and his own writing on the same level: as commentaries on his generation's historical situation and on the general condition of human existence. Yet in doing so he claims to be able to say more than psychoanalysis, which provides, despite its usefulness to Kafka, no magic key for us to interpret his work.

In constructing his characters Kafka undoubtedly drew both on Freud's analyses of the mechanisms of sexuality. Kafka's texts are laden with explicitly sexual scenes that sometimes verge on obscenity. In The Metamorphosis, Gregor's partially undressed Mother rushes toward the Father, "embracing him, in complete union with him" (CS 122). This should not lead us to conclude that his stories deal ultimately with sexual drama; rather, they are existential dramas. The sexual scenes ultimately direct the reader's attention to the text's existential meaning.

Kafka's female characters exemplify the function of sexuality in his work. The women are all associated with the hero's goal; they direct him to it. Fräulein Bürstner in The Trial—the name alludes to the verb bürsten, an obscene word for sexual intercourse—has an intense erotic attraction for K. and belongs to the sphere of the court, as do the wife of the court usher and Leni. In the final execution scene,

Fräulein Bürstner gives K. a "warning" to die. In *The Castle* Frieda
wants to hold onto K. but becomes aware of the castle official Klamm.
Rosa in *A Country Doctor* is a symbol of beauty and erotic life but her
name also alludes to the red of Christ's mortal wound—again dem-
onstrating the close and complex association of the two drives in Kafka's work.

The absolute claims of love and erotic submission anticipate the
absolute demands of existence, the final existential act of submission
to death. Thus, the judges in *The Trial* are described as skirt-chasers,
and the law books contain not laws but obscene, "dirty" drawings.
One can say that Kafka took seriously the ancient metaphor of the
Liebestod (love-death) in *The Castle* when he has K. experience
death in an embrace with Frieda on the floor "among the small
puddles of beer and other refuse," as the fulfillment of his unconscious
wishes:

> There hours went past, hours in which they breathed as one, in which
> their hearts beat as one, hours in which K. was haunted by the feeling
> that he was losing himself or wandering into a strange country, farther
> than ever man had wandered before, a country so strange that not even
> the air had anything in common with his native air, where one might
> die of strangeness, and yet whose enchantment was such that one could
> only go on and lose oneself further. (C 54)

Eroticism entices Kafka into other regions from which there is no
return. An entry in the third octavo notebook examines this ambivalence toward love. Kafka quotes the platonic distinction between
earthly and heavenly love: "Sensual love deceives one as to the nature
of heavenly love; it could not do so alone, but since it unconsciously
has the element of heavenly love within it, it can do so" (DF 42). In
another note he equates the seductiveness of woman with the seductiveness of the world:

> This world's method of seduction and the token of the guarantee that
> this world is only a transition are one and the same. Rightly so, for only
> in this way can this world seduce us, and it is in keeping with the truth.
> The worst thing, however, is that after the seduction has been successful
> we forget the guarantee and thus actually the Good has lured us into
> Evil, the woman's glance into her bed. (DF 47)

The equation of woman and world recalls one of the great visual motifs in the tradition of asceticism: the world as a woman who both
allures and repels. In Kafka's work women tempt the protagonist into
a realm beyond themselves, into death. The women tempt him to
perform a *Stoss*, a "thrust"—a common symbolic term in Kafka's
work. The "thrust" signifies sexual intercourse—and thus salvation
and death, the "thrust" out of life. At the end of "The Judgment,"
Georg Bendemann's death coincides with the endless, transcendent
"intercourse" (*Verkehr*) of traffic, streaming over the bridge.

Translated by Neil Donahue

KAFKA'S EGOLESS WOMAN: OTTO WEININGER'S *SEX AND CHARACTER*

Reiner Stach

WITH THE IDEA OF MYTH, the Feminine gained entry into the realm of theory—but only as another myth. The familiar images of woman as natural being, primal mother, vampire, sphinx, or the promise of happiness, were not disavowed but rather conceptualized into theory. However, the very continuity of these cultural projections allows us to decode prevalent sexual myths in their theoretical, largely affirmative reformulations. Besides psychoanalysis, the most influential attempt to develop a theory of sexuality was Otto Weininger's dissertation, which was published under the title *Sex and Character* in 1903.[1] The extent to which the struggle between the sexes had become the subject of scholarly research can be gauged by the case with which Weininger refers at central points in his argument to everyday erotic phenomena such as cosmetics, fashion, coquetry, and prostitution, apparently assuming that such discussions would not cause his examiners to question the seriousness of his work. Even his completely unfounded aesthetic and moral invectives against women escaped academic censure.[2]

Today it is difficult to comprehend the enormous success of his work, although traces of its influence can be found throughout the century. Fed by the sensational suicide of its twenty-three-year-old author (a convert from Judaism to Christianity), interest in the work increased steadily through the 1920s, but was eventually suppressed under pressure of anti-Semitic cultural politics in Germany and Austria. The twenty-fifth edition of *Sex and Character* appeared in 1923, and translations were published in eight languages. In 1926 and 1932 there even appeared popular "folk editions" with fewer notes; a collection of quotations for salon society also found a market.[3] What might appear to be merely a "popular" reception is misleading, though, for the book had a strong influence on contemporary writers and intellectuals, especially in Austria, but also in Italy, for example, where for a time a Weininger cult raged.[4] The popular topoi "genius" and "insanity" around the turn of the century served to further Weininger's notoriety and interest in his fate. As late as 1949, Gottfried Benn counted the author of *Sex and Character* among the three Jewish geniuses he had encountered; Kafka he praised merely as a "talent of the first order."[5]

The extent of Weininger's influence indicates a strong need for such theories, a need that undoubtedly originated in the incipient breakdown of traditional sex roles. To bourgeois men, it seemed incomprehensible that women, who had begun to enter the spheres of production and culture, could or would want to abandon their previously well-protected positions. As fear of feminine domination spread, Weininger promised complete enlightenment, a solution to these mystifying developments. In Kafka's case one must also add his curiosity (perhaps as a result of his own fear of sexuality) about theories positing an inherent polarity between the sexes or, more generally, the conflictual nature of sexuality—as his interest in psychoanalysis suggests.

There is no direct documentation available to establish how and at what point Kafka became acquainted with Weininger's theories.[6] It seems inconceivable, however, that he could have ignored such a well-known and controversial theory, especially one whose appeal derived from its claim to liberate men, through analysis, from their fear of femininity and simultaneously excuse this fear as an entirely natural *horror vacui*.[7] But here the biographical question of influence is secondary, and in any case an answer would require an exact, methodological definition of "influence." More important is the profound similarity between Weininger's theoretical description and Kafka's aesthetic projection of femininity, a similarity indicating that both authors shared a common fund of social and cultural experience.

This similarity is by no means readily apparent, and requires inter-pretation as well as methodological discrimination. Before discussing the function of the female figures in Kafka's texts, it is essential to clarify the female characterology they embody, either implicitly or explicitly. In Weininger's *Sex and Character* one can distinguish be-tween his model of the feminine and his moral judgments, which constantly influence his explication of the model. Explication is for Weininger always "deduction," and his concept of "woman" an at-tempt to use a pure Kantian category, without regard for the history of women in society. Even when introduced as the logical conse-quence of the model, his moral judgments are thinly, if ontologically, disguised polemics and invectives, which today make the book un-bearable; as a result, its cultural significance has been underesti-mated.[8] Contemporary readers dismissed his vehemently misogynist rhetoric as youthful excess, while devoting much attention to those sections of the book that—by comparison—seemed to be analytical. Karl Kraus's message to Weininger is characteristic: "An admirer of women concurs with the arguments of your contempt for women."[9]

Weininger begins with a grand thesis and devotes much space to establishing its scientific foundation: the fundamental bisexuality of human life and the existence of a graduated scale of intermediate sexual forms between male and female. More exactly, there are *only* intermediate forms, mixtures of the two "types" of "ideal man" (M) and "ideal woman" (W), which exist only in theory. Bisexuality, for-merly a mild variant of homosexual perversion, is advanced to the status of an anthropological constant: "The fact is that males and females are like two substances combined in different proportions, but with neither element ever wholly missing. We find, so to speak, never either a man or a woman, but only the male condition or the female condition" (8).

Someone unfamiliar with the history of male projections of femi-ninity might believe that such an acknowledgment of fluid sexual boundaries is progressive per se because it questions rigid sex roles and undercuts the logic for stereotypes which degrade and marginalize women. The opposite, however, is true. With his tactic of "sexual mixtures," Weininger avoids two old methodological difficulties of misogynist theories without altering their repressive nature. The first concerns the epistemological justification of male judgments about the female psyche: How can the (male) observer gain access to those emotional fluctuations that, as is well known, the woman never discloses? Weininger answers: Through introspection, since each man carries a portion of femininity within himself.[10] The second difficulty is the sheer impossibility of proving empirically the inferiority of women. After all, more than a few men displayed "female" characteristics such as passivity, sentimentality, and conceptual weakness, whereas women were already being recognized for their scientific and artistic achievements. Weininger responds that the "mixture coefficient" of these men and women tends in each case to the opposite sexual pole, as is evident in their external features: the feminine is by definition passive, whereas active women are simply masculinized women.

Such maneuvers, long known as the hypostatization of femininity, find their purest and most perverse expression in Weininger's work: he does not theorize about empirical women but about the typological *ideal* of womanhood, about "W," the "Feminine," "woman." This hypostatization protects his theory from social reality: as an "investigation of principles"—this is Weininger's subtitle—the work remains impervious to empirical observation or experience. However, his subject matter is empirical, and the ethical, cultural, and political consequences of his theory of femininity affect real women, not femininity.

Characteristic of this manner of specious rationalism, which dominated the discussion of femininity around the turn of the century, is the brutally systematic approach with which Weininger believes himself able to specify every aspect of that puzzling substance W. One learns that the purely Feminine is a negative syndrome, a syndrome of defects and deficiencies: essentially, it is defined by what it is not.[11] Positive (male) traits of differentiation, such as individuality and personality, are weak in W. Weininger claims the existence of a central empty core: "The absolute woman has no ego" (186). And insofar as Weininger understands the "self" as the stronghold of regulative, strictly conceptual ideas—the result of his psychologized reception of Kant—he merely needs to develop a complete canon of these rules in order to arrive at an equally complete negative canon for W.

Accordingly, in his view, woman has no conception of *truth*. She can relate to this concept neither affirmatively nor negatively, to say nothing of critically. If she speaks truth, then it is not for the sake of truth; if she lies, it is not for the sake of lying: thus, "the woman always lies, even if, objectively, she speaks the truth" (287). Weininger continues in this vein, to the point of complete nonsense, speaking of an "ontological untruthfulness of women" (264).

Among the analogous defects, woman suffers with respect to a concept of morality and guilt, which has the interesting consequence that a woman cannot sin. Weininger solves the old problem of why woman, traditionally the embodiment of sin, is statistically underrepresented in all categories of crime: "I am not arguing that woman is evil and anti-moral; I state that she cannot be really evil; *she is merely non-moral*" (197). For the same reason—a claim with important implications for *The Trial*—she also knows no self-doubt: "Women are convinced of their own integrity without ever having sat in judgment on it" (196). In this tone he traverses the firmament of ideas about bourgeois emancipation. W has no sense of beauty as such, only the effect of attractiveness on men, the "social currency" of beauty. Freedom, necessity, and causality are unknown to women; thus, they lack not only all insight into their own "destiny" (to be a woman), but also the capacity to arrive at such an insight through analytical, logical thinking. Finally, Weininger denies women the capacity to conceive of property—private, of course—as a genuine quality of the self, thus providing himself with an excellent explanation of female kleptomania (205–206).[12]

To understand the social behavior of W, it is essential to note that, since W is itself undifferentiated, it has no access to concepts of individuality and subjectivity. Women can relate to themselves only as things; they are without dignity. For women, self-consciousness, pride, and vanity depend only upon external qualities—an unblemished bodily appearance, fashionable attire, and so on (210–12). Women measure the significance of all others according to the same criteria. Since the subjectivity of others, as well as their own, is beyond their comprehension, women remain excluded from meaningful social achievement. "W is at most in love; M loves," Weininger claims. "Female friendship means merely sticking together" (288).

For Weininger the woman is a cheat of nature, who becomes

sphinxlike because man does not wish to admit that there is nothing
to discover:

> Women can appear everything and deny everything, but in reality they
> are never anything. Women have neither this nor that characteristic;
> their peculiarity consists in having no characteristics at all; the com-
> plexity and terrible mystery about women come to this; it is this which
> makes them above and beyond man's understanding—man, who always
> wants to get to the heart of things. (294)

Weininger deals in this passage only with the static aspect of the Feminine, affirming that W is without structure. Actual women in
society, however, are not simply diffuse, amorphous, ungovernable
creatures. They are neither fully passive nor malleable at will; goal-
oriented, "active" women also exist. What, then, takes the place of
male "ideas"?

Here Weininger invokes the ancient myth of woman as sexuality
incarnate—to provide support for his rigid, formal model. Sexual desire is the incomprehensible, vital, regulating factor of all female
thought, volition, and behavior. The woman is formless matter, is
nothing, but sexuality colors this nothingness, which shines forth
from every female action.

Female social activity is the atrophied, but sexually charged vestige
of male sociality—its caricature, in fact. The female, who knows no
self, and thus no "Thou," can perceive and acknowledge neither herself nor an other as a unique, defined, and differentiated being. Her
longing is directed not at man, but at a particular man's masculinity;
therefore, her sexuality is always reifying and instrumental. She en-
croaches upon the male ego, destroys it, dissolves its boundaries; his
ego, however, is capable of mixing with an other (without destroying
it). The woman wants the couple, wants to couple.[13]

Female interaction is thus always a form of sexual reification. Female desire, which is never anything other than sexual, is directed
entirely toward the condition of mixing and merging, which it tries
to achieve without exception in each physical, psychological, and
social action. Not only love or coitus offer women the possibility of
fulfillment; the extending of sympathy, caring, mothering, touching

other and touching herself, as well as participation in the coitus of others through gossip and matchmaking, also provide this fulfill-ment.[14]

Two apparently irreconcilable and radical forms of this kind of de-sire appear in society—motherhood and prostitution. It is perhaps Weininger's most popular thesis that these two boundaries mark the spectrum for the "empirical" character of all women. Each feminine display of affection is at once erotic and maternal. Yet these compo-nents are compatible since both "types" represent both the desire to merge as well as the deindividualized arbitrariness of this desire: on the one hand, "absolute mother" whose love is independent of the personality of her child or the husband she has accepted as a child, and on the other, the "absolute whore," whose promiscuity is likewise indiscriminate. Despite their completely different status in society, these two variants always appear together and in a nearly inextricable ambiguity.

It quickly becomes clear that this schematization of female defi-ciency is a theoretical system with striking similarities to the practice of Kafka's literary characterization of women. Heinz Politzer has noted that at least two women in *The Trial*, the usher's wife and Leni, correspond entirely to Weininger's mother-whore type; in particular, their offers of help display "an exemplary mix of the maternal and the whorish."[15] This approach can lead much further, however, to reveal a profound affinity between Kafka's portrayal of the Feminine and Weininger's model of female deficiency, which, because of his typol-ogy, I will henceforth refer to as the "feminine type."[16] [. . .]

Perhaps as a result of the passive core of their constructions, Kaf-ka's female characters act entirely as variations on Weininger's femi-nine type—not with respect to their narrative function but instead on the level of a feminine characterology. Several figures appear who clearly represent the model in toto, while others illustrate in varying degrees certain aspects of the model such as egolessness and passive activity. Therefore, an approach is required that is not simply de-scriptive or chronological; rather, we must establish correspondences between Kafka's female protagonists *through* the model of the femi-nine type, and thereby show the figures in a series extending beyond individual characters in individual works.

Weininger deserves credit for having formulated with previously unparalleled directness two characteristics of antifeminine resentment. First, that masculinity is law, measure, rule, territory—entities that are threatened by, and antagonistic to, whatever is without order, exceptional, unbounded. The feminine draws the masculine beyond its own limits and is, in the language of Deleuze and Guattari's *Anti-Oedipus*, the agent of "deterritorialization" itself. Second, that antifeminine resentment is totalitarian and paranoid. The more it braces itself against the hated exception, the more reason it has to fear contamination. To those under the spell of this resentment, any discussion or compromise appears as a dangerous blurring of boundaries, as "destruction." Since only a single form of confrontation is imaginable without redefining boundaries—namely, the systematic and complete destruction of the other—Weininger's line of reasoning devolves into fantasies of annihilation that throw a grim light on the motives behind his brutal system: the essence of woman, the substratum of the feminine, must be obliterated.[17]

However, this directness has been achieved with a degree of abstraction that can hardly be imitated in aesthetic terms. Strindberg, who was a devoted follower of Weininger in later years, made this clear with a series of entirely schematic and bloodless thesis-characters that depart from the traditional portrayal of femininity, but only manage to reproduce the negative canon partially, and out of context at that: his women sponge off others, lie, squander, and speak stupidities.[18]

Admittedly, for Weininger, women have at their disposal a broad palette of social graces—tactics which, on the one hand, make them dangerous and, on the other, allow them to correspond to male projections. However, the inner point where all these threads meet is presumed to be simply an emptiness, a barren nothingness dominated by an uncontrolled sexual appetite. Weininger initially avoids the precipice of women's unconstrained sexuality by separating the concept of feminine nature from any specific cases of individual psychology, thus making the problem ontological.[19] In contrast, the dramatist must work with a particular individual, whom he can of course invent, but cannot reduce to a bare concept. His character can never be transparent, she remains open to interpretation and unfolds sensual, gestural, and discursive qualities which the spectator is free to make sense of. The difficulty for the misogynist author, which Strindberg clearly did not resolve, would be to compose a believable female character whose interpretation and reconstruction *reveal* this inner nothingness.

In his prose Kafka developed a number of characterization techniques that achieve this requirement. Conclusions about his model of the feminine and its moral consequences can be drawn only very indirectly, as will become clear. Yet one must see that he held on to such deindividualizing techniques even when the results became grotesque. This is already apparent in an early and still relatively rough effort, the figure of Brunelda in *Amerika*, upon whose sensual abundance the chapter "The Refuge" focuses. There are two linked processes here that amount to a virtual emptying of the female ego—reification of the body and psychic regression.

Brunelda's body, bathed in harsh light, appears as a monstrous, inanimate object, whose particular movements we learn about in the neutral tone of an instruction manual, and whose distinguishing features are primarily mass and inertness. Brunelda is almost entirely immovable and is not able to undress or wash herself (A 211). "Although she's so fat, she's very delicate" (A 215), and therefore spends her days lying on the sofa. When she must vacate her apartment, it takes her male companions hours to carry her down the steps. She eats and smacks her lips, breathes heavily, and while sleeping, sighs and snorts like a machine so that the whole room is filled with the sound of her breathing. Her very being, it seems, robs other occupants of the "refuge" of space and air. Delamarche, Robinson, and Karl crowd around Brunelda; they lack even the freedom of movement needed to clean the room. When she forces the young but strong Karl against the balcony railing, he cannot avoid a tender hug by her "soft, fat little hands that immediately crush everything" (A 236).

Brunelda's sexuality is radically externalized in her bodily appearance, in pure passivity, uncontrollable states and theatrical posturings. Inexplicable attacks of feverishness are apparently characteristic—"I can't bear this heat, I'm burning, I must take off my clothes" (A 210)—as is her repeated spreading of her legs "so as to get more room for her disproportionately fat body" (A 210–11). A diffuse shamelessness, with no identifiable goal, appears as the

expression, even as the demand, of her bodily mass. And as if reification were not carried far enough, Kafka illuminates this figure with
the colors of bordello eroticism; the room is suffused with "dim red
lighting" (A 239); of her many possessions, she prefers a red dress,
which "suits her far the best of them all," and which is mentioned
repeatedly in the text (A 214–15). When she meets Delamarche, she
is dressed in white and carrying a red parasol, with which she points
out to her new lover the way to her apartment. Kafka's use of color
signals is extraordinarily precise here: in a fragment* he has Brunelda
run "her fat red tongue back and forth between her lips"; her "very
loose dress" is nevertheless now only "pale pink," an indication of her
diminishing sexual powers. In fact, another fragment assumes that
her friend Delamarche has taken off or been put in jail, so that her
only remaining means of survival is prostitution (for which she, oddly
enough, is already officially registered). While she has Karl cart her
to "Enterprise Number 25," she covers herself with a *gray* cloth.[20]

This monster in apparent decline has established a tortuous tyranny, but is not really dangerous. Brunelda is not erotically attractive;
her body is too strictly circumscribed by its animal needs. Her atrophied psyche, barricaded within her like a vestigial organ, does not
lead one to look for a communicative ego or the "heart of things"
denied women by Weininger. Here we find pure regression: willful
desires (such as that for perfume) appear suddenly, are enforced by
laments and crying, and disappear a moment later when some new
bodily need occurs to her. Brunelda sits in her bathtub and hits the
water with her fists, she drums on the sofa with her hands and
screams senselessly until she passes out. No doubt a somatic will-
power is at work here, as if the body knows nothing but its own
corporeality. Brunelda throws her weight around against Karl and
threatens Delamarche that she will run naked in the street. Only in
one passage does this animalistic and infantile behavior reflect a
threatening authoritarianism where it sharpens to an aggressive, aso-
cial gesture. When Brunelda's former husband, disdained but still
slavish, leaves her a luxurious present made of porcelain, she breaks
it and urinates on it.

---

* Not translated in the English edition. —TRANS.

We will not learn from Brunelda herself who or what she really is. There is no "herself." There is a body, whose lament sounds to the world like a poorly tuned instrument.[21] We get everything else—her experiences and opinions—third hand, but nevertheless are forced to accept their legitimacy. It is characteristic that everything Karl explains to himself about Brunelda must be pedantically completed by Robinson: "Sometimes she actually does what she says, but mostly she lies on the couch the same as before and never moves" (A 213). And when Brunelda cries for help, "she doesn't mean it." Kafka describes the feminine as a discontinuous, illogical being, approximating here the technique of Strindberg, who both shows the woman and interprets her at the same time.

Certainly this is one of the reasons that Brunelda has received little scholarly attention. The reader's curiosity receives little nourishment from this figure, whereas the women in The Castle are supposed to be more profound and difficult. If one ignores the simple narrative function of these figures—Brunelda is of course conceived as a contrast to Karl's innocence—one can indeed perceive an increasing refinement in Kafka's characterization skill. The crude portrayal of the body, which stands out in Amerika (1912) in high relief, has already been replaced in The Trial (1914) by subtler signals that render the body less material, thus freeing it as a surface of projections.[22]

An analysis of the usher's wife and the erotic disruptions in the courtroom in The Trial (chapter two; A 37–48) provides all the static and dynamic elements of Weininger's feminine "type": prominent, above all, is the diffusion of traits denounced by him as "egolessness" and experienced by the hero K., who searches for the "inner core" of things, as a bottomless surge in the ocean. The usher's wife is passive insofar as she seeks her "consummation as object." She offers herself to the gaze and grasp of the judge, the student, and K. Only when she disappears does K. notice her body. This body is constantly present when they sit together, as the unnoticed center of language, gesture, and promise, with the ambiguous suggestion that it is both the promise and what is promised. K.'s subliminal wishes and projections, which gradually spin out of control, anticipate the woman's sexual advances, indeed, actually initiate them. The feminine nothingness that produces this appeal does not, as in Brunelda's case, stem from regression or a lack of psychological acuity. The nothingness of the usher's wife is not revealed through the narrator's instructive interventions but through her own numerous meaningful ambiguities, her persistently vague mode of expression.

In accordance with the logic of *The Trial*—the logic of a failure whose cause becomes more apparent with each repetition—the episode with the usher's wife is repeated in another seduction that follows a similar course and leads to similar results. Leni, the nurse and lover of the lawyer Huld, is a character no less puzzling than the usher's wife—even if her function with respect to the accused is more clearly marked, as critics have not failed to emphasize. Her offer of help, expressed in her gesture of covering K.'s hands with her own, appears alternately erotic or motherly. Her diffuse opportunism, which demands K.'s subjugation; her naïve coquetry ("But you didn't like me at first and you probably don't like me even now" [T 107]); her little lies and deceptions—these are all repetitions. In addition, her relation to the similarly accused salesman Block also oscillates between solicitude and sadism. Finally, she has an ambiguous relationship to Huld, exchanging secret caresses with K. in order to "entertain" Huld later, behind K.'s back, with details of this liaison.

It is worth noting that Kafka's narrative technique now supports the woman's reifying and reified self-presentation by breaking down her bodily image into a series of isolated features which are fraught with symbolism. Leni's "two great, dark eyes" have apparently impressed K.—as well as Kafka the narrator—since he later recognizes her by the "dark, somewhat protuberant eyes" (T 99). The sight of her face, which seems to have no expression, intimates the nature of his opponent:

> K. was still glaring at the girl, who turned her back on him . . . she had a doll-like, rounded face; not only were her pale cheeks and her chin quite round in their modeling, but her temples and the line of her forehead as well. (T 99–100)

Again we encounter that same fragmenting gaze, which paralyzes its object. The notion here of a doll elicits similar threatening associations by indicating a danger that is both supraindividual and oblivious to direct communication. This threat closes in on K. when Leni shows him her "pretty little paw" (T 110), two webbed fingers connected by skin, like an amphibian. Adorno noted rightly that this detail is more important than, for example, the excursus about the law, because such a concrete detail contains much experience that has been lost in conceptual language and even more so in the discourse between the sexes.[23] Benjamin had the same thing in mind when he spoke of the "bog" of unsettling experiences in Kafka, out of which climb "swamp creatures like Leni."[24]

Such images of the body, borrowed from dream symbolism, can be integrated only with difficulty into a naturalistic representation. Their frequency gives rise to moments of abstraction and deindividuation, as if primal, not yet individualized forces were breaking in upon the everyday play of personal relations:

> Now that she was so close to him she gave out a bitter exciting odor like pepper; she clasped his head to her, bent over him, and bit and kissed him on the neck, biting into the very hairs of his head. (T 110)

Here Leni appears completely banished from the level of aesthetic characterology. A dense net of material ciphers covers the text, leading Walter Sokel, for example, to draw the conclusion of Leni's pure functionality within the narrative. One might object, however, that Kafka's abstract manner of characterization follows entirely the logic of the feminine type: if the female is a generic being, then no feminine individual can be more precisely characterized than through the supraindividual, feminine "essence" it shares. Viewed positively, abstraction is the sole means of characterization appropriate to the feminine character and to feminine nonindividuality. And indeed, the tendency of Kafka's abstract characterization corresponds to a precise ideological premise that puts the coded female body into an empty ego. Her body is her essence.

The shift from the usher's wife to Leni does not negate psychological realism in favor of a strict narrative economy, but instead orders and compresses experience through repetition. K.'s seduction of Leni proceeds more quickly, but its completion has a compulsive and mechanical quality. The woman herself no longer speaks of her body, the author does. Seduction and subjugation no longer need to be painstakingly deciphered from her obscure, slow language. The struggle is conducted in the open: Leni's attributes are preverbal, but all the more direct.

The necessity for this compression is well founded. On the one hand, in the text itself, K. is already worn down. He has recognized that he has to stand trial but that, emerging from his isolation, he will barely be able to endure it. He is now more susceptible to offers of help and attention, even openly sexual ones, than he was immediately after his arrest; that saves the woman words and digressions. Furthermore, the reader has been prepared for their encounter. The outcome of the struggle over reciprocal instrumentalization is already known. Only in a superficial sense does K. achieve more with Leni than with the wife of the court usher. His defeat is not, as he first believes, that at the last moment the woman chooses the bed of someone more powerful than himself; rather, his defeat is the sober realization that the woman, whether before or after coitus, is neither inclined nor able to keep her promise. Thus, tormented by the estrangement and senselessness of these love affairs, K. is more distracted and fragmented than before, and even further removed from his trial. In her vampiric, depersonalized obtrusiveness, Leni remains incomprehensible to him; the motherly care he receives from her (the most personal treatment he experiences in the novel) is not exclusively his. Kafka's text doubly and firmly disavows the ludicrous male turn of phrase to "possess" a woman. Leni is indeed "to be had," but she is nevertheless—as K. finds out in passing, and too late—innocently promiscuous. She likes all accused men. This "dirty creature" only gains human traits of trustworthiness and intimacy in the dim glow of the courtroom. Just as the unattainable body of the usher's wife is suddenly "illuminated" in the courtroom, so Leni's flickering femininity takes on a calmer, more definite form, her individual features combining into a beautiful whole when K. sees her in the distance, close to her lover, Huld: "Then Leni, displaying the fine lines of her taut figure, bent over close to the old man's face and stroked his long white hair" (T 193).

The figure of Leni with her openly declared sexual availability seems to mark a limit in Kafka's works. The ideal form of the feminine type is tangibly near. Feminine nullity and voraciousness are covered by a social veneer so thin that further abstraction would lead either to a completely automated woman or to a pornographic scenario—neither of which the author has in mind, since his texts deliberately leave such matters in obscurity. Nevertheless, in *The Trial* one encounters figures that clearly announce the author's intention to portray if not the source, at least the phenomenology of such matters with extreme precision. These are the girls of the court, whom K. meets when he climbs the long stairway to the painter Titorelli's atelier. Here Kafka has found the way out: he prevents any individuation of the feminine by using multiple figures, similar to his frequent use of pairs or triads of characters; but he manages to depict their characteristic gestures by plucking a single protagonist indiscriminately from the crowd:

> "Does a painter called Titorelli live here?" The girl, who was slightly hunchbacked and seemed scarcely thirteen years old, nudged him with her elbow and peered up at him knowingly. Neither her youth nor her deformity had saved her from being prematurely debauched. She did not even smile, but stared unwinkingly at K. with shrewd, bold eyes. "I want him to paint my portrait," he said. "To paint your portrait?" she repeated, letting her jaw fall open, then she gave K. a little slap as if he had said something extraordinarily unexpected or stupid, lifted her abbreviated skirts with both hands, and raced as fast as she could after the other girls. (T 141–42)

Here Kafka achieves the most extreme compression; in two sentences he presents the entire litany of female seduction techniques: the girl's look, flirtatious touch, and display of legs. At the same time, her "handicap" evokes again the radical, threatening strangeness and autonomy of her body, which lend her coquetry a shade of obscenity. But this concretization of erotic terror lasts only a second; then the girl sinks back into the feminine horde, of which she is the leader:

> They stood lined up on either side of the stairway, squeezing against the walls to leave room for K. to pass, and smoothing their skirts down with their hands. All their faces betrayed the same mixture of childishness and depravity which had prompted this idea of making him run the gauntlet between them. (T 142)

This gauntlet, which might be the memory of a bordello experience (see D 458–59), creates the atmosphere of an entirely abstract threat, no longer tied to coitus. No external attack actually threatens K. here—what could happen if he took the begging girls into Titorelli's room? He is faced rather with the fragmentation, degradation, and painful dissipation of his male ego. Something alive and insect-like, without consciousness or visible individuation, incites in K. mortal dread, perhaps also the fear of a previously unknown desire for self-dissolution. Kafka uses subtle means to make the feminine approximate animalistic and even blindly vegetative forces. The girls' erotic play—one of them already uses lipstick—is harmless compared to their abstract presence, which literally seeps in through the cracks in Titorelli's room. They quiet down for a while in front of the door, but "one of them had thrust a blade of straw through a crack between the planks and was moving it slowly up and down" (T 150). When K. takes off his coat, he provokes renewed commotion: "he could hear them crowding to peer through the cracks and view the spectacle for themselves" (T 156). And when, panic-stricken because of the unbearable warmth, K. tries to get past the door, almost fleeing, the girls begin to scream, a childish squeaking to be sure, less ill-natured than Brunelda's but still enough to terrify him: "K. felt he could almost see them through the door" (T 162).

It is difficult to understand how critics have consistently overlooked the gender-related aspects of this nightmare; Emrich and Politzer even concentrate exclusively on the relation of the girls to the "artist" Titorelli. The analysis of female figures in terms of their feminine characteristics, including the male reactions they provoke, points in a different direction. The usher's wife, Leni, and the girls at court form a chain which links narrative and characterological aspects. We will discuss the significance of this chain later, but here it is worth noting the women's increasing proximity to the court: the usher's wife flirts with revolt, Leni demands K.'s confession of guilt, the girls "belong" to the court. This increasing proximity, which K. perceives as a growing animosity toward him, corresponds to a mental and social reduction of the narrative. The figures become more and more abstract; an amoral, unconscious, sexually aggressive entity progressively emerges in their place, and not only at the cost of their discursive and social dimension, but of their human individuality as well. At the end of the chain their individuality is entirely done away with and femininity expresses itself only in gestures and in the collective practice of the horde.

The idea of the feminine type, which leads not to an empirical but to an essentialist portrait of the feminine, is doubly reinforced by this transition to the collective. First, in the text the horde of girls represents the biographical lineage of women. Out of this "bog" of non-individuality will be recruited the next generation of court mistresses. The transition is the biographical commentary on the giddy promiscuity of the Usher's wife. Moreover, the girls at court provide an image of the essential origin of femininity itself. In contrast to Leni and the Usher's wife, who already possesses the complex social techniques of flirting and a sort of façade-self, the court girls reveal the feminine in its elemental, not yet socialized form. The historical, fearful question of essence—What is woman *before* her socialization?—is replicated here in an image whose clarity omits nothing: corporeality, lust for life, sexual aggression, animalistic collectivity.

"She did not even smile" (T 142), we read of the hunchbacked girl whom K. looks in the eye. The traps of erotic hypnotism designed to overcome the male's guardedness have not yet been set. Even the moral camouflage of the female desire for sexual merging is not invoked: the girls show—rare for Kafka—not the slightest trace of motherliness. In place of social grace they show intensity, in place of social role-playing they band together freely. Deleuze and Guattari are on target when they remark that the court girls are not a childhood memory but a childhood block, that is, the fear of the return of a greater, antifamilial, emotional intensity. One must add, however, that this intensity only returns in order to congeal into the form of the feminine.

Only in The Trial does Kafka use the horde as a narrative technique of feminine depersonalization to this degree of radical, almost archaicizing stylization. The reason may be that this tendency toward dramatic dialogue, which emerges with increasing clarity in his work, resists such diffuse, incommunicable elements. With the court girls, as well as with Brunelda, no understanding is possible; language as the medium of figuration, which even in its misuse and decay would allow for moments of truth, has been omitted. The double or multiple figure will not admit distinct, individual voices. When his assistants speak for the first time *not* in chorus, the Land Surveyor K. in *The Castle* says: "You're already trying to dissociate yourselves from each other" (C 26).

This formal conflict is even more complicated in the case of Kafka's female voices, since they are not centered on an individual ego but, rather, on a general and transsubjective entity: feminine language is the language of the body. In his treatment of the girls in *The Castle*, Kafka is reluctant either to let the discursive incompetence of women speak for itself—which would appear as the paradoxical utterance "I am mute"—or to let it persist in its silence. The nameless girls, whom K. treats (like his assistants) as an indistinguishable pair, work as maids in the inn, where they share a room, bed, and blanket. For his quarters K. is given a miserable, cramped room, still in the squalid condition the maids left it in. Two days later K., who in the meantime has gotten together with Frieda, wants to change to a supposedly better place to stay, and an odd scene takes place: just as he and Frieda are about to move out, the maids appear at the door with packed bags, ready to reclaim their room: " 'You're surely in a hurry,' said K., who this time was very pleased with the maids, 'did you have to push your way in while we're still here?' " (C 125). The critical edition of *The Castle* reveals three different continuations to this passage:

(1) "Embarrassed, they gathered their bags together and said . . ."
(2) "They didn't answer. K. appeared. . . ."
(3) "They didn't answer and fidgeted in embarrassment with their bags, from which K. saw the familiar dirty rags protruding. . . ."

The gesture that is supposed to be reinforced by their verbal answer in (1) completely replaces it in (3). The maids remain mute. K. is still not satisfied:

"You probably have never washed your things," said K. He didn't say it angrily but with a certain tenderness. They noticed it, opening their hard mouths at the same time, displayed their beautiful, strong, animal-like

(1) teeth, and laughed silently.
(2) teeth and red gums high above the teeth, and laughed silently.
(3) teeth and laughed silently. [25]

One cannot mistake Kafka's intention here not only to depersonalize the women but to shift them into an intermediate realm between humans and animals. His hesitation concerns only the degree of characterization: the "hard mouths" and the teeth, reinforced with three strong adjectives, are united in a vulturelike grimace (2); but this accentuation proves unnecessary for the already grotesque image and is deleted.

Kafka clearly had difficulty in balancing the doubleness of his characters: their deindividualized nature is pushed to an inhuman extreme. Yet the last step must be taken by the reader: only in one's imagination does the range of associations elicited by the female characters' corporeality and inscrutable psychology overlap with the idea of animality, an ambiguity which is both traditional in Western culture and problematic from a moral standpoint.

The motif of filth that commonly clings to Kafka's female characters as a sign of the asociality is effective as well in rendering them animalistic. Brunelda, the Usher's wife, and the "filthy creature" Leni all feel quite at home in unclean surroundings. The court girls mess up "every corner" (T 144) of Titorelli's atelier. The maids' room is reminiscent of a stall, "filthy and stuffy." The bed has no sheets, merely a horsehair blanket, the table is encrusted with dust, their few belongings are in a "filthy pile" (C 115).

This persistent accumulation of filth around marginal figures, each of whom takes up hardly more than a page of print, is profoundly alienating. The maids serve no recognizable purpose in the world surrounding the castle.[26] They remain foreign bodies, external elements that disappear like apparitions from the text without in the slightest changing the dramatic situation, the relations between characters, or K.'s consciousness. They remain without depth and without the possibility of developing further. Exemplars of a certain phenomenology of the feminine, their presence in the text can only be explained by their thematic function as women, not as characters important for the narrative.

This view can be proven. In the dialogue from his diary (DF 339–42), dated the end of 1920, Kafka sketched a female couple that must be seen as a variation or even, because of verbal correspondences as a draft for the maids at the inn, who were conceived a year later.[27]

These women appear to represent ironic, puppetlike versions of the single feminine type. Unrestrained by a narrative context (the dialogue has a self-reflexive quality), the text offers an entire arsenal of depersonalizing techniques and achieves a degree of stylization that depicts the female body as a mythical force breaking into quotidian life. Above all, one notes Kafka's technique of doubling, which aims (as with the maids) not at differentiation but at unidentifiability. The women have names, Alba and Resi, but the man with whom they live cannot tell them apart and does not need to, since "jealousy is entirely foreign to them." Their bodily fullness, which causes them to breathe heavily, reminds us of Brunelda, to whom they are also related by their insatiable eating and all-day lounging around on the sofa. Although they are "very receptive to reasonable discussion"—an ironic example is given of their being persuaded to do nothing—their corporeality clearly dominates the scene, though as animalistic immediacy rather than erotic promise. They run around "almost naked," "laugh with throaty noises" (the first such reference), and are sexually unrestrained: "they storm in, hot, with torn shirts and the stinging smell of their breath." If visitors are expected, they clear away their "filthy rags." Otherwise, they save their energies during the day for their long private cult of evening coitus, which, as always with Kafka, takes place on the floor, in filth: "For instance, they think they clean the apartment well, and yet it is so dirty that it disgusts me to step over the threshold. . . ."

"A foreigner," Kafka himself says, "could be frightened by it." By what? It is not only the *horror vacui* that these texts elicit; that would be comprehensible, if Kafka, as Weininger continually claims, had natural history on his side. But Weininger's ontological conclusion that women represent nothingness because they are without an ego too clearly bears the marks of a self-placating rationalization. His conclusion covers over the fact that women's "amorphousness," which supposedly fills the gap left by the lack of feminine identity, is more frightening than a presumed feminine nothingness ever could be. Kafka's female characters show that the male figures must ward them off as if in flight from something that is too strong, too ubiquitous, completely *different*. The feminine horde and aggressive female corporeality transform the woman into something suprapersonal and natural by destroying her identity: the feminine no longer appears as a tangible adversary, nor as a simple deficiency, but as an engulfing, viscous medium that the male ego can no more avoid than a swimmer can avoid water. This is the meaning of the symbolism of water, fire, and light that is so consistently attached to the feminine in European literature. In its opulent illumination of formlessness, this symbolism reinforces the impotence of merely formal representation. The theft of feminine identity avenges itself: whatever is without form can adopt any form and gains new power from its previous lack.

The animalization of women—likewise an ancient topos that has survived most obviously in present-day advertising—fits itself seamlessly into these transformations. Its purpose is not the slick hypostasis of danger—which wouldn't be very convincing, since Brunelda, for example, is more pig than predator—but rather the further embedding of the feminine in nature, or even (as Spengler claimed) in the cosmic universe.[28] From these spheres, however, the feminine returns as a danger of a higher order, an eternal residue of civilization, and an avenging spirit for the abomination committed against nature. Nietzsche, who himself remains caught in this ideology, was also the first to give it precise formulation. His commentary, metaphorically naïve, just barely misses camouflaging his own projection:

> That in woman which inspires respect and fundamentally fear is her *nature*, which is more 'natural' than that of the man, her genuine, cunning, beast-of-prey suppleness, the tiger's claws beneath the glove, the naïveté of her egoism, her ineducability and inner savagery, and how incomprehensible, capacious and prowling her desires and virtues are. . . .[29]

The important quality here is woman's uncontrollable elusiveness, her amorphousness and omnipresence. Nothing stays "pure," her animal nature intrudes everywhere. The leitmotiv and source of this paranoid stream of images is, as one would guess, sexuality as a destructive principle. One similarly finds in Kafka that women bond into sibling groups and series, which prefigure the mingling of the sexes, the liquefaction of all form, dissolution and decline. Kafka's erotic fantasies reveal that he, like Weininger, feared this dissolution of boundaries as something irreversible and deadly.

Translated by Neil Donahue

SADISM AND MASOCHISM IN "IN THE PENAL COLONY" AND "A HUNGER ARTIST"

Margot Norris

BECAUSE OF THEIR PUZZLING NATURE, and because they fall into chronological clusters, Kafka's fictions are usually read in thematic or allegorical groups. According to this method, "In the Penal Colony" belongs with the law and punishment works of Kafka's earlier period ("The Judgment," *The Trial*, "The Stoker"),[1] while "A Hunger Artist" belongs with the art and asceticism theme of his later works ("Investigations of a Dog," "Josephine the Singer, or the Mouse Folk"). Whatever the merits of this method, it obscures the striking structural symmetry of these two stories: in each, a fanatical believer in meaningful suffering reenacts a spectacle that in an earlier age drew huge, festive crowds but now results only in sordid death and burial. Allegorical readings mask this symmetry by giving the stories different ideational contexts derived from the idea that governs the suffering in the work: the Law in "In the Penal Colony," and the Ideal in "A Hunger Artist." Reading the stories as companion pieces, however, suggests a new way of assessing the pain, one that renders the ideational contexts of the works wholly ironic. If suffering is seen as a means whose end is not the Law or the Ideal but pleasure, then Law and Ideal become mere pretexts, fraudulent rationales in a pornological fantasy.

On the status of pain in his writings, its transcendence or lack of it, hinges the question of whether Kafka is a religious or a pornological writer. He never depicted himself as spiritually as Max Brod depicts him. Not only did Brod's own religious zeal color his perceptions of Kafka's imagination, but his evident discomfort with "*das Peinliche*" (the pornological elements in Kafka's work, both painful and embarrassing) led him to find in religion a handy means of cloaking them. "This humor, an essential ingredient in Kafka's poetics (and his life style), indicates a higher essence beyond the weave of reality,"[2] Brod writes of "the most gruesome episodes" in "In the Penal Colony" and the "Whipper" chapter in *The Trial*. In his later years, Kafka became decreasingly abashed about his knowledge of pornological writing and his appreciation of its importance. "The Marquis de Sade, whose biography you lent me, is the actual patron of our time,"[3] he reportedly told Gustav Janouch. To Milena Jesenská he admitted, "Yes, torture is extremely important to me, I'm preoccupied with nothing but being tortured and torturing." As evidence of his obsession he sent her sketches of hideous execution devices invented in his imagination. As Klaus Wagenbach demonstrates, Kafka need scarcely have resorted to his imagination, since gruesome material for his stories abounded: New Caledonia and Devil's Island, penal colonies for the Paris Communards and Dreyfus respectively; the "Rotary Machine" of J. M. Cox, using torture to cure insanity; the documents of industrial mutilation Kafka himself compiled for the Workers' Accident Insurance Institute; and Octave Mirbeau's translated *Garten der Foltern* (Garden of Tortures).[4]

Viewing Kafka as writing in a modern void of faith, most commentators eschew Brod's frankly religious interpretation of Kafka's works: "Since the biblical Book of Job, God has not been so wildly quarreled with as in Kafka's *Trial*, and *Castle*, or in his 'In the Penal Colony.'"[5] Walter Sokel, for example, finds in Kafka the "negative transcendence" of unpleasure that Lionel Trilling describes in *Beyond Culture*;[6] pain as an antidote to bourgeois torpor, a willingness (in "Penal Colony") to suffer "*Schrecken und Grauen*" rather than "*seelisch zu versumpfen*" in frivolity and utilitarianism.[7] J. M. S. Pasley finds in "In the Penal Colony" a nostalgia for "what Nietzsche called 'the ascetic ideals': deprivation and abstinence, punishment and suffering, discipline and self-discipline, as paths to purity and salvation."[8] Yet if

Kafka derived his philosophy of punishment and asceticism from
Nietzsche's *Genealogy of Morals*, as Bridgwater demonstrates,[9] then
he derived it with Nietzsche's irony intact and, like Nietzsche,
exposes the fraudulent modern teleologies of suffering. Nietzsche
writes, "It is today impossible to say with certainty why there is
punishment"[10] and goes on to give a list of "uncertain," "secondary,"
and "accidental" "meanings" of punishment. "What then do ascetic
ideals mean?" he asks. "In the case of the artist, we now realize, nothing at all."[11]

Kafka's process in his stories, like Nietzsche's in *The Genealogy of
Morals*, entails not only a historical reconstruction but also its simultaneous critique. Critics too often see in Kafka's evocation of a golden
age of penal severity and hunger art a nostalgia for apotheosized pain.
Rather, his "history," like Nietzsche's ironic genealogy, exposes the
falsehoods and deceptions that constitute the civilizing process. Officer and hunger artist are robbed of a transcendence that was always
fraudulent, and their carcasses are therefore disposed of with the un-
ceremonious dispatch of animal burial, tossed into a ditch with dirty
rags and batting, buried in a hole with the filthy straw of the cage.
Nietzsche also uses the "education" of the animal as a mocking illustration of the civilizing process with its spurious "ascetic" rationalization of pain. " 'I suffer: someone must be to blame for that'; thus
thinks every sickly sheep. But its shepherd, the ascetic priest, says to
it, 'Quite right, my sheep! Someone must be to blame: but this someone is you yourself. . . .' That's quite daring, and quite false."[12] Bridgwater attributes to both Kafka and Nietzsche an asceticism rooted in
the desire to destroy the animal in man, since "obviously man has no
particular significance as an animal, unless it be as the most vicious
and unprincipled predator of all."[13] But Kafka's tortured *Tier-
menschen* are often already domesticated, like the "submissive dog" of
a condemned man in the penal colony, so docile "it seemed as though
one could let him run free on the neighboring slopes and then only
whistle, to make him return for the beginning of the execution" (CS
140). Kafka wishes to recover pain—untranscended, mute, "animal"
pain, stripped of *alatheia* and *telos*—from its cultural falsifications.
"Looked at with a primitive eye, the real, incontestable truth, a truth
marred by no external circumstances (martyrdom, sacrifice of oneself
for the sake of another), is only physical pain" (D 410). This is also

Nietzsche's enterprise. "Apart from the ascetic ideal," he begins the last section of the *Genealogy*, "man, the animal *man*, had until now no meaning." It is Nietzsche's task to de-moralize suffering as an ascetic ideal, to explain its function, but without acceding to its pretensions. "But any meaning being better than no meaning, the ascetic ideal was in every sense the best 'lesser evil' that ever existed."[14]

What makes Kafka's two "histories" pornological while Nietzsche's "genealogy" is not, is a narrative and dramatic form that manifests the particular structural and expressive elements found in their pornological writings. The researches of Gilles Deleuze demonstrate that the symptoms of the psychological conditions known as sadism and masochism are literary rather than behavioral, and that their study requires a textual analysis. As Deleuze proceeds to discover in the works of Sade and Masoch a new language, invented to give expression to inarticulate drives and needs, the works of Kafka provided him with a modern perspective elaborated in his collaborative study with Félix Guattari.[15]

According to Deleuze, sadism and masochism always have a conscious and an unconscious component, philosophical and psychoanalytical, an understanding and manipulation of the effects and an ignorance of the causes of that compulsion to construct certain fantasies and write pornological texts. He is able, thereby, to shed new light on the ideational contexts in Kafka's works, to show, for instance, that tyranny is not merely a symbolic expression of the paternal role, the superego function, in sadism but that the sadist uses tyranny subversively to expose the absurdity of the Law, by enacting an extreme application of "the letter of the law," for example, as in "In the Penal Colony."

Deleuze argues that sadism and masochism are not subject to transformations into the Freudian complex, and that there is therefore no such thing as sadomasochism. He then distinguishes the two perversions according to a system of philosophical and formal oppositions that include their philosophical antecedents (respectively, Spinoza / Kant), political structures (institutions / contracts), intellectual operations (demonstrative / dialectical), expressive modes (mathematical / aesthetic), temporal structure (cumulative repetition / suspense), and formal models (perpetual motion machine / frozen tableau). These distinctions help to elucidate the symmetry of Kafka's two stories "In the Penal Colony" and "A Hunger Artist." Besides de-moralizing pain and suffering, like Nietzsche's *Genealogy*, Deleuze's symptomatological model also provides a philosophical rationale for the "doubled" language in the stories, the language of hypocrisy and delusion, ulterior motives and deceptions. The irony in Kafka's stories emerges from the discrepancy between the "rational" and obsessional aspects of the discourse and is aimed like a blow at reason itself, specifically, the "rationalization" of suffering. By examining the ideational contexts of the two stories, "punishment" and "asceticism" as deceptive valorizations of pain consistent with the enterprise of sadism and masochism, their true subversive thrust can be salvaged from the critical tendency to make of Kafka one of the great religious writers of the century.

In both "In the Penal Colony" and "A Hunger Artist," execution and fast are doubled so that they occur twice, in past and present time, history and act, idealized and vulgarized form. But this "doubling" is not mere repetition, but repetition with a turn or a twist like a Moebius strip, to reverse our normal response to torture and thereby subvert the pretensions of justice and art that govern the event. Deleuze describes the "perversion" implicit in our attitude toward "perversion."

> Nietzsche stated the essentially religious problem of the meaning of pain and gave it the only fitting answer: if pain and suffering have any meaning, it must be that they are enjoyable to someone. From this viewpoint there are only three possibilities: the first, which is the "normal" one, is of a moral and sublime character; it states that pain is pleasing to the gods who contemplate and watch over man; the other two are perverse and state that pain is enjoyable either to the one who inflicts it or to the one who suffers it. It should be clear that the normal answer is the most fantastic, the most psychotic of the three.[16]

The theatricality of the public spectacle in older times guarantees the community's assent to a Law and an Ideal that require public torture as proof ("Now Justice is being done" [CS 154], the crowd thinks, as the execution begins). The society colludes with enthusiasm, filling the valley of the penal colony a day early to secure good seats, subscribing to season tickets at performances of hunger art, and offering (in both stories) front-row seats to the children, in the penal colony by order of the old Commandant himself. The children's participation stamps public torture as an edifying, educational experience and enshrines the Law and the Ideal that require it. In fact, in both stories, unpleasant scenes of torture are narrated as though through the eyes of the children, clasped in the officer's arms at the execution (CS 154), or standing, "open-mouthed," before the cage of the hunger artist, "holding each other's hands for greater security" (CS 268). The officer, who has a passion for theater (like the Marquis de Sade),[17] runs the execution like a one-man theater company, tending the props, giving stage directions, badgering a prospective patron to support a failing show, and eventually serving as an understudy for the lead.

Theater translates the abstraction into an action (justice = execution), and it is the incommensurate relationship between the two that reveals the irrationality of the proceeding. This discrepancy is not one of specificity, as Deleuze points out. For a Law or an Ideal that is never named and appears to have no content, a suffering is extracted that is obsessively specified as to duration (twelve hours for the execution, forty days for the fast), equipment (machine, cage), setting (hollow, dais), and quantity (the suffering of the criminal measured by precise observation of its physiological effects, the policing of the hunger artist to ensure his freedom from "cheating"). The Ideal of a hunger artist is as indeterminate as "to astound the world" (CS 274). The Law in the penal colony is also indeterminate, replaced by flimsy pretexts contrived to create an almost certain occasion for punishment (saluting a door every hour during the night).

The machine and the fast are not arbitrary means of inflicting or enduring pain. Because the actual nature of the violence in sadism and masochism is not physical but intellectual ("What happens in a novel by Sade is strictly fabulous," writes Roland Barthes),[18] the forms of the perverse fantasies are designed to serve subversive ends: specifically, to disavow the violence, make it impersonal and abstract, subordinated to a higher purpose, as though the sadist and the masochist had no hand in it.

The apparatus in "In the Penal Colony" is therefore metaphorically related to another machine designed by the old Commandant's mathematical diagrams. The apparatus, he tells the explorer "works all by itself even if it stands alone in this valley," and he describes the old Commandant's political organization as so perfect "that his successor, even with a thousand new plans in his head, cannot change anything of the old way, at least for many years" (CS 141). The use of machines and mathematical diagrams in torture serves to render the violence completely impersonal and thereby signifies a commitment to the "Idea of pure reason."[19] Both Deleuze and Barthes stress that the subordination of personal lusts and passions to a sham rational system, the phenomenon of "reasoned crime"[20] is the violence behind the violence in sadism.

The forms of masochism (art, suspense, contract), like those of sadism (machine, perpetual motion, institutions), serve to have suffering executed in the interest of all Idea (Law or Ideal), as though without the intervention of human desire and will. Fasting becomes hunger art when the point of view shifts from sufferer to spectator (since spectators can only see pain, not feel it) and thereby assumes an aesthetic form whose essence is stasis, like painting or sculpture. In other words, the torture of the hunger artist takes the form of waiting and suspense (how long can he fast?) until he becomes a frozen *tableau vivant*, a human being who never eats and therefore virtually never moves, His aesthetic effect is heightened by means of theatrical lighting, such as the illumination of torches at night. Appropriately, the impresario displays photographs (still shots) of the hunger artist to the crowd. The masochist disavows his own need and will to suffer by turning the execution of his suffering over to someone else by means of a contract. "The masochist appears to be held by real chains," writes Deleuze, "but in fact he is bound by his word alone."[21] Since the contract still implies his consent, the masochist attempts to undermine the volitional element by signing a "blank paper,"[22] like the hunger artist, who, upon joining the circus, avoided looking at the conditions of his contract.

The idealized historical accounts of executions and fasting in the two Kafka stories are the product of a rhetorical intention to persuade or educate someone about the desirability of such spectacles. The tacit assumption behind this rhetorical effort is that torture in its meaningless (unvalorized) state is unacceptable to the rational mind unless it is justified by an Idea. Consequently, persuasion and education become exercises in hypocrisy, discourses fraught with ulterior motives and devious intentions that constitute a form of intellectual violence—the use of "reason" to assault reason.

Instead of convincing the explorer that Law requires punishment in the form of torture, the officer's discourse betrays the hidden "rationale," namely, that torture requires Law to "justify" it (make it just) as punishment. The most concrete of human experiences, physical pain, is put in the service of the most abstract of principles, mathematical precision and engineering efficiency. The tribute paid to "mind," the mathematical and mechanical mind, fails to convince the explorer or the reader. Deleuze writes of the "demonstration" in sadism, "But the intention to convince is merely apparent, for nothing is in fact more alien to the sadist than the wish to convince, to persuade, in short to educate. He is interested in something quite different, namely to demonstrate that reasoning itself is a form of violence, and that he is on the side of violence, however calm and logical he may be."[23]

The officer's demonstration of the machine is itself a deliberate act of apathy toward the condemned man. The officer explains the prisoner's crime only at the insistence of the explorer, and then only as an irritable and reluctant digression from his demonstration of the machine. "But time is passing; the execution should be started and I am not yet finished explaining the apparatus" (CS 146). The prisoner's status in the demonstration is mere machine fodder. He is rendered depersonalized, arbitrary, interchangeable (as we see when the officer takes his place) and his pain is of less interest than the workings of the machine (during the officer's execution the explorer's interest is captured entirely by the self-destructing mechanism). Apathy is part of the intellectual violence of sadism because it totally negates the pain extracted from the victim.

Apathy in "In the Penal Colony" also takes the form of a rigid complementary distribution of language whose function is to render the officer as total subject and prisoner as total object. Barthes writes, "The master is he who speaks, who disposes of the entirety of language; the object is he who is silent, who remains separate, by a mutilation more absolute than any erotic torture, from any access to discourse, because he does not even have any right to receive the master's word."[24] The prisoner's crime, the verbal threat that appropriates language, and thereby dominance, from his superior, is scheduled to be redressed by a total linguistic exclusion, from the discourse of his judicial process (charge, defense, sentence), the demonstration of the apparatus (conducted in French), and the message that will transform him into a human text, until the moment of his transcendence, when he will decipher the script on his body, and, presumably, reenter the universe of discourse. The officer, on the other hand, uses language demonstratively and speculatively, to construct entire scenes complete with imaginary dialogue, which he projects as models for the explorer's meeting with the new Commandant.

The officer's verbal demonstration of the apparatus is related to the actual execution that is supposed to follow as mimesis to praxis, to borrow the terms Barthes applies to the procedure at the Château de Silling: "The story being told [by the enthroned storyteller] becomes the program of an action [by the libertines]." In the same vein, the officer tells the explorer, "I'm going to describe the apparatus first before I set it in motion. Then you'll be able to follow the proceedings better" (CS 142). The officer's own execution is itself only a narration for the reader, however, and we find in Kafka's story the same "reversion of texts" that Barthes finds in the writings of Sade: "The image appears to originate a program, the program a text, and the text a practice; however, this practice is itself written, it returns (for the reader) to program, to text, to fantasy."[25] The sequence of program, text, and practice obtains in the penal colony, where the old Commandant's program is literally committed to the mathematical text of his drawings ("I am still using the sketches of the former Commandant" [CS 148]), which in turn is translated onto the (precomputer) program of the apparatus, to be translated once more into the living text on the condemned man's body. In this way, "the reasoned crime" of the penal colony emerges from the reversion of texts, the final version being Kafka's story itself.

As the Law is fraudulently invoked in the penal officer's "persuasion" (which is ultimately autotelic and functions as a form of intellectual violence) so the hunger artist uses "education," ostensibly in the service of the Ideal, but in fact in order to usurp the impresario's role and become the architect of his own suffering. Deleuze writes,

"The masochistic contract implies not only the necessity of the victim's consent, but his ability to persuade, and his pedagogical and judicial efforts to train his torturer."[26] The hunger artist strains mightily, but with little success, to "train" his torturers in the role of policing his fast, ostensibly to render the achievement of the ascetic Ideal perfect. He sings when they refuse to watch him, tells them jokes and anecdotes to keep them awake during their vigil, feeds them at his own expense and before his eyes, and himself dictates a toast ("supposedly prompted by a whisper from the artist in the impresario's ear" [CS 272]) drunk to the public, not to himself. The stasis of his art dooms the control of the fast to failure. "No one could possibly watch the hunger artist continuously, day and night, and so no one could produce first-hand evidence that the fast had really been rigorous and continuous; only the artist himself could know that, he was therefore bound to be the sole completely satisfied spectator of his own fast" (CS 269–70).

Deleuze writes, "While Sade is spinozistic and employs demonstrative reason, Masoch is platonic and proceeds by dialectical imagination."[27] The hunger artist's ostensible ideal is asceticism, the triumph of spirit over flesh, of human over an animal nature ruled by Freud's "pleasure principle," and therefore organized to avoid pain. But the hunger artist's asceticism is beset by a masochistic paradox that reveals its fraudulence: the hunger artist, like the masochist, desires pain and finds the fast easy to endure: "It was the easiest thing in the world" (CS 270). The unnatural is natural to him, and the hunger artist, troubled by his hypocrisy, launches a two-pronged strategy to maintain the validity of his ideal: he confesses that his fast costs him no effort of will, and he transforms his ideal from a qualitative to a quantitative goal, the achievement of a world record that can be measured in temporal form, with clocks ("the only piece of furniture in the cage" [CS 270]), calendars ("the little notice board telling the number of fast days achieved, which at first was changed carefully every day" [CS 276]), and vigils. By abolishing the forty-day fast limit (which had only catered to the public's short attention span rather than to his welfare anyway), his ideal can be rendered absolute by an achievement of *never* eating again. The hunger artist's dying confession is therefore not a punch line, a surprise ending, but merely the fulfillment of his lifelong ambition, the completion of an absolute fast and its simultaneous disavowal: "But you shouldn't admire it. . . . Because I have to fast, I can't help it" (CS 277).

The hunger artist's ideal, like the masochist's, is frustrated by his dependence on the collusion of others. In accordance with his strategy, this collusion takes dual forms: he needs the public to measure his fast in order to believe its authenticity and simultaneously to believe his disavowal of effort. In other words, he requires recognition of both his physical and his moral achievement, a recognition that his public withholds. They police him carelessly, then accuse him of charlatanism. They disbelieve such desperate proofs of his rigor as his singing ("They only wondered at his cleverness in being able to fill his mouth even while singing" [CS 269), and reject his confession, holding that he was "out for publicity or else was some kind of cheat who found it easy to fast because he had discovered a way of making it easy, and then had the impudence to admit the fact, more or less" (CS 270). These conflicts result in a series of dialectical reversals that continually shift the hunger artist's suffering from site to site, from physical endurance to mental anguish, from positive asceticism to negative frustration. The public functions like an analogue to Kafka's own personal spiritual "Negative," a power that neutralizes every achievement, "For if I have gone the tiniest step upwards . . . I then stretch out on my step and wait for the negative, not to climb up to me, indeed, but to drag me down from it" (D 410).

Both penal officer and hunger artist fail to convince the public of the value and meaning of suffering. The significance of their common failure is obscured by allegorical interpretations that deride the penal officer as a tyrant and exalt the hunger artist as a saint, that congratulate the explorer on his enlightenment and condemn the hunger artist's public for its secularism and philistinism. Such readings prejudge the issue by invoking accepted teleologies of suffering that generate a whole vocabulary to express mediated pain, pain subordinated to a higher (abstract) value: punishment, atonement, sacrifice, martyrdom, discipline, immolation, and so on. The failure of Kafka's protagonists in "In the Penal Colony" and "A Hunger Artist" to win adherents to Law and Ideal reflects a philosophical dismantling rather than nostalgia—a reversal of the processes of valorization (giving values), rationalization (making rational), justification (making just), and mythification (creating a system of belief)—that make pain acceptable to the human mind. Kafka restores physical, "animal" pain to its real and incontestable "truth" by de-moralizing, demythifying, and de-signifying it.

Kafka's two stories, like sadism and masochism, have a conscious and an unconscious level, philosophical and psychoanalytic purposes. In other words, sadists and masochists know that they construct mythologies to justify their enjoyment of pain, although they may not know why they do so. Although the causes ascribed to Kafka are most often religious and moral, Kafka himself, it seems, delved into the psychological realm for an explanation of mastering pain that rather approximates Freud's explanation of the repetition-compulsion of children in *Beyond the Pleasure Principle*.[28] "Don't you feel the desire to exaggerate painful things as much as possible?" Kafka wrote to Grete Bloch. "It often seems to me the only way people with weak instincts can exorcise pain; one cauterizes the wound, as medicine, otherwise bereft of all good instincts, does. Of course, nothing final is accomplished in this, but the moment itself . . . is almost experienced pleasurably" (F 378).

Deleuze, however, offers a psychoanalytic explanation that would account for the erotic element in "In the Penal Colony," and would allow us at least to speculate about the hidden fears and tensions that control "A Hunger Artist." According to Deleuze, the erotic pleasure in sadism and masochism depends on a dialectical process of desexualization and resexualization that begins with the fusion of ego functions and the role of the parents. "Sadism is in every sense an active negation of the mother and an exaltation of the father who is beyond all laws."[29] The old Commandant's inflation as an autocrat, as well as his overdetermination ("Did he combine everything in himself, then? Was he soldier, judge, builder, chemist, draughtsman?" [CS 144]), are manifestations of his superego function. This superego serves to desexualize the subject by suppressing all feeling. However, once desexualization is complete, the libidinal energy that is unbound from feeling is cathected onto reason and the mind. "At the culmination of desexualization a total rexsexualization takes place, which now bears on the neutral energy or pure thought." In other words, although one is tempted to suppose that the torture itself (naked man, "bed," harrow as symbolic rape) is the eroticized element, the contrary is true: it is the intellectual process, the "rational" discourse, the officer's demonstration of the machine and his defense of the autocratic system that are eroticized. "The essential operation of sadism is the sexualization of thought and of the speculative process as such, in so far as these are the product of the superego."[30]

The problem that remains is finding an explanation for the ending of the stories. In each of the two Kafka stories, the lament for a lost golden age of apotheosized suffering is followed by a tarnished reenactment of the torture (machine befouled and broken, cage uncleaned, signs unpainted, calendar unmarked), robbed of its glory. This transition, which was earlier described as a movement from story to action, from demonstration to praxis, is also a movement from theorizing or fantasy to "reality," a disillusionment that Deleuze calls "disphantasization" in describing the ending of Masoch's novels.[31] In other words, the idea or fantasy is never entirely convincing to the sadist or masochist, who, in any event, "knows" their fraudulence: the disavowals, disguises, and displacements that constitute them. The discrepancy between fantasy and "reality" becomes in Kafka's fiction a temporal gap, the unhappy transition from a glorious, severe past to a squalid and lax present.

In "In the Penal Colony," the disillusionment of the officer results from the universal rejection of the superego function as new Commandant and explorer refuse to support the old regime, and the officer takes upon himself an overdetermined role as executioner and victim. If old and new Commandant here represent a "symbolic" and "real" father, particularly a "real" father who refuses to assume symbolic superego functions, then their relationship provides a bridge to the biographical situation of Herrmann and Franz Kafka. In Kafka's "Letter to His Father," we find both processes in evidence: Kafka inflating his father to global and autocratic proportions, then (imaginatively) letting his father decline the honor by insisting, in his defense, that Franz has hypocritically foisted the superego function onto him. "For example: when you recently wanted to marry, you wanted . . . simultaneously not to marry, but wanted, in order not to have to exert yourself, that I help you with this not-marrying, by forbidding this marriage" (DF 195). Kafka here recognizes the difference between the "symbolic" father in his fiction, the man who shies apples at his son or who condemns his son to death by drowning, and the "real" father, the baffled Prague merchant who never understood the superego functions he was made to bear by his writer-son: "You asked me recently why I maintain that I am afraid of you" (DF 138).

The disillusionment in "In the Penal Colony" expresses this recognition, and the officer's autoexecution is an appropriate ending, as the explorer himself notes. But Kafka discovered this solution only after much experimentation. In unused versions of the story in Kafka's diary, the characters shift in their principal roles as executioner, condemned man, and witness, roles first occupied by the officer, prisoner, and explorer respectively. The shift occurs when the explorer discovers that the executed man is not the prisoner but the officer himself, who (spike through forehead) accuses the explorer of murder: "I was executed, as you commanded" (D 382). This shifting of executioner, victim, and witness resembles the "modification of the utterance" that brings to light "the grammar of the fantasy" in Freud's 1919 essay, "A Child Is Being Beaten."[32] In other words, Kafka's indecision and experimentation with the subject / object category ([SOMEONE] executes [SOMEONE]) may betray similar repressions, projections, and evasions with respect to the sadistic fantasy.

Perhaps the most intriguing clue to "the grammar of the fantasy" is the snake, "the great Madame" who appears to enter the penal colony as a potentate of sorts, according to a fragment in the diary.

"Now!" our Commandant called out, blithely as always, "go to it, you snake-fodder!" Immediately we raised our hammers and for miles around the busiest hammering began. No pause was allowed, only a change from one hand to the other. The arrival of our snake was promised for the evening, by then everything had to be crushed to dust, our snake could not stand even the tiniest of stones. Where is there another snake so fastidious? She is a snake without peer, she has been thoroughly pampered by our labour, and by now there is no one to compare with her. (D 380–81)

"The great Madame" is clearly a figure from a different fantasy, the severe, cruel woman of the masochistic fantasy, Masoch's Wanda or Kafka's pampered, tyrannical Brunelda in Amerika, and her appearance in the sadistic fantasy is anomalous. One complicated explanation might account for her, namely Jacques Lacan's principle that something abolished on the "symbolic plane resurges in 'the real' in a hallucinatory form."[33] In other words, the mother, banished in the sadistic fantasy of the penal colony (the only women, the new Commandant's ladies, subvert and threaten the autocratic order of the inflated father) here reappears (literally, since the fragment tells only of her expected approach down the road) in the hallucinatory form of the snake.

"The great Madame" was omitted from the final version of "In the Penal Colony," and, according to Deleuze's formulation of the psychoanalytic configuration in masochism (a model based on Masoch's work), the oral mother is missing in "A Hunger Artist" as well, if that work is to be considered a masochistic fantasy. Yet at the risk of raising phantoms or filling gaps that don't exist, I would like to speculate that the oral mother lurks invisibly behind the starving artist and that a hidden dialectic of oral fantasies (Who eats whom?) governs "A Hunger Artist" as surely as the superego fantasy (Who executes whom?) governs "In the Penal Colony."

If we return for a moment to the patterns of misunderstanding in "A Hunger Artist," we find that the Christian elements in the work belong among them. Deleuze explains Christology as providing a mystical justification for the masochist: man is "reborn" through pain inflicted by the oral mother, for example, the crucifixions in Masoch's work.[34] In "A Hunger Artist," Kafka alludes to Christ's asceticism plagued by temptations including, presumably, the temptation to turn stones into loaves of bread and eat them. The hunger artist's tempters are the ladies, "apparently so friendly and in reality so cruel" (CS 271), who lead him to the unwelcome food out of misplaced sympathy and concern. The threat that women pose to a necessary and desired asceticism has numerous analogues in Kafka's own life, with the same result: an everpresent torment intensified by misunderstanding. In the running dispute with her son over his vegetarian diet, Kafka's mother once tried to enlist Felice Bauer's aid in bringing Franz to more robust fare. "Franz's mother loves him very much, but she hasn't the faintest inkling who her son is and *what he needs*," Max Brod subsequently advised Felice. "Frau Kafka and I have often had words over this. All the love in the world is useless when there is total lack of understanding. . . . After years of trial and error Franz has at last found the only diet that suits him, the vegetarian one. For years he suffered from his stomach; now he is as fit and healthy as I have ever known him. Then along come his parents, of course, and in the name of love try to force him back into eating meat and being ill" (F 57). If Kafka intended Christ's fasting and temptation to serve as an analogue to his own dietary abstentions and ensuing family squabbles, then he clearly seems to aim at a humorous deflation of the saintly pretensions of his own "magnificent, inborn capacity for asceticism" (F 304). At the same time, his parents' confusion about the sources of his suffering, blaming Kafka's vegetarianism and "literature" rather than his frustration at being unable to eat and write as he wished, to structure and control his own deprivations and sufferings, conforms to the same dialectical conflicts depicted in "The Hunger Artist." "This perversion of the truth, familiar to the artist though it was, always unnerved him afresh and proved too much for him. What was a consequence of the premature ending of his fast was here presented as the cause of it!"(CS 273).

If Kafka's mother is a nurturing, oral mother, urging unwanted food on her son, then we find in a small detail in "A Hunger Artist" an allusion to her monstrous opposite, the cannibalistic mother. The hunger artist "stretching an arm through the bars so that one might feel how thin it was" (CS 268) unmistakably recalls Hänsel in the Grimms' fairy tale (also caged, but to be fattened rather than to hunger), extending a chicken bone through the bars of his cage to convince the wicked witch that he is too thin to be eaten. If "A Hunger Artist" is in any sense an "anti-Märchen"[35] of "Hänsel and Gretel," then the meaning of the fasting becomes clear: fasting is a defense against being eaten.[36] If this seems far-fetched, one should remember the frightful fantasies of forced feeding and butchering that dot Kafka's personal writings. For Milena he conjures up a sanitarium that won't allow a vegetarian diet. "What shall I do there? Have the head doctor put me between his knees, and gag on the meat clumps he stuffs into my mouth with his carbolic fingers and then presses along my gullet?" (M 237). In his diary he writes, "Always the image of a pork butcher's broad knife that quickly and with mechanical regularity chops into me from the side and cuts off very thin slices which fly off almost like shavings because of the speed of the action" (D 221).[37] Images of monstrous devouring occur throughout Kafka's fiction as well, in "An Old Manuscript" and "Jackals and Arabs," to name only two. Nor is the guise of the oral mother as a devouring monster in-compatible with the masochistic fantasy, since in Masoch's works the women hunt the animals and the men,[38] thereby posing a similar danger.

Kafka's two stories "In the Penal Colony" and "A Hunger Artist" are complements, then, pornologically and philosophically (sadism and masochism, Law and Ideal) as well as psychoanalytically (the son's relationship to the father and the mother respectively). Reading them in this way reveals in Kafka a subversive tendency that little supports pious notions of his own atonement and asceticism. Rather, he offers us a bestial gesture in the form of anatomizing an antibestial gesture: he unmasks the twin demigods of culture, rationalism and idealism, by exposing to us their double cruelty (simultaneous sanc-tion and apathy toward the infliction of pain), their double violence (the simultaneous practice and denial of cruelty), and their double perversity (libidinous pleasure derived from the abolition of libido).

KAFKA, CASANOVA, AND *THE TRIAL*

Michael Müller

IN A LETTER PROBABLY written on July 28, 1920,[1] Kafka asks his correspondent Milena Jesenská, "Do you know of Casanova's escape from 'The Leads'?" * He immediately answers his own question, "Yes, you know it," meaning that Milena must know this story even without having read it, since her letters to him are full of similar tales. Kafka finds in the Venetian adventurer's autobiographical report

> the most horrifying form of imprisonment . . . briefly described there—down in the cellar, in the dark, in the humidity, on a level with the lagoons. One cowers on a narrow board, the water reaching almost up to it, at high tide it actually does reach it, but the worst are the wild water rats, their screaming at night, their tugging, tearing and gnawing (I believe one has to fight them for one's bread), and above all their impatient waiting for the weakened man to fall from his little board. (M 145)

Moreover in another letter written to her on July 30, 1920, Kafka uses the expression "the Meran Leads" to characterize his confine-

---

* Reference here is to the prison in Venice, called "the Leads" because of its lead roof.—TRANS.

ment at a health spa in Meran (from April until June 1920). These two letters contain the only direct evidence that Kafka had read Casanova's memoirs—if not the complete, comprehensive *Memoirs of My Life*,[2] then at least the story "Casanova's Imprisonment and Escape from the Leads of Venice."

This story is one of Casanova's best-known adventures, and he is said never to have tired of relating the episode at social gatherings; he eventually put it into writing, and it became a best-seller especially in the eighteenth and nineteenth centuries, going through more than fifty editions and translations into many languages.[3] The tale first appeared in Prague in 1788, and numerous German editions would have been available to Kafka;[4] most, though, were reworked in some way and thus shared the same fate as most of Casanova's writings, which until recently were deemed unfit for public consumption unless they had first been "sanitized."

Judging from the passage cited above, Kafka had read Casanova's "Escape" some time before writing the letter to Milena, but precisely when he became acquainted with the work is not known. He mentions Casanova one other time when writing to Felice Bauer on January 20–21, 1913, but it remains unclear in the letter whether he already knew any of Casanova's writings at the time. It is quite possible that the brief discussion in his correspondence with Felice (who, apparently, had compared Casanova's stories with Martin Buber's edition of *Chinese Ghost and Love Stories* [F 163]) itself prompted Kafka to read Casanova for the first time. In any event, as the following discussion will show, Kafka must have read the "Escape" before August 1914, the month in which he began to write his novel *The Trial*.

The passage of time does not seem to have diminished the effect that Casanova's report had on him, and the strong impression made by this account of the "most horrifying form of imprisonment" is still evident in the 1920 letter to Milena. It should also be noted that in Casanova's report, Kafka would have found only a "brief" description of these prisons "on a level with the lagoons," since these are the *pozzi*, the Wells, and not the *piombi*, the cells under the lead roof of the Doge's palace where Casanova was actually imprisoned. The Venetian mentions these dungeons only in passing to give his readers a general picture of the horrors that might await anyone who fell into the hands of the Inquisition.

Kafka's interest in a story of "imprisonment and escape" is revealing. This author who repeatedly thematizes the most diverse punish-
ments—letting "judgments" be passed, visiting "penal colonies," and
populating his poetic world with judges, lawyers, and executioners—
held in his hands the authentic account of a punishment that had
been carried out. And it was not just any punishment but one of the
most "horrifying" imaginable. Casanova's little story deserves to be
considered a source for one of Kafka's large-scale penal fantasies, his
novel The Trial; indeed, it influenced The Trial to an even greater
extent than those works already recognized as sources, such as Dostoyevsky's Crime and Punishment and his letters from the internment
camp.[5] Proof of this source may also suggest several new possibilities
for interpreting the novel. Kafka appropriates several elements of
plot, and was also inspired by Casanova's rendering of particular milieux. Further, Kafka gives his protagonist Joseph K. certain personality traits of Casanova, a figure whom we not only identify as the
"adventurer," but who might even be seen as the purest expression of
this character type.

   The first noticeable parallel between Casanova's "Escape" and The
Trial occurs right at the outset of both works. The two beginnings, in
which the first sentence sets the entire subsequent plot into motion,
are quite similar:

Someone must have been telling lies about Joseph K., for without having done anything wrong he was arrested one fine morning. (T 1)

The date was July 25th, 1755. Next morning at day-break who should
enter my room but the awful Messer-Grande. . . he told me to rise, to
put on my clothes, and give him all the papers and manuscripts in my
possession, and to follow him.[6]

The situation in which both protagonists find themselves is the same:
Casanova and Joseph K. are arrested in bed: from a position of utter
helplessness, they are delivered naked, as it were, into the clutches of
the authorities. Getting dressed thus plays an important role for both:
it is the symbolic act of arming oneself, and at the same time signals
the acceptance of a challenge: "K., opening the wardrobe . . .
searched for a long time among his many suits, chose his best black

one, a lounge suit which had caused almost a sensation among his acquaintances because of its elegance, then selected another shirt and began to dress with great care" (T 9). Casanova puts on "a laced shirt" and his "holiday suit," as if he were "going to a wedding."[7]

This almost defiant attitude, which derives from an unawareness of impending dangers, characterizes both the author of the autobiographical report and the protagonist of the novel, and implies a shared outlook. One is tempted to put into the mouth of Casanova— born in 1725 and thirty years old at the time of his arrest—the words of Joseph K.: "when one has lived for thirty years in this world and had to fight one's way through it, as I have had to do, one becomes hardened to surprises and doesn't take them too seriously" (T 11). Kafka's characterization of Joseph K. in the opening chapter of the novel could be applied in part to Casanova, or at least to the cliché of Casanova as an "adventurer" and "ladies' man."

Although he is a respected attorney at a bank, Joseph K. does not conform entirely to the norms of bourgeois society. Having shed his familial bonds, he has not seen his mother for a long time, and has all but forgotten the niece supposedly in his charge. His only ties to anyone outside his professional sphere are to a group that meets regularly in a neighborhood café and to "a girl called Elsa, who was on duty all night till early morning as a waitress in a cabaret and during the day received her visitors in bed" (T 17). K.'s professional status does not conflict with this lifestyle; on the contrary, it forms the very basis of his independence as a bachelor, and thus he "had always been inclined to take things easily, to believe in the worst only when the worst happened, to take no care for the morrow even when the outlook was threatening" (T 4). This carefree life comes to a sudden halt on a particular day: the warders enter K.'s apartment on his thirtieth birthday, just as Messer-Grande and his forty *sbirra* (men-at-arms) forcibly enter Casanova's dwelling on the feast day of his patron saint.

K.'s story is familiar: Although he has been arrested, he is allowed to continue moving around freely. Only his inner freedom has been lost, and by the end he is completely preoccupied with his battle against the invisible authorities who are to pass judgment on him. Casanova, by contrast, is led away immediately following his arrest. Yet if we trace his path into the Leads, we discover in it a physical parallel with the path that Joseph K. follows—seemingly on his own initiative—in his search for the highest judicial authorities: we find that Kafka's hero gets to know his own "Leads." Casanova reports:

> After climbing several flights of stairs we crossed a closed bridge which forms the communication between the prisons and the Doge's palace, crossing the canal called Rio di Palazzo. On the other side of this bridge there is a gallery which we traversed. We then crossed one room, and entered another, where sat an individual in the dress of a noble, who, after looking fixedly at me, said, "É quello, mettetelo in deposito." . . . Messer-Grande then made me over to the warden of the Leads, who stood by with an enormous bunch of keys and, accompanied by two guards, made me climb two short flights of stairs, at the top of which followed a passage and then another gallery, at the end of which he opened a door, and I found myself in a dirty garret, thirty-six feet long by twelve broad, badly lighted by a window high up in the roof.[8]

K. goes through two similar stages. The Court of Inquiry in which his first hearing takes place is located on the fifth floor of an apartment building, and is accessible only by way of many stairs that weave a labyrinthine path through the house:

> K. turned toward the stairs to make his way up to the Court of Inquiry, but then came to a standstill again, for in addition to this staircase he could see in the courtyard three other separate flights of stairs and besides these a little passage at the other end which seemed to lead into a second courtyard. (T 35)

Later he manages to gain entry to the offices above the examination room; in his description of these offices, Kafka captures and compresses in a few short pages the impressions that Casanova conveys of the Leads in the course of his hundred-page account. The offices themselves recall a kind of prison:

> some of the offices were not properly boarded off from the passage but had an open frontage of wooden rails, reaching, however, to the roof, through which a little light penetrated and through which one could see a few officials as well, some writing at their desks, and some standing close to the rails peering through the interstices at the people in the lobby. (T 63)

Whenever Casanova boasted of his successful escape from the ducal palace, he was said to have described the cells under the thick leaden roof for hours on end, in order to exaggerate his feat. In the following, I will restrict myself to his literary account of the dungeon. The first cell assigned to Casanova was the worst of all, and was called the *Trave*, since a beam that ran the length of the ceiling made it impossible for a prisoner to stand upright in his cell. Casanova ceaselessly describes the horrors of this place, mentioning that enormous rats fill the garret next to his cell, and complaining of the dust that collects in the prisoners' lungs. He also laments the dimness of his cell even during the day, and above all, of the heat under the lead roof that makes breathing impossible: "The strength of the sun's rays upon the roof made my cell like a stove, so that the streams of perspiration which rolled off my poor body as I sat quite naked on my sofa-chair wetted the floor to the right and left of me."[9] Finally he is seized by a violent fever.

Almost all of these elements recur in similar or slightly altered form in Kafka's description of the attic offices. K. sees other defendants there: "They did not stand quite erect. Their backs remained bowed, their knees bent, they stood like the street beggars" (T 63); disoriented, he stumbles through the dimly lit room, and must depend on the court usher and the girl for help. In the end, he too is seized by a feeling of uneasiness that forces him to sit down in a chair. The girl consoles him: "Don't worry . . . That's nothing out of the common here, almost everybody has an attack of that kind the first time they come here. . . . The sun beats on the roof here and the hot roof-beams make the air stuffy and heavy" (T 67).

Like Joseph K., Casanova remains ignorant of the reason he has been imprisoned in this hell. Never allowed to see his judges face-to-face, nor hearing a sentence passed, Casanova reflects: "My investigation as to what I had done to deserve such a fate was not a long one, for in the most scrupulous examination of my conduct I could find no crimes."[10] Initially, then, he hopes that each new day will bring freedom; later he speculates that his incarceration will last only as long as the present Inquisitors are in office, and expects to be released when the new Inquisitors begin their term. In retrospect, he takes an ironic view of his optimism:

I was so certain that I had right on my side, that I reasoned accordingly; but this was not the attitude I should have assumed towards a court which stands aloof from all of the courts in the world for its unbounded absolutism. To prove anyone guilty, it is only necessary for the Inquisitors to proceed against him; so there is no need to speak to him, and when he is condemned it would be useless to announce to the prisoner his sentence, as his consent is not required, and they prefer to leave the poor wretch the feeling of hope. . . . The guilty party is not required to have any share in the matter; he is like a nail, which to be driven into a wall only needs to be struck. *[11]

Yet Casanova refuses to submit to the unseen court as if he were a creature or an object without a will. He decides to obtain justice for himself, and with ingenuity and his last ounce of physical strength he engineers his first escape attempt. With an improvised tool he digs a hole in the floor of the cell, through which he plans to lower himself into the Inquisitors' hall below. His plan fails, however, because on the day he has finally managed to make the opening large enough to fit through, he is transferred to another cell.

Casanova leaves behind this sign of his unbroken will, and we find it not only in the Leads. It also appears in the attic chambers that Joseph K. learns of as the lawyer complains to him about the inhumane conditions in the offices, even in the lawyers' chamber, a "small and cramped room":

It was lit only by a small skylight, which was so high up that if you wanted to look out, you had to get some colleague to hoist you on his back, and even then the smoke from the chimney close by choked you and blackened your face. . . . There had been for more than a year now a hole in the floor, not so big that you could fall through the floor, but big enough to let a man's leg slip through. (T 116)

Has Casanova preceded K. in the Court offices? He has done that and more: he even seems to put in a personal appearance in Joseph K.'s waking dreams. Casanova, we recall, enters prison elegantly dressed

---

* The German text, which Kafka would have read, reads slightly differently for this final sentence: "The prisoner is not a person, merely a thing that need not directly intervene in its own case."—TRANS.

in a cloak, a "fine suit" and a hat "trimmed with a Spanish point and
adorned with a beautiful white feather."[12] Just such an exotically
dressed Latin figure continues to haunt Joseph K. as he lies half-
waking, half-sleeping on the sofa. Overwrought from his trial, K.
fantasizes that all sorts of people—not just those "persons who were
connected with the Court"—mingle together, as in his thoughts he
hurries through the court buildings:

> He knew his way about all the rooms very well; remote passages he could
> never have seen in his life seemed as familiar to him as if he had always
> lived there, and details kept on impressing themselves on his mind with
> painful clarity. For instance there was a foreigner strolling about in the
> antechamber dressed like a bullfighter, with a wasp waist and an abbre-
> viated little coat of coarse yellow lace standing out stiffly; this man,
> without pausing for a moment in his perambulations, allowed K.'s as-
> tonished gaze to follow him unremittingly. Stooping low, K. circled
> round him, gaping at him with wide-open eyes. He knew all the pat-
> terns of the lace, all the torn fringes, all the oscillations of the little
> coat, and still he couldn't see enough of it. Or rather, he had seen
> enough of it long ago; or better still, he had never wanted to look at it
> at all, and yet he couldn't tear himself away. What masquerades foreign
> countries provide, he thought, and opened his eyes wider still. And he
> kept on following this man about until he flung himself round on the
> sofa and pressed his face into the leather upholstery. (T 248)

". . . he had never wanted to look at it at all, and yet he couldn't tear
himself away." Perhaps here we may dissolve the initial K. into Kafka,
and we may interpret the passage as a covert representation of Kafka's
meeting with Casanova, the writer whose book describes "the most
horrifying form of imprisonment."

How can one explain that both K. and Kafka continue to "follow
this man about," and that, unable to "tear himself away" from the
story of Casanova's escape from the Leads, Kafka recalls its particulars
even six years after ceasing work on The Trial? Aside from the obvious
theme of punishment, where lies the deeper connection between the
tale of the Venetian adventurer, the story of a bank attorney, and, by
extension, the personal history of the writer Franz Kafka? Critics
have already investigated the biographical components of The Trial.
However close a parallel one wishes to draw between the events in

the novel and Kafka's personal experiences, no one will dispute the fact that his break with Felice Bauer in June 1914 helped to trigger his writing of *The Trial*, which he began one month later. Casanova, K., and Kafka all find themselves in a similar situation at the beginning of their respective trials. With his break from Felice, Kafka cuts himself off once again from bourgeois society, and does not take the step toward integration expected of him. He has a secure professional position, yet precisely because of this guaranteed security, he commits a social offense and breaks a taboo by continuing, in his own words, his "monotonous, empty, mad bachelor's life" (D 303). In opposition to the bourgeois moral code, he makes no provisions for the future, does not plan, "establishes" nothing. An outsider, he leads the eccentric life of a writer—exactly the existence he sought in breaking off his engagement and giving up a marriage that would have threatened his writing. Numerous entries in Kafka's diaries during this time express his ambivalence toward a life that concentrates all his energies on writing. On the surface, his separation from Felice means complete freedom; and yet, from the very start he mixes metaphors of captivity with his remarks on bachelorhood. As is well known, Kafka described the ceremony marking the official cancellation of his engagement (which took place in a Berlin hotel) with the key phrase "the tribunal in the hotel" (D 293). Newly won freedom seems to lead directly to a new form of imprisonment.

Kafka's biographical situation is reflected in both *The Trial* and in the "Memoirs of the Kalda Railroad," which for a time he wrote concurrently with the novel. The story's narrator enters voluntarily into a state of total isolation when he journeys to a remote area in the interior of Russia, and he explains at the outset: "For various reasons that do not matter now, I had been looking for just such a place at the time; the more solitude ringing in my ears the better I liked it" (D 303). Later in the story, however, he remarks: "I perceived that I was not particularly suited to stand a condition of utter solitude" (D 305).

The key term "solitude" leads us back to Casanova, who stresses repeatedly that it was not so much the physical torments that made his stay in the Leads so unbearable, but rather the loneliness. Initially he views it as a privilege that he has been assigned his own cell, but his watchman explains that he is mistaken; solitary confinement is a more, not less severe form of punishment:

The fool was right, and I soon found it out. I discovered that a man imprisoned by himself can have no occupations. Alone in a gloomy cell where he sees only the fellow who brings his food once a day, where he cannot walk upright, he is the most wretched of men. He would like to be in hell, if he believes in it, for the sake of the company. So strong a feeling is this that I got to desire the company of a murderer, of one stricken with the plague, or of a bear. The loneliness behind prison bars is terrible, but it must be learnt by experience to be understood, and such an experience I would not wish even to my enemies. [13]

Kafka also has this experience, also enters into a place where solitude is "ringing in his ears." On August 3, 1914, he writes in his diary:

Alone in my sister's apartment. It is lower down than my room, it is also on a side street, hence the neighbors' loud talking below, in front of their doors. Otherwise complete solitude. No longed-for wife to open the door. In one month I was to have been married. The saying hurts: You've made your bed, now lie in it. (D 301)

In this complete solitude his study threatens to become a cell, and only writing can save him from imprisonment. On August 15, 1914, the diary reads: "I have been writing these past few days, may it continue. . . . I can once more carry on a conversation with myself, and don't stare so into complete emptiness. Only in this way is there any possibility of improvement for me" (D 303).

By writing he hopes to discover a partner in himself, and in this way break through the isolation. At the end of the diary entry for August 29 he issues the following warning to himself: "But I must not forsake myself, I am entirely alone" (D 313). And on September 1 he writes: "if I wish to transcend the initial pangs of writing (as well as the inhibiting effect of my way of life) and rise up into the freedom that perhaps awaits me, I know that I must not yield" (D 313–14).

Of course, writing at this time means primarily writing *The Trial*, the story of a lonely man who, after initially seeing his lack of ties or commitments as a privilege, is suddenly pulled up short by his isolation. Finally, when he is fully conscious of both his arrest and his social responsibilities* he tries desperately to establish contact with,

---

* The term *Verhaftung* means both "arrest" and "security."—TRANS.

and thereby find, a foothold in the society that appears to him a hostile, self-enclosed entity. The character who at first never thinks of his future and takes everything lightly ultimately directs all of his thoughts toward winning his "trial"—just like his creator. At one point in the novel, Kafka clearly gives a portrait of himself in Joseph K., when K. decides to submit a written petition in his defense:

> In this defense he would give a short account of his life, and when he came to an event of any importance explain for what reasons he had acted as he did, intimate whether he approved or condemned his way of action in retrospect, and adduce grounds for condemnation or approval. (T 113)

> . . . the plea simply had to be drawn up. If he could find no time for it in his office, which seemed very probable, then he must draft it in his lodgings at night. And if his nights were not enough, then he must ask for furlough. Anything but stop halfway, that was the most senseless thing one could do in any affair, not only in business. (T 128)

K., Kafka, and Casanova—three prisoners, who day and night strive untiringly to win their freedom. Yet only the latter is successful, since he alone has the necessary physical and mental resources: "The situation of a man who had to act as I had, is an unhappy one, but in risking all for all, half its bitterness vanishes," he asserts in one passage of the memoir.[14] In another he declares:

> It has always been my opinion that when a man sets himself determinedly to do something, and thinks of naught but his design, he must succeed despite all difficulties in his path: such a one may make himself Pope or Grand Vizier, he may overturn an ancient line of kings—provided that he knows how to seize on his opportunity, and be a man of wit and pertinacity.[15]

Casanova makes a second attempt, and the seemingly impossible happens: through the lead roof of the Doge's palace he is able to escape to freedom.

The progress of Kafka's struggle for freedom can be traced in his diary entries as well as in his novel. After an initial period of successful work, the stream of writing begins to slacken, and on November

30 he notes: "I can't write any more" (D 94). The negative end of his—Joseph K.'s—trial is now in sight. In chapter nine of the novel, the Cathedral chapter, the priest asks Joseph K., "Do you know that your case is going badly?" and K. answers:

> "I have that idea myself. I've done what I could, but without any success so far. Of course, my petition isn't finished yet." "How do you think it will end?" asked the priest. "At first I thought it must turn out well," said K., "but now I frequently have my doubts. I don't know how it will end. Do you?" "No," said the priest, "but I fear it will end badly. You are held to be guilty. Your case will perhaps never get beyond a lower Court." (T 210)

Thus, both of Kafka's "trials" come to an end: Joseph K. is killed, and it becomes increasingly clear to Kafka himself that he will not rise above the "initial pangs of writing" into a higher "freedom." Instead, he has only become lonelier and more entrapped: "my sleep, my memory, my ability to think, my resistance to the tiniest worries have been weakened past all cure—strangely enough, the consequences of a long period of imprisonment are about the same" (D 320).

What fascinates Kafka about Casanova's story is perhaps the fact that it is only a tale of imprisonment but also one of escape, of a successful act of liberation. Compared with Kafka and Joseph K., Casanova is a positive hero who actually completes what he set out to do. It almost seems as if Casanova had learned that the specific kind of freedom he idealized before his ordeal in the Leads must at some point necessarily end in solitude and incarceration. His warning to a fellow prisoner reads: "Nature, when a man listens to her and nothing else, takes him from one folly to another, till she puts him under the Leads."[16]

Translated by Elizabeth Bredeck

III.

TEXTS, LETTERS, AND AUTOBIOGRAPHY

THE ACT OF WRITING AND THE TEXT: THE GENESIS OF KAFKA'S MANUSCRIPTS

Malcolm Pasley

YEARS AGO A BOOK on Kafka appeared which claimed that his well-known story "The Judgment" had been written on an overnight train trip. How could this be? Did he really write the story on a train? Puzzled, I reached for the diary from 1912 and . . . almost agreed with the author. He wrote the story, he says, "*in einem Zug*"—a phrase that can mean either "in a train" or "in one sitting"—"during the night of the 22nd–23rd, from ten o'clock at night to six in the morning"(D 212). Had Kafka in fact written "The Judgment" on a train rather than at his desk, we would have *quite* a different story before us. Because for Kafka—and one needn't be a positivist to recognize this—circumstances such as his immediate surroundings, pen, and paper were essential to the form and substance of what he wrote. "Writing's lack of independence of the world," Kafka wrote in his diary on December 6, 1921, "its dependence on the maid who tends the fire, on the cat warming itself by the stove; it is even dependent on the poor old human being warming himself by the stove. All these are independent activities ruled by their own laws; only writing is helpless, cannot live in itself, is a joke and a despair" (D 398).

Among the external objects on which his writing depends, Kafka mentions (but characteristically only in last place) "the poor old

human being warming himself by the stove," that is, Franz Kafka
himself, the consumptive, melancholy, flesh-and-blood person upon
which that other, less tangible figure, Franz Kafka the writer, partially
depends. For without a body, without a hand one cannot write. But
this dependence, the necessity of a physical being, is mentioned only
in passing at the end of the entry, as if it were an inconvenient precondition for writing, and would ideally disappear, completely sup-
planted by the writer. In a letter to Max Brod Kafka claims that the
writer "isn't present" in the work and that, furthermore (a warning,
perhaps, for biographical critics), "When we write something, we
have not coughed up the moon, whose origins might then be investigated. Rather, we have moved to the moon with everything we
have. . . . we have lost ourselves for the sake of a homeland on the
moon" (L 204). Of course, the immediate conditions of writing also
include the writer's mood and psychic disposition, which only in the
rarest cases can be reconstructed. For "The Judgment," I believe these
conditions can be determined with some precision. Certainly, one
may assume that on the September evening in question Kafka felt an
especially intense (because repressed) desire to write. (In 1912, Yom
Kippur, during which Jews are prohibited from writing, fell on September 22.[1]) It seems to me, however, that attempts to reconstruct
the psychological preconditions for writing should be made with extreme care and then only tentatively. In any case, I will limit myself
in the following to more obvious and even more direct connections
between the manuscript and the work, that is, between the act of
writing and the finished text.

To begin with, even the writing instrument used for each manuscript is not without importance: consider Kafka's preference for
fountain pens, which are characteristically fluid, or his antipathy to
typewriters, which fascinated him technically but which he used only
rarely. If one reads, for example, the prose piece "Seek Him with
Pointed Pen . . ." (DF 264), one might guess that he wrote it with a
fountain pen—and one would be right, as the manuscript shows.
Wherever Kafka mentions a writing instrument in his texts one can
be fairly sure that his own instrument has occupied him in some way
shortly beforehand. This is certainly the case in the passage in *Amerika* when Karl Rossmann scribbles in his notebook a list of errands
"with a fountain pen which the Manageress had given him in reward

for drawing up methodically and writing out neatly a long inventory of hers" (A 157). Shortly before writing this passage, as one can see from the manuscript, the novelist clearly had to struggle with, and replace, a malfunctioning fountain pen. Here we see how closely the written text—the work—relates to the physical act of writing and even to the small calamities that can occur during the writing process. We can also see how literary invention depends on immediate circumstances, "ruled by their own laws," for setting words to paper.

In the story "In the Penal Colony," texts are inscribed in human flesh by a horrible writing machine, and in the story "A Dream" the fictional artist writes with a pencil that magically produces gold letters on stone. What is Kafka's actual relationship to his writing materials? He didn't use loose sheets of paper but wrote directly into notebooks, which lent his activity a school-like or business seriousness. For whatever is entered into a notebook, even a schoolboy's notebook, cannot be easily removed. The choice of a set frame discourages uncontrolled experimentation with the pen. Even early in his life Kafka conceived of writing more as self-discipline than as self-expression, which probably accounts for his life-long habit of writing his texts directly into notebooks. For the diary he began in 1910 he bought himself quite beautiful quarto oilcloth notebooks, which immediately imply permanence. For *The Metamorphosis* and *Amerika*, more demanding works, he also selected similarly grand notebooks. On the other hand, his choice of the modest little notebooks for his writing during the winter of 1916–1917 (the "eight blue octavo notebooks") coincides with his turn toward short, parable-like pieces such as "The Bridge," which he brought to paper in this reduced framework. His decision to experiment, for the first time since his early collection *Meditation*, with short, even tiny pieces conditioned, one can truly say, his choice of the diminutive manuscript. One could extend the notion of the writing "frame" even further to include the tiny room on the Alchimistengasse where he wrote in the miniature notebooks; this too reflects the reduced format in which his short pieces originated.

The clear correspondences between the format of his materials and the form of his work, though, should probably not be understood as a prerequisite for the form he had in mind, but as a kind of support and encouragement. The reduced space would help him write in a more concentrated (and aphoristic) fashion.[2] This is especially evident in the single piece of paper that he set before himself in order to write, with the tiniest of strokes, his story "First Sorrow"—thus allowing himself only the most confined space for his difficult and frightening literary acrobatics, which the story both portrays and embodies as an act of writing. After studying this manuscript page, one is hard put to distinguish between the genesis of the story and the genesis of the material text.

Intriguing evidence of the effects that the writing material exerted on the text (and therefore its genesis) can be found throughout Kafka's novel *The Castle*, which he composed in six quarto notebooks. The manuscript indicates that Kafka's uncertainty in writing something down (thus, his uncertainty in narrating the story) apparently increased whenever he approached the end of a notebook and, therefore, had to confront the frightening prospect of the open, unknown space of the next, empty, notebook. Toward the end of the second notebook, for example (which corresponds roughly to the end of chapter nine), the story loses direction; he crosses out several attempts to continue the story before finding the right transition to the next subject in the new notebook. We find similar hesitation at the end of the third notebook, where, on the last page, following the significant words "he apparently trembles with fright" (C 238), the text dissolves into chaos. One crossed-out passage follows another well into the fourth notebook until the disruption of changing notebooks is finally overcome; and so too with the beginning and the end of the fifth notebook. Regardless of how one interprets Kafka's general fear of beginnings and endings, this fear informs the writing process of his longer works in this way. As soon as he is faced with an unavoidable transition to a new notebook, disruptions appear almost regularly in the manuscript.

In general, it seems reasonable to take literally Kafka's own definition of his literary activity as "writing." It is often assumed that a literary work originates in an author's mind and is then translated to the page. In Kafka's case this model—the egg-laying model, if you will—should be used with great caution. Especially with his stories and novels, we repeatedly encounter the question of how far, or even whether, the genesis of the work can be distinguished from that of the handwritten manuscript. In other cases it might be appropriate to "divide" the author into a creator/inventor with legislative authority and a scribe with executive powers. With Kafka, however, this distinction is clearly alien, a counterproductive intrusion. Rather, one might punningly label him a *Konzipist*—on the one hand (in the Austrian sense of the word), one who drafts legal and official documents and on the other, one who "conceptualizes" a work.* It is precisely this sense of constant conceptualizing in the very act of writing, which normally characterizes Kafka. His extant manuscripts, which substantiate his comments on his writing method, give us the clearest idea of *how* he wrote.

Although there are clean or second copies of some of his works, for the most part we have only first drafts; these, however, allow us to follow the continuous (often surprisingly so) development of a story. The integral relation between creation and notation is manifest, as is the way in which imagined scenes are transformed into pen strokes that continuously give fixed form to literary idea and guide, even alter, its next direction. Only through the act of writing itself do the fixed preconditions for the story's progress gradually emerge; the story determines itself, as it were, from "behind," from its fictional past, evolving—as it is brought to paper and arises as a tangible object—into a text. The story draws its borders into ever-smaller circles, takes on a literally more fixed form under the writing hand, increasingly makes use of every possible change in direction or escape, and finally (like the reader, who at times experiences horror at the repetition of this process while reading) is propelled to its unalterable endpoint by the very letters which can no longer be erased or taken back. It is truly a redemptive moment when manuscript and story (usually this means manuscript and fictional autobiography) arrive at their destination simultaneously, as it were, with a sigh of relief. At the conclusion of the story "A Dream," as the hero sinks into his grave, "his head still straining upwards on his neck," he sees his name race "across the stone above him in great flourishes" (CS 400–401). The successful conclusion of the manuscript must wait for the protago-

---

* Kafka, of course, worked as an insurance official in Prague, and was quite familiar with the exigencies of bureaucratic composition.—ED.

nist's burial, for the end of his life story; only when his name has been written into the gravestone does the hero receive his own happy— that is, redemptive—burial.

My thesis (which, by the way, makes no claim to being new) is as follows: The genesis of the narrative works Kafka wrote after "The Judgment" (1912) is bound closely to, if not identical with, the genesis of the manuscript itself to an uncommon degree. In fact, the bond between the narrative and its recording is so close in Kafka that one could almost claim that the texts "wrote themselves." To vary Kleist's expression, we see in Kafka's later works "the gradual completion of a story as it is being written."[3] Kafka's own comments on his work habits support this thesis, but stronger evidence is to be found in the implicit testimony of his manuscripts. If this thesis holds true, it would have important consequences for the understanding and interpretation of these works. For it would mean that Kafka's narratives, including his novels, essentially arose without a specific or premeditated goal, without any predetermined plot line or choice of characters, arose simply *along the way*. Further, even, that at the beginning of a text practically *nothing* existed except (for we must assume at least this) a volatile cluster of images, an invented scene which carried within itself a wealth of dynamic possibilities. And if this were in fact the case, how could anyone claim that Kafka used such-and-such book as a "pre-text," a source for his writing? Could we even speak of these books in conventional terms as "literary sources," or would we have to say that long before Kafka's text existed, such "sources"—which do of course exist in a certain sense—had flowed along the most varied and elusive paths into the inner sea from which his story then originated?

The same might be said about the author's actual life experiences, those so-called biographical moments, which of course in some form entered the work as it developed. Could the claim still be made that any given experience in Kafka's life is directly "represented" or "finds an echo" in one or another story? Perhaps we would have to consider the matter in another way, namely, that Franz Kafka's relevant or important empirical experiences had already been digested, transformed, combined with other elements, even mythologized and intertwined with his "dreamlike inner life" *before* the story had been conceived. Perhaps biographical data entered the work in such a mediated, labyrinthian fashion that not even the cleverest psychologist or the most industrious biographer could draw convincing and *productive* parallels between life and work. We should recall what Kafka once wrote to Felice Bauer:

> Writing that springs from the surface of existence—when there is no other way and the deeper wells have dried up—is nothing, and collapses the moment a truer emotion makes that surface shake. This is why one can never be alone enough when one writes, why there can never be enough silence around one when one writes, why even night is not night enough. (F 156)

The above passage already indicates what, in my opinion, must inevitably follow if my thesis of the "gradual completion of the story as it is being written" is basically correct. Kafka's own statements seem to support this thesis.[4] First of all, we have the important diary entry of November 15, 1911—from the period before the "breakthrough," before "The Judgment"—where Kafka speaks of a difficulty and a disturbing deficiency in his work habits up to that point:

> It is certain that everything I have conceived in advance, even when I was in a good mood, whether word for word or just casually, but in specific words, appears dry, wrong, inflexible, embarrassing to everybody around me, timid, but above all incomplete when I try to write it down at my desk, although I have forgotten nothing of the original conception. This is naturally related in large part to the fact that I conceive something good away from paper only in a time of exaltation, a time more feared than longed for, much as I do long for it; but then the fullness is so great that I have to give up. Blindly and arbitrarily I snatch handfuls out of the stream so that when I write it down calmly, my acquisition is nothing in comparison with the fullness in which it lived, is incapable of restoring this fullness, and thus is bad and disturbing because it tempts to no purpose. (D 118)

What Kafka laments here is a mode of literary production in which the conception of a work and its written execution are still far apart. What he conceives of "in advance," "away from paper," proves itself to be "wrong" and "inflexible," "embarrassing to everybody around me," and "incomplete" (later he will often describe this as "patchwork"). Kafka's inspired conception "away from paper"—in its over-whelming "fullness"—is at odds with his "calm" writing and can be forced only with difficulty into the confining forward progression of the written text. One may venture to say that he recoginzes here the real origin of his literary block: he has not yet learned to entrust himself and his conception of a work to the *act* of writing, integrating conception and writing as closely as possible. Even at this early point, Kafka rejects the Romantic notion of a divine, perfect birth of a lit-erary work in the author's mind, which his pen, as a dutiful secretary, merely translates or transcribes. Not until "The Judgment" does Kafka succeed (and here we find the real significance of this "break-through") in seamlessly combining conception and execution, work and text, *in einem Zug*. (Of course he later admits the dangers of the opposite situation in which the writing pen appropriates too much control and becomes "arrogant." Thus, in 1914 he complains to Grete Bloch that writing itself often seduces him into incorrect for-mulations because "sentences have their own force of gravity from which one cannot escape" [F 389].)

"The Judgment" is certainly the best-documented example of Kaf-ka's unprepared (or rather, not consciously prepared) literary crea-tion, in which conception and execution of the material text coincide perfectly. And partly for this reason, it remained exemplary for him. In detailed accounts of its composition, he uses the images of a birth and an opening wound. His first image, however, which is perhaps more revealing, is that of a consuming and creative fire, which excludes all possibility of preplanning: "How everything can be said, how for everything, for the strangest fancies, there waits a great fire in which they perish and rise up again" (D 213). What is most surprising is that, when he took pen in hand, whatever idea he did have about how plot and characters would develop was *utterly* transformed by the act of writing. "When I sat down to write . . .," he wrote to Felice Bauer, "I meant to describe a war; from his window a young man was to see a vast crowd advancing across the bridge, but then the whole thing turned in my hands into something else" (F 265).

In writing "The Judgment" it became clear to Kafka how impor-tant it was to complete a text, if possible, "in one sitting." A story like *The Metamorphosis*, he later wrote, "should be written with no more than one interruption, in two 10-hour sessions" (F 64). Any longer interruption could be fatal for the story because that would mean being wrenched away from the stream and having to step back on land, as it were, or—to use a more common metaphor—having to emerge from a sort of subterranean tunnel or labyrinth into the light of day. In the abovementioned letter to Felice, Kafka combines metaphors of water and of the underworld: the "deeper wells" flow *down below;* only when they are silent is it necessary (and deleterious to the story) to draw down something from the "surface" into the writing.

Kafka's comments on his writing method reveal three things he considers important: first, *spontaneity,* the greatest abbreviation of the passage from an idea to its written form; second, *fluidity,* the un-interrupted movement of writing; and finally, the *open, unprejudiced* quality of writing that doesn't know where it is going and lets itself be carried along by the developing story. He expressed this best in a remark reported by Max Brod: "One must write as if in a dark tunnel, without knowing how the characters are going to develop."[5]

The manuscripts offer further support for our thesis of the "gradual completion of the story as it is being written." The original manu-scripts' most striking feature is probably their sequential linearity. The work itself (including finished texts, the much more frequent fragmentary pieces, and even the shortest beginnings) appears as a *series of entries,* usually in bound notebooks, though in some rare cases on loose papers (which, however, are arranged together, like a notebook). Almost never is a shorter work written on a separate sheet of paper chosen only for this purpose. ("First Sorrow" is a striking exception.) These chronologically ordered entries, which look ex-actly like diary entries, follow one another and are separated only by a short horizontal slash. Quite economically, there is no space be-tween them—hence, no space for later additions or attempts to con-tinue a story that has been broken off. Where a story has been broken off one finds hardly any corrections which might indicate that Kafka considered alternatives, that is, attempted to make the abandoned narrative seaworthy again. Instead, the text simply comes to an end, sometimes in midsentence; below it the horizontal slash is firmly drawn and the author never returns to this unsuccessful work. It is as if the pen simply did not want to write further and this refusal was interpreted by Kafka as an unmistakable sign that the story was stunted beyond repair. In looking at these notebooks, this series of successfully completed works and abandoned ruins, Schiller's characterization of "naïve poetry" comes to mind: "It is a happy throw; it needs no correction when it succeeds, but suffers none when it misses."[6]

This brings me to the second chief characteristic of the manuscripts, namely their lack of signs of subsequent rewriting. The manuscripts exhibit astonishingly few revisions that were not definitely or in all probability made at the very moment of composition. Only rarely can one be certain that a particular correction was inserted at a later time, when the text could no longer be experienced as something caught in the original flow of writing. And even when such corrections can be identified, they are almost always grammatical or stylistic revisions; they recall the animal's final cosmetic touches in "The Burrow," the "pressing and smoothing" which can only be done once a new passageway has been completed. In other words, the changes in the original manuscripts are almost always part of the original writing process. They show that Kafka recognized and corrected false starts, that he abandoned some passageways in order to continue in other directions. Alternative formulations are never allowed to remain: all decisions regarding the plot have to be made as quickly as possible and cannot be reversed, and nothing is left unresolved for later consideration. Kafka apparently felt the need to secure a story's passageway as quickly as possible once he entered it. This is also true of the larger structural changes that appear in the manuscripts: they too can be characterized as "original corrections," for they *had* to be completed before the story could continue. Two examples from his novel *The Castle* will illustrate this point.

At the beginning of the fifth notebook, at the point in the novel where K. has finally disengaged himself from Olga's stories and finds himself on the street with his former assistant Jeremiah (Frieda's new lover), Jeremiah says: "But all the same it wasn't necessary for you to take the roundabout way through the next-door garden, I know that way" (C 304).[7] What originally followed this scene—as the manuscript shows—is the beginning of a new chapter, which was to take place in the empty schoolhouse vacated by Frieda: "The door stood wide open, they hadn't even bothered to close it after leaving; K.

alone was responsible after their departure. The evacuation had been complete, nothing remained behind except the backpack with a few undergarments, even the cane seemed to be gone, as if it had been planned that he would bring along the unused willow rod as a substitute." This passage was then deleted and the novel continued in the way we know it today: K. learns the details of Frieda's flight not through his own observations in the schoolhouse, but from Frieda herself. Moreover, her account is not quite the same: the school gate, we now learn, was never actually opened; instead, the enterprising Jeremiah broke open a window and stole Frieda from the school in a dramatic manner.

The second example concerns the passage in the manuscript corresponding to the beginning of chapter five, "At the Mayor's." As is well known, in the final version of the novel the land-surveyor meets the Mayor in bed; the latter, plagued by sore feet, directs from his bed the whole ludicrous search for the papers concerning K.'s supposed employment. Two assistants, his wife Mizzi and the teacher, are there to help the Mayor with his paperwork. Mizzi, who will be mentioned later in the novel, plays an important role in this chapter because of the Mayor's illness. However, when Kafka first put pen to paper for chapter five, neither Mizzi nor the Mayor's illness had apparently occurred to him; evidently, they had not yet been invented. This means that all the preparations for the grand comic scene in the Mayor's chamber were still to be made. Originally, the new chapter began as follows: "When K. entered the room the Mayor was sitting with the town scribe, busy with the duties of his office." At this point the first version breaks off and is crossed out. There is no wife Mizzi who assists the Mayor as a secretary but a scribe (who will disappear from the story, never to be seen again). Also, the Mayor does not lie in bed, groaning in pain, but is working happily away at his desk. In such passages we have Kafka's continuous, nonteleological writing manner directly before us: "One must write as if in a dark tunnel, without knowing how the characters are going to develop."

This method is connected with the fact that Kafka never (as far as I can tell) gave a story a title before writing it out.[8] To have done so would have been surprising for an author who took seriously the venerable idea of artistic paternity—for how can a child be baptized before it is born? Of course, a child's name can hover in a parent's mind beforehand (and with it a vague notion of how the desired child might develop), but the christening itself must wait for the child's birth. For Kafka, a story had to exist as a completed whole, a fully developed entity, before it could be given a title and thereby equipped for the journey into the wide world. One can generally say that Kafka titled only those manuscripts which he had successfully completed and judged worthy of publication. Of course the novels pose a somewhat different problem, but even here the principle of a belated christening is evident. The chapters that were given titles at all received them only after Kafka considered them finished. Chapters seventeen through twenty of *The Castle*, for example, apparently received their title—"Amalia's Secret," "Amalia's Punishment," "Petitions," and "Olga's Plans"—only after this entire section (the evening with the Barnabas family) had been completed. In line with this principle, by the way, none of the three novels ever received a definitive title, because none of them was ever finished.

Production and product, writing and the finished text, appear to be connected even more closely—and in a more subterranean fashion—in Kafka's case than I have intimated until now; his narratives simultaneously *represent* and *enact* a process of searching and researching. The story's tentative progress forward, in which it materializes even as Kafka writes, does not *represent* the fictional hero's tentative progress but, rather, runs parallel to it: there are two related, ongoing searches and we become aware of both while reading. The hero digs himself forward and his writing creator does likewise; together they grope their way forward, like the land-surveyor and the story in which he finds himself. The two analogous searches intersect and condition one another, and sometimes seem surprisingly united. When the land-surveyor reflects upon his situation in the schoolhouse and the text reads, "For it must not be forgotten that this reception had perhaps determined the course of events" (C 215–16), he is surely thinking of his arrival in the village at the beginning of the novel, and of how he was received by the innkeeper, by the castellan's son Schwarzer, and by the group assembled at Lasemann's. However, something else appears to resonate here: the author's "reception" of this rich opening scene, the original idea that would point the way to all the following material—a way that he had scarcely imagined, which was only revealed to him as he wrote. Thus the reader gains the impression, at least subliminally, of being involved not only in a momentous fictional process of searching but also in the quite real, exhausting writing process of a man who explores the world with his pen and for whom this writing—and the almost desperate hope accompanying it—was the most important thing in life.

The thesis of the gradual completion of a work through the act of writing, the "tunnel-thesis" which I have tried to illustrate here, relates in its full sense only to Kafka's narrative fictional work, to his stories. In conclusion, however, we should at least mention that other category of his work which might be termed reflections or meditations. This category includes—besides those melancholy short pieces from his early period which appeared in *Meditation*—above all the plotless pieces from the years 1916 and 1917 ("The New Advocate," "Up in the Gallery," "The Cares of a Family Man," "Eleven Sons," and "A Crossbreed"), those from 1920 (such as "Poseidon," "The City Coat of Arms"), and a text like "A Little Woman" in *A Hunger Artist* from 1922. These static reflections represent and meditate upon enigmatic objects or figures, they circle abstractly around something meaningful but puzzling. One certainly cannot describe them as spontaneous, nor can one claim that they lack a preconceived plan, as if written by someone feeling his way forward in a dark tunnel. With these pieces we obviously are dealing with a different kind of literary production. For unlike the stories, these pieces not only have a recognizable, given *object*—a fixed point outside themselves which is constantly referred to—but they also appear to follow a preconceived plan of how the object is to be examined in the course of writing and interrogated about its secret meaning.

If, as the stories unfold, an internal process is seized and then guided by the act of representation, in his meditations the author already has some existing object in sight which he then investigates in an artful game with his pen. This object, which Kafka always understood as the embodiment of something spiritual (since, as we know, he believed that "nothing other than a spiritual world" exists [DF 41]), had to remain immediately present to him while he was writing, whether as a clear image hovering before him or, apparently more often the case, as a tangible object on his desk or in his study. The object in question could thus very well be something literally *present*, some "small thing" which could "easily" be covered up by the

writer "with his hand" (for example, "A Little Woman").[9] Consequently, in the meditative pieces—where one can hardly speak of
"exaltation" or an inspired kind of writing and where, as it were,
those "deeper wells" that Kafka mentions are silent—something from
the "surface" world of the writer can still be brought down into the
writing which, as in "Eleven Sons," structurally determines the work.

To summarize: Kafka's texts depend to an extreme degree on the
concrete circumstances in which they were written. Precisely because
the person of the author was completely shut out in favor of the writer
while a story was being fashioned, the activity of "placing text"
(Schriftstellen)—the actual writing act—took on greater significance. And precisely because Kafka's works shut themselves off so
emphatically from the empirical realities of life, as well as from everything "in the air" around him, precisely because they originated in a
hermetically sealed space, in "solitary confinement," they often get
caught up (as paradoxical as this may sound) in the *manual* conditions of their creation. Kafka's texts lack any conscious reference to
an "outside," to actual events in the world, and are thus all the more
dependent on Kafka's actual workshop and its conditions. For this
reason, they bear the indelible traces of his tangible, yet elusive
writing.

Translated by Susan Lhota

"THE JUDGMENT," "LETTER TO HIS FATHER," AND THE BOURGEOIS FAMILY

Gerhard Neumann

KAFKA'S EXPERIENCE of his own identity in writing "The Judgment" exemplifies a contradiction that, as the French philosopher Jacques Derrida has shown, has formed an explicit part of European culture and its essential discursivity at least since Rousseau—the contradiction between writing as a liberating act that expresses the individual's particular identity (*Eigentümlichkeit*) and writing as a form of enslavement to the disciplinary norms of a society in which even a schoolboy learns to measure his identity in terms of the ability to write correctly. Traces of Kafka's traumatic experiences with the bourgeois educational system can be found throughout his work, perhaps most poignantly in his autobiographical sketch "Every human being is peculiar . . ." (DF 201–6) and in the later "Letter to His Father." One symptom of a reversal of the writing ritual from emancipatory act into forced confession is the letter of November 16, 1912, that Kafka's mother wrote to Felice Bauer. In it she makes an attempt, at once helpless and effective, to turn Kafka the writer back into Kafka the schoolboy, to force him back into the norms of supervised writing within the scope of the family's discipline:

I have known for many years that [my son] spends his leisure hours writing. But I assumed this to be a mere pastime. Actually, this occupation would not harm his health if only he would sleep and eat like other young people of his age. But he sleeps and eats so little that he is undermining his health, and I am afraid he may not listen to reason until, God forbid, it is too late. I would therefore very much like to ask you if you could somehow draw his attention to this fact, question him about the way he lives, what he eats, how many meals he has, and about his daily routine in general. On the other hand, he must not suspect that I have written to you, nor must he learn that I am aware of his correspondence with you. Should it be within your power to change his mode of life, I would be greatly in your debt and you would be making me very happy. With the expression of my great esteem,

Julie Kafka (F 46)

Kafka never observed anything more carefully than this paradox of language acquisition: language provides the only means for human beings to emancipate, realize, and define themselves culturally, and yet also inevitably forces them to efface their individuality. It functions, on the one hand, as an autonomous vehicle for personal fantasies, but on the other, as a disciplinary machine. For Kafka the prime example of these conflicts was the confrontation in his own family between a writing son and an authoritarian, vocally powerful father.

Significantly, in his own texts Kafka never contrasts this rebellious, antiauthoritarian "writing" with the activity of daily life, but merges them in a highly questionable fashion. "Poets" do not appear in his work; "artists" are figured at best in the dubious form of cabaret acrobats, talking animals, or hunger artists. Thus Georg Bendemann attempts to emancipate himself in "The Judgment" by writing an "everyday" letter. Only from the later vantage point of November 1919 did Kafka explicitly articulate the theme of a child's emancipation from the family through literary expression: the "Letter to His Father" recapitulates the constellation of writing son and speaking father from an autobiographical perspective.

The two texts belong together because they treat the same problem from two (different) perspectives: the problem of the individual's "second" birth once he or she has left the family to enter society. This passage from the "family" into "life" is made possible by an upbringing in the family which, in view of its paradoxical nature, might be termed "education to freedom" (*Erziehung zur Freiheit*) or "discipline for the sake of autonomy." What the parents say is essentially: "Without our help, you will never become an adult." This classical form of a familial double bind is given literary form in "The Judgment" in the paradox of Georg's apparently senseless acceptance of his father's death sentence. In the "Letter to His Father" it is subjected to explicit and masterful analysis, its genesis and power at once described and exposed: he provides us here with an interpretation of his upbringing whose insightfulness can scarcely be overemphasized. A sketch of his arguments will make this clear.

WORDS AND CONCEPTS

On the most rudimentary level of the text—that of words and ideas—there are numerous cross-references between the "Letter to His Father" and "The Judgment." The very word "judgment" and its derivatives sustain the entire text of the letter like a pedal point; legal terms are everywhere woven into the text, accompanying the entire argument like leitmotivs. On the very first pages one finds the words "your judgment of me" (DF 139). The father is granted the power to legitimate all processes of self-realization, as if this were self-evident.

Kafka's sister Ottla appears to be the one person in the family unit capable of "judging" for herself: as the youngest, she was the last to enter a family situation "where the balance of power was already established." Hence, she is able "to form her own judgment from the large amount of material at her disposal" (DF 167). A second important term in the conceptual system of the letter is that of "intercourse" (*Verkehr*) in the sense of human communication—precisely the word that also mysteriously concludes "The Judgment." Thus, Kafka reproaches his father for "never learning anything about my association with other people [*Menschenverkehr*]" (DF 171) and complains: "The impossibility of getting on calmly together [*Verkehr*] had one more result, actually a very natural one: I lost the capacity to talk" (DF 150). Finally—along with the two main ideas of "judgment" through discourse (*Rede*, a word also meaning "speech" or "conversation") and "intercourse" between human beings—little figures of speech, as so often in Kafka, act as connectors between the early story and the later essay in autobiography. Thus, in the letter Kafka supplies his father with a fictional tirade addressed to his son, which makes use of the same metaphorical expressions that old Bendemann uses to reproach his son: "You are unfit for life; but in order to be able to settle down in it comfortably, without worries and without self-reproaches, you must prove that I have deprived you of all your fitness for life and put it into my pockets" (DF 195). Precisely this motif of pockets crops up twice in "The Judgment": first, as the pocket into which Georg puts his letter; second, as the "pockets" in the father's nightshirt which Georg tries to ridicule (CS 80, 86). This is a characteristic example of a verbal invention that develops out of a proverbial figure of speech—"I shall have you in my pocket" ("Ich stecke dich allemal in die Tasche"). The perspective supplied by a verbal image reproduces within the family strategic ploys of enfranchisement and disenfranchisement.

LEARNING AT HOME

The argument of the "Letter to His Father" has a further goal: to depict those processes in the family meant to teach the child to realize himself or herself—that is, the situation ultimately arising under the pressure of family feelings and family bonds, in which the child learns to think within the disciplinary rituals devised and endlessly repeated by the father:

> In all my thinking I was, after all, under the heavy pressure of your personality, even in that part of it—and particularly in that—which was not in accord with yours. All these thoughts, seemingly independent of you, were from the beginning loaded with the burden of your harsh and dogmatic judgments; it was almost impossible to endure this and yet work out one's thoughts with any measure of completeness and permanence. I am not here speaking of any sublime thoughts, but of every little enterprise in childhood. (DF 145–46)

What Kafka is describing here is the pragmatic aspect of human communication: thought content is determined less by its conceptual content than it is by its function within a relationship. The decisive factor in this mode of learning is the readiness of the dependent partner in the communication to submit to the rules of learning rather than jeopardize his or her relationship to the dominant partner. This is exactly the Kafka family situation as described by Franz.

THE FAMILY DOUBLE BIND

This way of learning to realize oneself through paternal instruction within the family takes place, above all, at the dinner table. Kafka writes:

> But that was what your whole method of upbringing was like. You have, I think, a gift for bringing up children; you could, I am sure, have been of use to a human being of your own kind with your methods; such a person would have seen the reasonableness of what you told him, would not have troubled about anything else, and would quietly have done things the way he was told. But for me as a child everything you shouted at me was positively a heavenly commandment. I never forgot it, it remained for me the most important means of forming a judgment of the world, above all of forming a judgment of you yourself, and there you failed entirely. Since as a child I was together with you chiefly at meals, your teaching was to a large extent teaching about proper behavior at table. What was brought to the table had to be eaten up, there could be no discussion of the goodness of the food—but you yourself often found the food uneatable, called it "this swill," said "that brute" (the cook) had ruined it. . . . Bones mustn't be cracked with the teeth, but you could. Vinegar must not be sipped noisily, but you could. The main thing was that the bread should be cut straight. But it didn't matter that you did it with a knife dripping with gravy. One had to take care that no scraps fell on the floor. In the end it was under your chair that there were most scraps. . . . These would in themselves have been utterly insignificant details, they only became depressing for me because you, the man who was so tremendously the measure of all things for me, yourself did not keep the commandments you imposed on me. (DF 147–48)

What Kafka characterizes in this scene is one of the core strategies of family education, the so-called double bind. His particular form of this conflict is rooted in the Enlightenment theorem of an "education toward freedom," the benevolent "compulsory acquisition of autonomy." The child, a dependent who can neither afford nor desire to end relations with its parents, is compelled to repress the content of the discourse—in this case, the very contradictions that constitute its pedagogical method—precisely in order to salvage the affective relation. By "following" the inherently contradictory demand for action, the child is forced "to disregard it or by disregarding it to follow it." It is essential to this aporia that the command—in this case, the father's "judgment"—be experienced simultaneously not only as absolute and universally binding but also as applicable solely to the individual. This same paradox is reproduced in the structure of the parable "Before the Law": the door to the Law, which by its nature can be comprehended only as something general, is closed the instant that the individual before it dies. By acknowledging this type of paradox, one can interpret Kafka's texts in a manner that does them least violence: language is experienced in affectively bounded situations as the vehicle of inherently contradictory demands for action; consequently, it compels paradoxical behavior. The aporetic mealtime situation so clearly depicted in the "Letter to His Father" finds its ultimate paradigmatic representation in "A Hunger Artist." On the other hand, "The Judgment" reproduces the inherent contradiction of a "law" that, paradoxically, applies only to the individual: the judgment is accepted although its legally binding character is not perceived.

Kafka portrays the primordial scene of the child's experience of the self in the famous "*pavlatche* scene," the paternal denial of a drink of water: "One night I kept on whimpering for water . . ." (DF 142). "The Judgment" reproduces this experience as a reversal: the father condemns the son to death by drowning. His sentence is the definitive revocation of what the family is supposed to teach: the art of survival.

LAW AS THE DISCOURSE OF THE OTHER

The functioning of this paradoxical law is described by Kafka once again with the greatest precision:

Hence the world was for me divided into three parts: into one in which I, the slave, lived under laws that had been invented only for me and which I could, I did not know why, never completely comply with; then a second world, which was infinitely remote from mine, in which you lived, concerned with government, with the issuing of orders and with annoyance about their not being obeyed; and finally a third world where everybody else lived happily and free from orders and from having to obey. (DF 148)

Kafka retrospectively articulates with considerable conceptual precision the conditions of a situation that in "The Judgment" he could only reconstruct from its symptoms. In the "Letter to His Father," he analyzes the origin of what in "The Judgment" appears sheerly incomprehensible. Someone does something of immense gravity which contrary to all reason he or she is forced to do by discourse alone. It is not an abstract ethical world which gives this law its prestige; it is, rather, the family constellation, the bounded communicative system between parents and children based on love as power, that produces this inherently contradictory world of laws. Hence, there is no longer a question of guilt in the usual sense. What "The Judgment" leaves open is very precisely diagnosed in the "Letter to His Father": only as an adult was Kafka able to perceive that the father's gesture of power as well as the "child's exclusive sense of guilt" merely hide the "helplessness" of both (DF 150). Further, the process that leads to such judgments additionally admits of no objective judge but only of interested parties. In "this terrible trial that is pending between us and you," Kafka writes, "you keep on claiming to be the judge, whereas, at least in the main (here I leave a margin for all the mistakes I may naturally make) you are party too, just as weak and deluded as we are (DF 167–68).

The "innocent guilt" of this situation results in the victory of the oppressive family discourse over the emancipatory discourse of the individual. It is the father who punctuates the speech acts of the family unit: "I," says the son, "lost the capacity to talk" (DF 150).

THE FATHER'S JUDGMENT

The strategic means of regulating the language, and hence, the reality of the family is the double bind. Kafka provides a classic example:

> You have always reproached me (and what is more either alone or in front of others, you having no feeling for the humiliation of this latter, your children's affairs always being public affairs) for living in peace and quiet, warmth, and abundance, lacking for nothing, thanks to your hard work. I think here of remarks that must positively have worn grooves in my brain, like: "When I was only seven I had to push a barrow from village to village." "We all had to sleep in one room." "We were glad when we got potatoes." "For years I had open sores on my legs from not having enough clothes to wear in winter." "I was only a little boy when I was sent away to Pisek to go into business." "I got nothing from home, not even when I was in the army, even then I was sending money home." "But for all that, for all that—Father was always Father to me. Ah, nobody knows what that means these days! What do these children know? Nobody's been through that! Does any child understand such things today?" Under other conditions such stories might have been very educational, they might have been a way of encouraging one and strengthening one to endure torments and deprivations similar to those one's father had undergone. But that wasn't what you wanted at all; the situation had, after all, become quite different as a result of all your efforts, and there was no opportunity to distinguish oneself in the world as you had done. Such an opportunity would first of all have had to be created by violence and revolution, it would have meant breaking away from home. . . . But all that was not what you wanted at all, that you termed ingratitude, extravagance, disobedience, treachery, madness. And so, while on the one hand you tempted me to it by means of example, story, and humiliation, on the other hand you forbade it with the utmost severity. (DF 158–59)

Here Kafka reconstructs the double bind step by step. First the father holds himself up as an example to the children: as a child he had to work in the snow with open wounds. The educational device at work here is that of a normative, exemplary previous life, in which deprivation is the precondition of emancipation. Obviously, though, the initial argument is reversed as the discourse proceeds: namely, as a result of suffering deprivation, the father has himself achieved status and affluence, and he is in a position to provide for—indeed impose upon—his children a life of material comfort. In this way he obligates them to be grateful, and precisely in this way prevents them from achieving the personal freedom that results from deprivation. The demand for action, which issues from the father in the form of educational maxims, is inherently contradictory and brings about total disorientation: "Emancipate yourselves by following my example and become adults" runs the one maxim; "yield through gratitude and remain children" runs the opposite one. The resulting educational discourse coagulates into an order that cannot be obeyed: "I order you not to be so obedient!" The astonishing thing is that the father's discourse contains both possibilities at once. Given this paradoxical demand for action, a breakthrough becomes possible only through revolution or madness—the Oedipal or the schizoid reaction. Kafka himself articulates this image:

> It is as if a person were a prisoner and he had not only the intention of escaping, which would perhaps be attainable, but also, and indeed simultaneously, the intention of rebuilding the prison as a pleasure seat for himself. But if he escapes, he cannot do any rebuilding, and if he rebuilds, he cannot escape. (DF 190)

Or again in conceptual language: "Such an opportunity would first of all have had to be created by violence and revolution, it would have meant breaking away from home" (DF 158).

The "Letter to His Father" develops in theoretical and almost systematic form a motif already found in "The Judgment." Here fantasies of breakthrough through revolution appear again and again—on the one hand, in the rejected passage concerning the depiction of a war and in the pogrom visions from Russia; on the other hand, in the increasing spiritual disintegration of the protagonist, the upshot of which is the powerful image of the lost thread:

> Georg shrank into a corner, as far away from his father as possible. A long time ago he had firmly made up his mind to watch closely every least movement so that he should not be surprised by any indirect attack, a pounce from behind or above. At this moment he recalled this long-forgotten resolve and forgot it again, like a man drawing a short thread through the eye of a needle. (CS 85)

FANTASIES OF EMANCIPATION

While in "The Judgment" the escape from the family situation, as a birth into the social world, misfires and is accompanied only marginally—metaphorically, as it were—by escape fantasies of revolution and madness, the "Letter to His Father" offers an entire series of such escape routes, all of which, of course, prove ultimately impossible. The weakest possibility of emancipation is conceived of simply as a form of growing into adulthood and is expressed as half-hearted trust in the biological process of maturation: "What you had to fight for we received from your hand, but the fight for external life, a fight that was instantly open to you and which we were naturally not spared either, we have to fight for only late in life, in our maturity but with only childish strength" (DF 159–60). The second possibility, basically just as unrealizable for Kafka, is that of a belated entry into the family situation, which, of course, had been the lot of the younger sister Ottla but not the firstborn son (DF 167). A third possibility is defined as the exile of the father as the all-powerful, ultimate seat of legitimation for all family discourse:

> I might go on to describe further orbits of your influence and of struggle against it, but there I would be entering uncertain ground and would have to construct things, and apart from that, the further you are at a remove from your business and your family the pleasanter you have always become, easier to get on with, better mannered, more considerate, and more sympathetic (I mean outwardly too), in exactly the same way as for instance an autocrat, when he happens to be outside the frontiers of his own country, has no reason to go on being tyrannical and is able to associate good-humoredly even with the lowest of the low. In point of fact, in the group photographs taken at Franzensbad, for instance, you always looked as big and jolly, among those sulky little people, as a king upon his travels. (DF 169)

This is Kafka's subtle diagnosis of how power—precisely, too, the power of discourse—remains bound to territoriality. We have both sides of a single, no-win situation: the father can be conceived of as powerless only in exile, while during his lifetime Kafka himself never succeeded in making the leap out of the territoriality of the family situation in Prague into the autonomy of another place abroad. The fourth possibility of emancipation considered by the "Letter to His Father" is the development of a negative sense of family "for breaking away from you" (DF 169); but it is Freud's achievement to have shown that such a reversal of affect in no way indicates a solution. Love and hate are but two sides of the same coin. Indeed, it is just this ambivalence of feeling that, from the beginning, has fueled the paradoxical demand for action within "the family animal" (L 294): it is the first to bind the partners indissolubly to each other, and hate enters where love fails. The fifth possibility of self-emancipation adduced by the letter is that of the development of a language of self-realization that would not be regulated exclusively by the paternal process of education, a sort of utopian establishment of a new system of communication. Here Kafka's attempts at writing, which again and again were introduced into the family battlefield as arguments, have their place:

> You struck nearer home with your dislike of my writing and all that, unknown to you, was connected with it. Here I had, in fact, got some distance away from you by my own efforts, even if it was slightly reminiscent of the worm that, as a foot tramples on the tail end of it, breaks loose with its top end and drags itself aside. To a certain extent I was in safety; there was a chance to breathe freely. The dislike that you naturally and immediately had of my writing too was, by way of exception, welcome to me. My vanity and my ambition, did suffer, it is true, under your soon proverbial way of hailing the arrival of my books*: "Put it on my bedside table!" (as it happened, you were usually playing cards when a book came), but fundamentally I was thoroughly glad of it, not only out of rebellious malice, not only out of delight at a new confirmation of my view of our relationship, but quite spontaneously, because to me that formula sounded something like: "Now you are free!" Of course it was a delusion; I was not, or, to put it most optimistically, was not yet, free. My writing was all about you; all I did there, after all, was to bemoan what I could not bemoan upon your breast. (DF 176–77)

The hopelessness of such an attempt to found a language of one's own—wrested from the sphere of family discourse—becomes clear in the fact that this discourse of freedom is no more than the recoding

---

* Kafka is speaking here particularly of A Country Doctor, which he dedicated to his father. —ED.

of the paternal judgment. It is a sort of palimpsest, on which the formula "Now you are free" is written on top of the paternal sentence "Put it on my bedside table." In precisely this way too the "Letter to His Father" refers back to "The Judgment": even the discourse of self-emancipation is still the discourse *on* this family and the victory of the father, who stays in power as its legitimator. This would have to be the final paradox of Kafka's work: that even the discourse of liberation in the form of the discourse of art can still be defined only as a carbon copy of the coercion machine of family language and of the rituals of self-realization acquired through it. A final attempt at liberation—one that was also considered in "The Judgment" and as promptly rejected—is alluded to in the idea of founding one's own family, of marriage as the opportunity for a new, not yet regulated family communications system.

> But I showed no foresight at all with regard to the significance and possibility of a marriage for me; this up to now the greatest terror of my life has come upon me almost completely unexpectedly. The child had developed so slowly, these things were outwardly all too remote from him; now and then the necessity of thinking of them did arise; but that here a permanent, decisive and indeed the most grimly bitter ordeal was imminent was something that could not be recognized. In reality, however, the plans to marry became the most large-scale and hopeful attempt at escape, and then the failure was on a correspondingly large scale, too. (DF 181–82)

The truth that does not clearly emerge in art, that is, in the writing of literature (that the language of coercion is inscribed in every attempt at liberation), is immediately evident in Kafka's attempts to marry, which were continually broken off:

> The most important obstacle to marriage however is the no longer eradicable conviction that what is essential to supporting a family and, more, to guiding it is what I have recognized in you, and indeed everything rolled into one, good and bad, as it is organically combined in you, that is to say, strength, and scorn of the other, health and a certain immoderation, eloquence and inadequacy, self-confidence and dissatisfaction with everyone else, a superior attitude to the world and tyranny, knowledge of human nature and mistrust of most people, then also good

> qualities without any drawback, such as industry, endurance, presence
> of mind, and fearlessness. (DF 192–93)

Liberation would only be possible through unconditional identification with the father's teaching: precisely this, however, appears as the
ultimate and final foreclosure of that individuality whose preservation was the goal of even the most helpless attempts at writing. Only
at the price of assuming the authority to establish the rules of family
discourse oneself would this sort of identity (as mere equality with
the father) be possible, indeed only at the cost of establishing oneself
as the most powerful party in the paradoxical structure of family relations. Together with this final attempt at liberation—and, of all of
the arguments advanced in "Letter to His Father," this is the dominant, the irrefutable one—the penultimate possibility of emancipation would also fail: writing in a language that would be free, not
governed by double binds. It is the hopelessness of this situation—of
needing to be solitary and, because of the social nature of language,
not being able to be solitary—that had already marked "The Judgment" and had given the "Letter to His Father" its tragic dimension.

  The characteristic literary form that records this sort of tragedy of
communication without communication is the letter. A letter is the
distinctive theme of "The Judgment," and the argument about this
judgment continues on its way in the letter form of the forever unsent
"Letter to His Father." The letter is the sole form of linguistic organization adequate to the aporia of solitude as communication and of
communication in solitude. Here the desperate attempt finds its distinctive form: keeping the rules of communication under control;
governing freely and controlling through a kind of literary "machine"
the distances between I and Thou, between the extremes of total
fusion and total self-assertion; surveying autonomously the distance
between I and Thou. To this extent the letter becomes purely and
simply a "transitional object." Only the letter makes possible that
government over the subject and its inherently paradoxical condition
of being at once producer and produced. Only in the letter is the
fantasy of a social birth possible—one free of the coercive mechanisms of a socially ritualized language. Only in this form, which in a
certain sense creates the interlocutor, can the fantasy of becoming a
self (by oneself) be organized as the mediation between two ques-

tions: between, on the one hand, that of producing oneself (by oneself) through discourse; and on the other, that of being produced
through others and their discourse. Only the letter is able to remain
suspended between these two impossibilities as the most paradoxical
form of identification through language situated within a social
context.

Translated by Stanley Corngold

THE LETTERS TO FELICE

Elias Canetti

So NOW THEY ARE IN PRINT, these letters, telling of five years of torment; and the first name of Kafka's fiancée—the only pointer to which was for a long time the discreet sign "F.," matching Kafka's "K.," so that for many years people had no idea what she was called and were kept wondering which of all possible names it might be, never guessing the right one, for to do so was quite impossible—this name now stands writ large on the cover of the book. The woman to whom these letters were addressed died in 1960. Five years before her death, she sold them to Kafka's publisher; however this may strike one, Kafka's "dearest businesswoman" certainly was showing for one last time that efficiency of hers, which meant much to him and even evoked feelings of tenderness in him.

True, Kafka had been dead for forty-three years when these letters appeared. Even then, because one revered the man and his misfortune, one's first response was a feeling of awkwardness and embarrassment. I know people whose embarrassment increased, the more they read, who could not help feeling that they were intruding precisely where they should not.

I respect these people, but I am not one of them. I found these letters more gripping and absorbing than any literary work I have read for years past. They belong among those singular memoirs, autobiographies, collections of letters from which Kafka himself drew sustenance. He himself, with reverence his loftiest feature, had no qualms about reading, over and over again, the letters of Kleist, of Flaubert, and of Hebbel. In one of the most harassed moments of his life, he took his cue from the fact that Grillparzer, when he was finally able to take Kathi Fröhlich on his lap, felt altogether indifferent (F 405). In the face of life's horror—luckily most people notice it only on occasion, but a few whom inner forces appoint to bear witness are always conscious of it—there is only one comfort: its alignment with the horror experienced by previous witnesses. One must accordingly be most grateful to Felice Bauer for keeping and preserving Kafka's letters, even if she did find it in her heart to sell them.

To call these letters a document would be saying too little, unless one were to apply the same title to the life-testimonies of Pascal, Kierkegaard, and Dostoyevsky. For my part, I can only say that these letters have penetrated me like an actual life, and that they are now so enigmatic and familiar to me that it seems they have been mental possessions of mine from the moment when I first began to accommodate human beings entirely in my mind, in order to arrive, time and again, at a fresh understanding of them.

It was in Max Brod's family apartment, on August 13, 1912, late in the evening, that Kafka first met Felice Bauer. Many remarks that he made at the time about this meeting have been preserved. The first occurs in a letter to Max Brod, dated August 14. Kafka here refers to the manuscript of *Meditation*, which he had brought to Brod on the previous evening; together they were to make a final arrangement of the texts in it. "Yesterday, when we were arranging the pieces, I was under the girl's influence, it is just possible that something foolish, some (secretly) comic sequence may have resulted" (L 84). He asks Brod to see that all is well, and he thanks him. The next day, August 15, the following statement appears in his diary: "Thought much of—what embarrassment before writing down names—F. B." (D 206).

Then on August 20, a week after the meeting, he tries to describe his first impression objectively. He describes her appearance, and feels that he is becoming a little estranged from her by "coming too close to her, physically," in this description. He found it natural that she, a stranger, should be sitting in this company. He got on well with her at once. "As I was sitting down, I looked at her closely for the first time, by the time I was seated I already had an unshakable verdict"* (D 268–69). The diary entry breaks off in the middle of the next sentence. All the weightier observations might otherwise have been set down; how much more might have been written becomes apparent only later.

He writes to her for the first time on September 20, and reminds her—five weeks have passed since their meeting—that he is the person at the Brods' apartment who handed to her, across the table, one by one, some photographs, "and who finally, with the very hand now striking the keys, held your hand, the one which confirmed a promise to accompany him next year to Palestine" (F 5).

The promptness of this promise, the certainty with which she made it, were what impressed him so strongly at first. He senses in this handshake an avowal, the word betrothal lying not far behind it, and quickness cannot but fascinate him, slow as he is at making decisions himself, for whom every goal he would like to approach removes itself in a thousand doubts, instead of coming closer. The goal of the promise, however, is Palestine; and at this stage in his life there could hardly have been a more auspicious word—it is the Promised Land.

The situation becomes still more significant when one considers what pictures he is handing across the table. They are photographs of a "Thalia" journey†: early in July, five or six weeks before, he had been with Max Brod in Weimar, where some remarkable events had befallen him in the Goethe House. Inside the Goethe House itself he had noticed the custodian's daughter, a beautiful girl. He had managed to converse with her, had been introduced to her parents, had photographed her in the garden and at the entrance to the house, was invited to return and so could visit the house freely, not only during official visiting hours. Also, he met her often, by chance, in the lanes of the little town, watched her anxiously in company with young men, arranged a rendezvous with her, which she did not keep,

---

* The word for verdict, "*Urteil*," also means "judgment," and is the title of Kafka's "breakthrough" story "The Judgment," written the following month.—Ed.
† Probably so named after the muse of comedy, since the trip was largely devoted to visiting cultural sights.

and soon came to realize that her preference was for students. The whole thing happened during a period of a few days; the encounter had gained in intensity by being part of the movement of travel, which makes everything happen at a quicker pace. Immediately after this, Kafka went alone, without Brod, to a sanatorium at Jungborn, in the Harz Mountains. There are wonderfully rich memoirs of those weeks, free from "Thalia" interests and pious respect for the dwellings of great poets. But he sent postcards to the beautiful girl in Weimar, and received answers. He copies out one of the answers verbatim in a letter to Brod, and adds the following remark—a hopeful one, considering his cast of mind: "For even if I do not displease her, yet she finds me utterly humdrum. But why then does she write, just as I want her to? Could it be that one can take a girl captive by writing?" (L 80).

So the encounter in the Goethe House gave him courage. Across the table he hands to Felice the pictures taken on that journey. The memory of his attempt to make contact, and of his doings at the time, which had led at least to the photographs he could now show, is transferred to the girl who sits facing him now: Felice.

Kafka also became acquainted with Ernst Rowohlt on this journey, which had begun in Leipzig, and Rowohlt had decided to publish his first book. The compiling of short prose pieces from his diaries, for the book *Meditation*, had been keeping Kafka very busy. He was hesitant; the pieces did not seem to him good enough. Brod pressed him and kept the pressure up; eventually the book took shape, and on the evening of August 13 Kafka brought the final selection with him, intending, as has already been remarked, to discuss the arrangement of them with Brod.

Thus he was equipped, on that evening, with everything that might bring him encouragement: the manuscript of his first book; the pictures of the "Thalia" journey, among them the pictures of the girl who had responded to him politely; and in his pocket an issue of the magazine *Palästina*.

Kafka felt at ease with the Brod family, in whose home the meeting occurred. He used to try, as he himself tells, to prolong the evenings spent with them, and when they wanted to get to bed he had to be driven away, albeit amicably. It was the family in which he took refuge from his own. Here literature was not taboo. Max Brod's parents were proud of their son and of the name he had already made as a writer, and they took his friends seriously.

It is also a time during which Kafka's notebook writings acquired a new scope and precision. The Jungborn diary entries—finest of all his travel diaries—testify to this. They are also the ones that relate most directly to his oeuvre proper, in this case to *Amerika*. [. . .]

The correspondence developed rapidly, with daily letters coming from Kafka and Felice soon replying at the same rate (only his letters are preserved). It has certain quite astonishing features: for an open-minded reader, the most noticeable is the amount of complaining, on Kafka's part, about his physical states. These complaints begin as early as the second letter, still somewhat veiled: "Oh, the moods I get into, Fräulein Bauer! A hail of nervousness pours down upon me continuously. What I want one minute I don't want the next. When I have reached the top of the stairs, I still don't know the state I shall be in when I enter the apartment. I have to pile up uncertainties within myself before they turn into a little certainty or a letter. . . . My memory is very bad . . . my halfheartedness . . . I remember that I once actually got out of bed to write down what I had thought out for you; but I promptly returned to bed, because—and this is my second failing—I reproached myself for the foolishness of my anxiety" (F 6–7).

One can see that what he is describing here is his indecisiveness, and with this his wooing begins. But soon everything is brought into relation to his physical states.

He begins the fifth letter with a reference to his inability to sleep, and he ends it with an account of interruptions in the office where he is writing. From now on, there is hardly a single letter without complaints. At first they are outweighed by interest in Felice. He asks a hundred questions, wants to know everything about her, wishes to be in a position to imagine exactly what goes on in the office where she works and in her home. But that sounds far too general—actually his questions are more concrete. He asks her to tell him when she arrives at her office, what she has had for breakfast, what sort of view she has from her office window, what sort of work she is doing. What are the names of her friends, men and women; who it is that is damaging her health with sweets—these are only the very first questions, countless others follow later. He wants her to be well and safe. He wants to know about the rooms she lives and works in, and no less about how she arranges her time. He will not let any contradiction pass, and he asks for immediate explanations. Of Felice he demands a precision equal to that with which he describes his own states of mind.

Let us keep in mind Kafka's deeper intent during the first period of this correspondence: he was establishing a connection, a channel of communication, between her efficiency and health and his own indecisiveness and weakness. Across the distance between Prague and Berlin he wishes to hold fast to her robustness. The weak words that he is permitted to address to her come back from her ten times stronger. He writes to her two or three times a day. He fights—contrary to his assertions about his weakness—tenaciously, even unyieldingly, for her answers. She is—in this one respect—more capricious than he; she does not have the same obsession. But he succeeds in imposing upon her his own obsession: soon enough, she too is writing him a letter a day, sometimes two.

The struggle to obtain this strength which her regular letters bring him does have meaning. It is no empty exchange of letters, no end in itself, no mere self-gratification: it helps his *writing*. Two nights after his first letter to her he writes "The Judgment," at one sitting, during a single night, in ten hours. One might say that with this story his self-assurance as a writer was established. He reads it to his friends, the story's authenticity is beyond doubt, and thereafter he never repudiated it as he did so many other writings. During the following week he writes "The Stoker," and then inside the next two months five more chapters of *Amerika,* making six chapters altogether. During a two-week pause in the writing of the novel, he writes *The Metamorphosis.*

So it is a magnificent period, and not only from our later standpoint; few other periods in Kafka's life can be compared with it. To judge by the results—and how else should one judge a writer's life—Kafka's attitude during the first three months of correspondence with Felice was entirely the right one for him. He was feeling what he needed to feel: security somewhere far off, a source of strength sufficiently distant to leave his sensitivity lucid, not perturbed by too close a contact—a woman who was there for him, who did not expect more from him than his words, a sort of transformer, whose every technical fault he knew and mastered well enough to be able to rectify it at once by letter. The woman who thus served his purposes had not to be exposed to the influences of his family, from whose proximity Kafka suffered greatly: he had to keep her away from them. She would have to take seriously everything he had to say about himself. Sparing of words as he was in speech, in writing he would expatiate upon himself to her, set forth his complaints regardless: he must hold nothing back, since that might disconcert him in the act of writing; he must tell her, in every detail, of the importance, the continuance, and the hesitations of this writing. His diary stops during this period—the letters to Felice are his expanded diary, with the advantage that he really does write an entry each day, that here he can repeat himself more frequently and thus yield to an important need of his nature. What he writes to her are not unique things which are set down once and for all; he can correct himself in later letters, he can confirm or retract. And even volatility, which with his controlled intelligence he begrudges himself in the single diary entries, because he regards it as being disorderly, is quite possible in the sequence of the letters. But doubtless the chief advantage, as already indicated, is that repetitions, veritable litanies, are possible. If anyone was ever cognizant of the need and function of "litanies," it was Kafka. Among his very pronounced characteristics as a writer, it is this that has most often led to the "religious" misinterpretations of his work.

The opening of this correspondence was so important for Kafka that its effects continued to be felt by him for three months; further, it led to works as singular as *The Metamorphosis*. Why then does his writing suddenly come to a standstill in January 1913? Statements about a writer's having productive and unproductive periods would not answer this question adequately. Productivity always has its determinants, and one should make the effort to find out what causes productivity to stop.

Perhaps it should not be overlooked that the letters of the first period, though they can hardly be viewed as love letters in the usual sense, do entail an element that pertains quite especially to love: for Kafka it is important that Felice *expects* something of him. At the first meeting, from which he drew sustenance for such a long time, he had the manuscript of his first book with him. Felice had made his acquaintance as a writer, not merely as the friend of a writer whose work she knew somewhat; and Kafka's claim to receive letters from

her is based on the premise that she regards him as such. The first
story with which he is satisfied, "The Judgment," is *hers*; he is indebted to her for it, and he dedicated it to her. Naturally he is not
sure about her literary opinions, and in his letters he tries to exert
some influence on them. He asks for a list of the books she has, but
he never receives one.

Felice was an uncomplicated person; this shows clearly enough in
remarks of hers that are quoted in Kafka's letters. The dialogue that
Kafka was conducting with himself by way of her—if such a standard
word as dialogue can be applied to something so complex and subterranean—might have been continued for a long time. He, however,
became bewildered by her craving for culture: she was reading other
writers and named them in her letters. He had brought to light so far
only a fraction of the tremendous world he felt to be in his head; and
as a writer he wanted to have Felice for himself.

On December 11 he sends her his first book; *Meditation* has just
been published. He writes: "Please be kind to my poor book! It consists of those few pages you saw me putting in order on our evening. . . . I wonder if you notice how the various pieces differ in age.
One of them for example is certainly 8 to 10 years old. Show the book
to as few people as possible, so as to avoid having your mind about me
changed" (F 100).

On December 13 he mentions his book again: "I am so happy to
think that my book, no matter how much I find fault with it . . . is
now in your possession" (F 104).

On December 23 the following lonely statement occurs: "Oh, if
Frl. Lindner [a colleague of Felice's] only knew how difficult it is to
write as little as I do!" (F 120). This alludes to the brevity of *Meditation* and can only be interpreted as a reply to an evasive remark in
one of Felice's letters.

And that is all, until his great outburst of jealousy on December
28, seventeen days after he had sent her the book: the letters of that
period, concerning matters of one kind and another, fill thirty closely
printed pages, and, as has been noted, only his letters survive. It is
evident that Felice expressed not a single serious opinion on *Meditation*. His outburst is now aimed against Herbert Eulenberg, about
whom Felice is enthusiastic: "I am jealous of all the people in your

letter, those named and those unnamed, men and girls, business people and writers (writers above all, needless to say). . . . I am jealous of Werfel, Sophocles, Ricarda Huch, Lagerlöf, Jacobsen. My jealousy is childishly pleased because you call Eulenberg Hermann instead of Herbert, while Franz no doubt is deeply engraved on your brain. (You like the *Silhouettes?* You find them pithy and clear?) 'Mozart' is the only one I know in its entirety, Eulenberg . . . gave a reading of it here, but I could hardly bear it, the breathless unclean prose. . . . But of course there is no doubt that in my present condition I am doing him a grave injustice. *But you ought not to read the Silhouettes.* And now I see that you are even 'very enthusiastic' about him. (Listen everyone: Felice is very enthusiastic about him, very enthusiastic indeed, and here am I raging against him in the middle of the night.) But other people are to be found in your letter as well; I want to start a fight with them all, the whole lot, not because I mean to do them any harm, but to drive them away from you, to get you away from them, to read only letters that are concerned solely with you, your family, . . . and of course, of course, me!" (F 129).

The following day he receives from her a letter that is unexpected, for it is Sunday, and he thanks her: "Dearest, once again this is the kind of letter that makes one go hot with silent joy. It is not full of all those friends and writers" (F 131).

That very night he finds an explanation for the previous day's jealousy: "By the way, now I know more precisely why yesterday's letter made me so jealous: You don't like my book any more than you liked my photograph. This really wouldn't matter, for what is written there is largely old stuff. . . . I feel your presence so acutely in everything else that I should be quite prepared . . . to be the *first* to kick the little book aside with *my* foot. . . . But why don't you tell me, tell me in two words, that you don't like it! It would be quite understandable if you did not like the book. . . . No one will know what to make of it, that is and was perfectly clear to me; the trouble the spendthrift publisher took and the money he lost, both utterly wasted, prey on my mind too. . . . But you said nothing, or rather you did once announce that something would be said, but did not say it" (F 132).

At the end of January he comes back to *Meditation:* the Viennese writer Otto Stoessl, whom he rates highly and likes personally, has written him a letter about it: "He also writes about my book, but with such complete lack of understanding that for a moment I thought the book must really be good, since—even in a man as discerning and experienced in literary matters as Stoessl—it can create the kind of misunderstanding one would consider impossible with books" (F 177). He copies for her the whole relevant section of the letter, which is fairly lengthy. There are astounding remarks it in: "It is full of very pertinent humor, turned inward as it were, not unlike the way in which, after a good night's sleep, a refreshing bath, and dressed in clean linen, one welcomes a free, sunny day with happy expectations and an inconceivable sensation of strength. The humor of a healthy frame of mind" (F 178). A mistake of monstrous proportions, every word utterly wrong; Kafka boggles at the phrase "humor of a healthy frame of mind," and later he quotes it again. But he also adds: "The letter, incidentally, goes rather well with an extravagantly favorable review published today, which finds in the book nothing but sorrow" (F 178).

It is clear that he has not forgotten her disregard of *Meditation*; the amplitude of his account of Stoessl's reactions—unusual for Kafka— covers a wound. He wants to teach Felice a lesson—she has made things too easy for herself—and he thereby betrays how hurt he has been by her failure to react.

The most violent outburst against another writer comes during the first half of February. Felice has asked him about Else Lasker-Schüler, and he writes: "I cannot bear her poems; their emptiness makes me feel nothing but boredom, and their contrived verbosity nothing but antipathy. Her prose I find just as tiresome and for the same reasons; it is the work of an indiscriminate brain twitching in the head of an overwrought city-dweller. . . . Yes, she is in a bad way; I believe her second husband has left her; they are collecting for her here, too; I have to give 5 kronen, without feeling the slightest sympathy for her. I don't quite know why, but I always imagine her simply as a drunk, dragging herself through the coffeehouses at night. . . . Away with you, Lasker-Schüler! Come here, dearest! No one is to be between us, no one around us" (F 191).

Felice plans a visit to the theater to see Arthur Schnitzler's *Professor Bernhardi*, and Kafka writes: "But if you go to *Professor Bernhardi*, dearest, you drag me along by that inevitable cord, and there is a danger that we both succumb to that kind of bad literature, which the greater part of Schnitzler represents for me" (F 193). So he goes, the same evening, to see *Hidalla*, in which Frank Wedekind and his wife are playing: "For I don't like Schnitzler at all, and hardly respect him; no doubt he is capable of certain things, but for me his great plays and his great prose are full of a truly staggering mass of the most sickening drivel. It is impossible to be too hard on him. . . . Only when looking at his photograph—that bogus dreaminess, that sentimentality I wouldn't touch even with the tips of my fingers—can I see how he could have developed in this way from his partly excellent early work (*Anatol, La Ronde, Lieutenant Gustl*).—Wedekind I won't even mention in the same letter.

"Enough, enough! Let me quickly get rid of Schnitzler who is trying to come between us, like Lasker-Schüler the other day" (F 193).

His jealousy of other writers, as far as Felice's interest in them is concerned, is just as strong as jealousy usually is; one is astonished and relieved to find Kafka being so naturally, wholeheartedly aggressive toward others. Throughout these numerous letters one can hear the better-known voice of the Kafka who is aggressive toward himself. Yet the unusual tone of these attacks on other writers, who are actually worlds apart from him, the murderous quality of the attacks, their crassness, are symptomatic of a change in his relationship with Felice. This change takes a tragic turn because of her failure to understand his writing. He needs her strength, as a steady flow of sustenance for his work; yet she is not capable of comprehending who it is that she is sustaining with her letters.

His situation, in this regard, is all the worse because of the nature of his first book. He is too sensible and too serious to overestimate the weight of *Meditation*. It is a book that announces many of his themes. But it is patchwork, still rather moody and artistic; it shows extraneous influences (Robert Walser), and it lacks, quite particularly, unity and urgency. For him it has significance because he had the manuscript with him when he first saw Felice.

But six weeks after that evening, directly after his first letter to Felice, he has become entirely himself, in "The Judgment" and "The Stoker." Almost more important here is the fact that he was seemingly quite aware of the value of these two texts. The correspondence with Felice was beginning, night after night he was writing his things, and after eight weeks, in *The Metamorphosis*, he is at the height of his mastery. He had written something he would never surpass, because there is nothing that could possibly surpass *The Metamorphosis*, one of the few great and perfect works of poetic imagination written during this century.

Four days after the completion of *The Metamorphosis*, *Meditation* is published. He sends this first book to Felice and waits seventeen days for a word about it from her. Letters are exchanged several times a day; he waits in vain and has already written *The Metamorphosis* and a large part of *Amerika*. It is enough to wring tears from a stone: he now realized that the sustenance given by her letters, without which he could not write, had been given blindly. His doubts, always present, became overwhelming; he was no longer certain of his claim to the letters he had extracted from her during the good time. And his writing, which was his very life, began to falter.

An indirect—but in its violence very striking—result of this catastrophe was his jealousy of other writers. Felice wounded him deeply with names of authors she was reading, names that kept coming up in her letters. In her eyes, all these were *Dichter* (poets, writers). But what, in her eyes, was he?

The blessings she had bestowed upon him thus came to an end. With his immense tenacity, the astounding reverse side of his frailty, he held fast to the form of the existing relationship, and from that standpoint looked longingly back upon the paradise of those three months that could never return. The equilibrium she had given him had been destroyed.

Translated by Christopher Middleton

UNSIGNED
LETTERS TO
MILENA JESENSKÁ

Mark Anderson

> Above all, consider that these lines are literature from
> beginning to end.
> —Kafka to Max Brod in reference to
> a postcard by Margarethe Kirchner (L 80)

THE RECENT RE-EDITION OF Kafka's correspondence with Milena Jesenská, one of his most intriguing works and a landmark of autobiographical confession in twentieth-century European literature,
contains more than a few surprises.[1] The only edition available until
recently was first published in 1952 by Willy Haas and was, as he
himself noted, seriously inadequate: the letters were largely undated
and their chronological order (as is now apparent) jumbled; a few
pages and letters had been lost; Milena had crossed out numerous
passages in ink before releasing the correspondence to Haas; and
Haas himself had omitted passages critical of persons still living at
the time of publication. Most disturbing, however, was his decision
not to indicate the location or extent of his deletions: "In order further to emphasize the non-scientific character of this volume, which
is concerned only with being readable, the deleted passages have not
been specially marked" (L 16; some translations have been slightly

241

altered). In reality an incomplete, dismembered, scrambled collection of papers, the correspondence was presented as a deceptively continuous whole.

Painstaking detective work by editors Born and Müller has allowed them to date almost all of the letters and establish a new, more probable order of succession than the one proposed by Haas. But aside from its valuable information, their work is significant because it questions the status of a text we have been using (and without much complaint) for over thirty years. By pointing out the mistakes, gaps, and confused sequence in Haas's edition, the new edition forces us to examine how these elements have conditioned our reading. And implicitly it raises the larger question any critical edition is confronted with: What are the uncertainties, the limits in establishing a "definitive" text?

Born and Müller see the value of the letters as primarily biographical: "Only now [that the letters have been dated] can one grant this correspondence, this crucial biographical document in Kafka's life . . . its proper significance. Only now can the individual letters be brought into relation with other personal documents from the years 1920 to 1923."[2] This attitude has predominated in the critical reception of the letters since their publication. Scholars value them for information about Kafka and his work, not for themselves and not as a whole. The letters are not related to one another but to other events and writings of the same period. They do not constitute the object of interpretation but the means to interpret someone or something else. Their meaning as a single, diacritical text, their own aesthetic form, the development of metaphors, images and themes throughout the letters—these questions have been conspicuously absent in the minor industry constituted by Kafka research.[3] As a result, the letters to Milena have remained largely uninterpreted, however widely read or quoted. For at the root of their nonreception is the deep-seated critical assumption that an author's private letters do not belong in the canon of his literary, interpretable works. Interesting, yes, important, yes, but in the end "merely" historical, autobiographical documents secondary to the aesthetic oeuvre proper, in Kafka's case, the novels and stories.

The scope of the present essay does not allow for a thorough discussion of the history, assumptions, and etymological absurdities implicit in this critical tendency. One might note in passing, however, the complex and ambiguous status of the Latin term "littera," which in its singular form means "letter" (of the alphabet) and in the plural, "litterae," signifies letter (as epistle), written document, and literature. Thus, the "letter" in its double meaning founds both the alphabet and literature, as is apparent in the phrases "a man of letters," "belles lettres," or "Faculté des lettres." Moreover, "littera" is the origin for both "literal" and "literary," terms which are often used as opposites. "Literal" refers to strict, material, "plain" meaning (as in "the letter of the law"), opposed to figurative, symbolic, or allegorical meaning. Yet the figurative, or the figure, constitutes precisely the domain of literature, of the literary. This confusion is augmented by the potential reference of both terms, literal and literary, to the alphabet and the epistle. Yet these coincidences are far from arbitrary, for precisely the ambivalence of the "littera," its hovering status between the material signs of the alphabet and their figurative use, between "litteralis" and "litterarius," is what makes literature possible.

That autobiographical and other historical writings were not sharply distinguished from the domain of literature before the nineteenth century can be seen in the success of the epistolary novel as a literary genre in the period of the Enlightenment. Private letters of the time were highly stylized, conventional, "literary." A European "man of letters" received his introduction to writing and literature by learning how to compose various types of letters, all subject to strict stylistic codes. Separation of the literary text from the "mere" document was encouraged by an increasingly historical mode of consciousness. If history was to constitute itself as a scientific discipline it had first to isolate its objects of study, the temporal and the particular, from the aesthetic. Further, the spread of literacy in eighteenth- and nineteenth-century Europe gave rise to a group of writers—journalists, teachers, business correspondents, and so on—who could not be considered authors, or who, as Roland Barthes has put it, were not "écrivains" but "scripteurs." The prevailing tendency among literary critics to separate an author's private writings from his literary works (which include an implicit hierarchical distinction) stems from these developments and was fostered by the attempt, largely within the confines of the university, to make the study of literature as objective, as scientific, as possible.

With regard to Kafka one can observe the beginnings of a break-down in the formerly rigid critical distinction between his work and life, his literary and his "private" texts. The studies of Maurice Blan-chot, Félix Guattari and Gilles Deleuze, Elias Canetti, and others, although widely divergent in nature, share a willingness to treat Kaf-ka's letters and diaries as not essentially different from or requiring different modes of analysis than the "literary" works proper.[4] The fol-lowing remarks in part derive from these studies and seek to interpret the letters to Milena as an enterprise in writing contiguous with sto-ries such as "A Hunger Artist" and "Josephine the Singer, or the Mouse Folk." They offer an interpretation of the letters as an en-semble, as a group, if not as a unified whole. And they take seriously the fact that Kafka's passion for Milena begins with her absence and ends with the threat of her proximity. Her absence, the distance be-tween Merano and Vienna, or later, Prague and Vienna, is the gap in which the letters are both necessary and possible. To close this gap would put an end to writing, as Kafka learned in his correspondence with Felice Bauer. Thus, the "condition of possibility" structuring the letters is Kafka's isolation. His passion remains "letterary," articulated and interpretable only within the peculiar space of writing.

> By the way, there is no more beautiful fate for a story than for it to disappear, and in this way.
> —Kafka to Milena, in reference to Grillparzer's *The Poor Fiddler*
> (M 97)

In a perceptive essay on Kafka and the problem of mimesis, Margot Norris notes that "the Kafkaesque performance always results in death or madness or effacement of some sort—a clue to its mediative position in a power conflict."[6] "A Hunger Artist" and "Josephine the Singer" involve performances of self-effacement; in both stories the main character disappears. The titles express the artist's identity, which is dependent on his or her activity—fasting and singing. But the bodies of both texts, at the same time as they describe the per-formers' bodies and the physical particularities of their performances, call into question the very identity from which they derive their ex-istence. For what are we to imagine as the spectacle of a man fasting or a mouse singing? Invisible or inaudible, untheatrical or non-performative, both "shows" undermine the expressive function and status of the stories into which they have been inscribed.

In "A Hunger Artist" fasting is made a public spectacle. Normally a private and essentially undramatic activity, the act of not eating can only be turned into a show by the aid of external props. A cage is set up to stage and frame the hunger artist. Guards are positioned around him, not (as the public might believe) to keep him from eating but as an indirect sign that "something is taking place." The number of days fasted is displayed and updated with ceremony. An impresario organizes publicity, sells photographs and stages the only dramatic event in the artist's show, the *breaking* of his fast: "So on the fortieth day the flower-bedecked cage was opened, enthusiastic spectators filled the hall, a military band played, two doctors entered the cage to measure the results of the fast . . . and finally two young ladies appeared . . . to help the hunger artist down the few steps leading to a small table on which was spread a carefully chosen invalid repast" (CS 270).

The actual performance of fasting is nothing the public can see. One can observe the static picture of his emaciated body but not watch anything temporally visual and hence dramatic. And because no one "could produce first-hand evidence that the fast had really been rigorous and continuous," the truth of his art is invariably questioned by his audience. The only true spectator to the art of going hungry is the hunger artist himself; he is both actor and public: "only the artist himself could know that, he was therefore bound to be the sole completely satisfied spectator of his own fast" (CS 270).

An undramatic art with no spectators—this is the hunger artist's predicament in the best of times. But the story begins with the decline in interest for hunger shows, the hunger artist's loss of fame, fortune, and his impresario, and his degradation to working in a circus. The story begins with the possibility of unlimited fasting, and hence with the death of art. For once the forty-day term of fasting is lifted the hunger artist is no longer representing, but merely presenting his own existence. The show has stopped before we begin reading, and what we watch as the hunger artist's body dwindles in size, finally disappearing under the straw in his cage, is the presentation of his life, which is simultaneously his death.

That he was *never* an artist, however, we learn only from his dying confession to the circus guards: "I always wanted you to admire my fasting. . . . But you shouldn't admire it. . . . Because I have to fast, I can't help it" (CS 277). According to German classical tradition, the aesthetic realm is defined as lying outside the domain of need or necessity. An artist produces or performs as an expression of personal freedom. The hunger artist's "I can't help it" (an allusion to Martin Luther's rebellion against the Catholic Church) erases his identity as an artist, and because he has no other identity, it erases him. The only true artist in the story is the "free" panther, which maintains the traditional master/slave dialectic of performance by capturing the very audience that once shunned the hunger artist: "The spectators . . . crowded around the cage, and did not want ever to move away" (CS 277).

Representation breaks down in "A Hunger Artist," as it does in so many of Kafka's works, because the traditional distinction between reality and art is denied or called into question. This is true of "Josephine the Singer," a text which also explores the dialectic of performance, of attracting, holding, and manipulating an audience. Its title also affirms the existence and identity of an artist: Josephine sings, and "anyone who has not heard her does not know the power of song" (CS 360). Yet again the body of the text progressively undermines and ultimately contradicts the affirmation of its title. We learn that Josephine's song is nothing special: "Among intimates we admit freely to one another that Josephine's singing, as singing, is nothing out of the ordinary" (CS 360–61). Then her coloraturas are shortened, although the narrator remarks: "I know nothing about coloraturas, and have never noticed any in Josephine's singing" (CS 374). Then the songs themselves are shortened, and finally, like the hunger artist, Josephine disappears: "Josephine has vanished, she will not sing . . . this time she has deserted us entirely." Physical effacement is then rendered absolute by the assertion that the mice keep no historical records. Not even the memory of Josephine will remain behind: "Since we [the mice people] are no historians, [Josephine] will rise to the heights of redemption and be forgotten like all her brothers" (CS 376).

Yet almost none of the narrator's affirmations can be held on to with assurance. The very origin of this story is troubled by paradox, since it presents itself as a "history" of Josephine written by a member of a race that keeps no historical records. Like Rotpeter, the eloquent ape who addresses a learned academy, the vermin narrator of "Josephine" comically exploits the reader's incredulity at watching an animal employ human categories of perception. Yet whereas "A Report to an Academy" still contains the rudiments of a psychophysiological explanation for this phenomenon, "Josephine" explicitly contradicts the notion that a mouse can do more than squeak. "Since we are no historians," (*Da wir keine Geschichte treiben*) also means "I cannot have written the story I have written."

What complicates the uncertainty of this narrative even further is that the narrator proves himself unreliable by contradicting and retracting his statements about Josephine's singing, finally voicing the doubt that she may never have produced any sounds, any audible art, anything more than the artifice of representation:

> How can our gatherings take place in utter silence? Still, were they not silent even when Josephine was present? Was her actual piping notably louder and more alive than the memory of it will be? Was it even in her lifetime more than a simple memory? (CS 376)

But if Josephine never sang, what is left of her story? By an elaborate strategy of retraction that includes contradictory assertions, hypothetical questions, and a thoroughly unreliable narrator, this narrative calls its own existence into question. Like a carpet rolling itself up, the story reduces itself to memory in a culture that signifies: the impossibility of memory. Josephine disappears; so too Kafka's text.

> *Only in this way* can writing be done, only with such coherence, with such a complete opening out of the body and the soul.
> —Kafka in reference to the writing of "The Judgment," Sept 23, 1912
> (D 213)

What kind of letters did Kafka write to Milena Jesenská? The common assumption, which has simultaneously enshrined the letters and prevented them from being interpreted, is that they are love letters, "the most personal and passionate document by Kafka in our possession."[7] Willy Haas was the first to speak of a "passionate relationship," of a "love" between Kafka and Milena, although he adds that "their love was essentially a letter-love, like the love of Werther or Kierke-gaard" (M 9). Yet one may ask whether the basic phrase of all love letters, the "I love you," can be used to characterize Kafka's relation to Milena. Not whether Kafka "really loved" Milena, but whether an "I" exists at all, whether it is single, identical to itself, whether it is strong enough to assume its active role. The conventional phrase of love presupposes two distinct, identifiable subjects, related to but separated by the verb "to love." Kafka's letters to Milena disallow precisely this assumption. They negate both the identity and the existence of such a writing subject, just as they throw into question the traditional limits of the body, of inside and outside, nominative and accusative. The two subjects merge, exchange positions, defy any stable relation to one another, not in the physical act of loving one another, but in long-distance forms of communication, letters, and dreams.

In their letter-love Kafka and Milena exist primarily as marks on a page, as written images. A thoroughly consistent thematic characteristic of the correspondence involves the merging of the body with the writing process or its products. Letters become things, either as a kind of appeasing drink: "nevertheless one leans far back and drinks in the letters and is aware of nothing but that one doesn't want to stop drinking" (M 36); as objects that the hands manipulate and play with; as a substitute for Milena's body; or like her face, as a blinding fire: "enough, this white paper, that won't come to an end, burns one's eyes out, and this is why one writes" (M 56). In an opposite but congruent gesture the body tends to become a form of writing. Kafka relates a dream in which he travels to Vienna, then to Prague to find Milena but forgets her name, address, "everything," except the name "Schreiber," that is, "Writer." Milena writes that "two hours of life are so certainly more than two pages of writing" (M 48), and Kafka protests. He is made of literature, he is his letters. "I'm nothing but one single word" (M 56).

Kafka's vision of Milena is strongly ambivalent, her face appearing now as indistinct, now as a blinding fire, now as a Medusa head, and in all cases impossible to see. In the postscript to the second letter,[8] Kafka notes:

It occurs to me that I can't remember your face in any precise detail. Only how you finally walked away between the tables of the coffee-house, your figure, your dress, these I can still see. (M 19)

The face Kafka "can't remember" quickly is transformed into one he cannot behold. Milena's first letter written in her native Czech gives Kafka a more precise image:

I see you clearer, the movements of your body, your hands, so quick, so determined, it's almost a meeting, although when I try to raise my eyes to your face, then in the flow of the letter—what a story!—fire breaks out and I see nothing but fire. (M 30)

In other letters she appears as a "living fire," a "storm," or with the "magnificent head of Medusa": "for the snakes of terror hiss around your head and indeed around mine the snakes of fear hiss even wilder" (M 59). Kafka's "fear" signifies a retreat, Milena's "courage" an advance, and in a passage reminiscent of *The Metamorphosis* he reiterates his ambivalence toward her letters: "I can't read them and yet read them I must, as a thirsting animal drinks, at the same time fear and more fear, I search for furniture under which I can hide . . ." (M 59).

Kafka is no Greek hero; unlike Theseus he has no polished shield to deflect Milena's gaze. In Freud's work on dreams the Medusa head is generally associated with the fear of castration. The image of snakes represents "the female genitals . . . probably those of an adult woman, covered with hair, in essence those of the mother," a view which is supported by the child/mother, student/teacher relations between the correspondents (cf. H. Böhme's "Mutter Milena," op. cit.). Yet castration also implies a disaggregation of identity. As with the *Doppelgänger*, the "double" of German Romanticism and *fin-de-siècle* psychoanalysis, more signifies less; a doubled or multiplied phallus calls into question the primacy of the single, unique subject. Freud noted in his essay on E. T. A. Hoffmann and the "uncanny": "A technical rule—that the proliferation of phallic symbols signifies castration—is here confirmed."[9]

The dispersal of Kafka's identity, the disaggregation of the proper noun "Kafka," is at work throughout the correspondence but can perhaps be most clearly observed in the way he signs, or rather unsigns, his letters. The first closings are conventional: "Kindest regards/ Kafka" or "Kindest regards/Yours Kafka." But soon the name starts shedding letters: "Yours Franz K.," "Yours Kafka," and then consistently "Yours F." or simply "F." In a short letter of June 15 the name is suppressed entirely and replaced by the possessive adjective "*Dein*," somewhat awkwardly rendered in English as "Thine." Below it, in parentheses, we read: "now I've lost even my name; it has been growing shorter all the time and now it is: Thine" (M 67). On July 29 (M 122) even this negative form of closure is repudiated:

(Franz wrong K wrong Thine wrong / nothing more, silence, deep forest).

Kafka defines himself negatively, in relationship to Milena, drawing from her the blood of his own identity like a vampire from its prey: "I see you bent over your work, your neck is bare, I stand behind you, you aren't aware of it—please don't be frightened if you feel my lips on the back of your neck" (M 157; see also Deleuze and Guattari, "What Is a Minor Literature?"). Kafka's existence is not so much dependent on as it is possible through Milena: "And perhaps it isn't you at all I really love, but the existence presented to me by you" (M 96). Yet the paradox of a self-effacing existence must continually be reexplained: "You don't seem to realize, Milena, that we're standing side by side, watching this creature on the ground which is me; but I, as the spectator, am then non-existent" (M 211). And in a nightmare reported on September 20 Milena and Kafka appear as interpenetrating forms of fire:

Last night I dreamt about you. What happened in detail I can hardly remember, all I know is that we kept merging into one another, I was you, you were me. Finally you caught fire. . . . I took an old coat and beat you with it. But again the transmutations began and it went so far that you were no longer even there, instead it was I who was on fire and it was also I who beat the fire with the coat. (M 207)

The conjunction of Milena, writing, fire, and either blindness or vision recurs throughout the letters and merits closer attention. Conflagrations are rare in Kafka's work. Death, if it is granted at all, usually comes by starvation, drowning, or at the point of a knife. But fire appears conspicuously in the famous diary entry of September 23, 1912, in which Kafka comments on the writing of "The Judgment":

How everything can be said, how for everything, for the strangest fancies, there waits a great fire in which they perish and rise up again. . . . *Only in this way* can writing be done . . . with such a complete opening out of the body and the soul. (D 213)

"The Judgment" is commonly regarded as Kafka's "breakthrough" story into the realm of his mature works (*The Metamorphosis*, and the bulk of his *Amerika* novel were composed in the same period). And, as critics have pointed out, it is intimately related to his relationship with Felice Bauer, to whom it is dedicated. In a diary entry of February 11, 1913, Kafka himself makes the connection at the same time as he demonstrates the importance of the signifier, the literality of the letters *F* and *B*:

Frieda has as many letters as F. and the same initial, Brandenfeld has the same initial as B., and in the word "Feld" [field] a certain connection in meaning as well. * Perhaps even the thought of Berlin was not without influence and the recollection of the Mark Brandenburg perhaps had some influence. (D 215)

Yet common to "Brandenburg" ("burning mountain") and "Brandenfeld" ("burning field") is the element of fire, the same element in

---

* Reference is to Felice's last name, Bauer, which also means "Farmer."—ED.

which Kafka's strange "fancies" are forged in the writing of "The Judgment." The female figure of Frieda/Felice is a "burning field," a source of both inspiration and fear. It is surely no accident that Georg Bendemann, the protagonist of "The Judgment," commits a water suicide. For in executing his father's "judgment" he is not only fleeing the Oedipal conflict but also his fiancée. He is putting out the fire.[10]

Milena occupies a congruent position in the history of Kafka's writing. Her fire frightens, blinds, consumes, but it also functions as a source of vision. In the same letter in which his name is reduced to the purely relational status of "Thine," Kafka relates the following memory:

> In this connection I remember something which I once read somewhere and which went vaguely like this: "My beloved is a fiery column which moves across the earth. Now it holds me encircled. It leads, however, not those encircled, but those who see." (M 67)

Presented as an incidental quotation, this image nonetheless speaks to Kafka's own situation. "My beloved" is clearly Milena (in Czech, the language she is writing in, her name means "beloved" or "loving one"), and again she is associated with fire. But Kafka is now inside the fire, not blinded and not consumed but "seeing." Milena gives this sight direction, she "leads."

We must remember that during the correspondence Milena is sending Kafka her Czech translations of his own work. She thus exists literally as his written double, a fact that underlies their constant play with and exchange of identities. Just as Kafka inhabits the words of her translations invisibly, so too in the above column of fire (strangely reminiscent of the pillar of fire that leads the Jews out of Egypt in the Book of Exodus) he has disappeared into her body without losing the faculty of sight. His body has been erased but not his consciousness (sight), his identity.

Precisely this paradoxical relationship, characteristic throughout the letters, is realized grammatically in Kafka's formulation of the phrase "I love you." In response to a question by Milena he wrote: "You always want to know, Milena, whether love you." Willy Haas published the sentence as: "You always want to know, Milena, whether [I] love you" (M 119), assuming that Kafka must have made a mistake. After all, a sentence without a subject, like a body without its head, makes no sense. Given Kafka's strategies of effacement, however, the "mistake" makes perfect sense. The "*ich*" ("I") has been erased, or rather it has migrated into Milena's body, the "*Dich*" ("You"), existing there as its double, simultaneously present and invisible. Kafka exists again as a parasite, the "*ich*" feeding on the body of its host and grammatical cousin, which in the relative clause assumes the subject's initial position. In the space of writing Kafka achieves what only the dream can imagine and what the physical merging of intercourse merely approximates.

If this claim seems excessive, one might consider Kafka's response to Milena's reproach that he lacks the "strength to love." He agrees (for a "beingless" subject cannot articulate the active phrase "I love you"), but insists that he can love in the passive voice. However, this linguistic explanation leads Kafka to the painful insight that his love doesn't exist outside the discursive space of language. He is not a lover, but the grammarian of love:

> What you wrote about the people, Milena—"nemate sily milovat"— "who haven't got the strength to love"—was correct, even though while writing it down you didn't consider it correct. Perhaps their talent for love consists only in the ability to be loved. And even in this there exists a qualifying distinction for these people. If one of them says to his beloved: "I believe that you love me," then this is something completely different and much less than when he says, "I'm loved by you." These, of course, are not lovers but grammarians. (M 203)

Looking back on his correspondence with Milena in the diary entry of February 12, 1922, Kafka sums up his grammatical discourse in the following words:

> The gesture of rejection with which I was forever met did not mean, "I do not love you," but: "You cannot love me, much as you would like; you are unhappily in love with your love for me, but your love for me is not in love with you." It is consequently incorrect to say that I have known the words, "I love you"; I have known only the expectant still-

ness that should have been broken by my "I love you," that is all that I
have known, nothing more. (D 413)

Kafka never writes "I love you," never possesses Milena, remains a
"socialist" in the peculiar usage he gives to that term: nameless,
homeless, without possessions. His mistake at Gmünd during their
second meeting involves a lapse into "capitalism": "fool that I was,
magnificently sure, . . . I arrived like a house-owner" (M 190). But
generally all his attributes, all of his identity have been sacrificed,
and so in breaking off the correspondence Kafka loses even more than
Robinson Crusoe: "He still had the island and Friday and many things
and finally the ship which took him off and almost turned everything
into a dream again—I would have nothing, not even a name, this too
I gave to you" (M 194). Yet for just that reason Kafka is in a certain
sense independent of Milena, "precisely because the dependence
reaches beyond all bounds." Because he is "nonexistent" the loss of
Milena is "not just bad but simply nothing . . . there is no jealousy,
no suffering, no anxiety—nothing" (M 167). This, he confides, is
Samson's secret, and now Delilah can cut off his hair.[11]

Structurally, the end of "The Judgment" can be related to the last
letters in the correspondence with Milena. Just as Georg Bendemann
falls into water and away from the fire of his fiancée, so is Kafka's
withdrawal from Milena figured in death scenarios involving weight,
vertical falling, and water. He repeatedly complains of being too
"heavy": "again and again that word, it's the only one that fits me, do
you understand this at all?" (M 202). Fleeing from the light of the
sun, he retreats into a deep forest (the same symbol of negation antic-
ipated in the final undressing of his name—"nothing more, silence,
deep forest"): "I had to return to the darkness, I couldn't stand the
sun, I was desperate, really like a stray animal" (M 199). And in one
of his most brutal visions, a re-imagining of Casanova's (!) under-
ground imprisonment in Venice, Kafka extinguishes Milena's fire:

Do you know the story of Casanova's escape from "The Leads"? Yes, you
know it. The most horrifying form of imprisonment is briefly described
there—down in the cellar, in the dark, in the humidity, on a level with
the lagoons. One cowers on a narrow board, the water reaching almost
up to it, at high tide it actually does reach it, but the worst are the wild

water rats, their screaming at night, their tugging, tearing and gnawing
. . . above all their impatient waiting for the weakened man to fall from
his little board. (M 145)*

It is characteristic of the rigor of Kafka's self-effacement that mere
physical disappearance will not suffice. The letters themselves must
be taken back, repudiated, unwritten. In a gesture that logically concludes the process of identity fragmentation we have witnessed in the
letters, Kafka explicitly denies to Milena the reality of any of his
former selves: "The reason I ask whether you won't be afraid is that
the person of whom you write doesn't exist and never existed, the one
in Vienna didn't exist, nor did the one in Gmünd, though the latter
one more so and he shall be cursed" (M 205). "Kafka" is only a proper
noun covering a vast assembly of nonexistent figures. Underneath
them all is "the real one—unknown to all and himself, existing less
than the others, but in his manifestations of power more real than all
the others." Kafka thus explicitly denies his letters a single, unified
author. The only "true" writer of the letters exists less than all the
others and must remain, even to himself, unknown. "Who is Kafka?"
asks Kafka in effect. By designating the fictional status of his own
name, the absence of its referent, he cuts the last ties of ownership
with his literary property. He unsigns the letters, bidding his reader
to consider them anonymous, their author dead.

The paradoxes that dwell in Kafka's last, self-effacing stories are
not greater than the ones we are confronted with in his letters. Like
Josephine and the hunger artist, the writer of the letters to Milena
constantly forces us to consider the impossibility of his writing "performance." Josephine's singing is reduced to the memory of song in a
context where cultural memory is excluded; Kafka's nameless letters
are said to have been written by authors who never existed. Were
these texts meant to disappear? These are not isolated paradoxes in
Kafka's work. The same uncertainty underlies all the writings he
asked Max Brod to destroy. For whose eyes were *Amerika, The Trial,*
and *The Castle* intended? Salvation, we learn at the end of "Josephine," comes in the denial of history, in erasing one's written tracks,

---

* On the subject of Kafka and Casanova, see Michael Müller's essay in this volume.—Ed.

in being forgotten like all of Josephine's mice brothers. In saving Kafka's texts Max Brod denied his friend that kind of salvation. We remember Kafka, and we continue to re-member, re-structure, change him. In essence we are still formulating the central question of the letters: Who is Kafka? And precisely because the Socratic injunction "Know thyself" proves unfeasible, because Kafka himself cannot answer, his texts remain enigmatic, slippery, perhaps ultimately indecipherable. And for those reasons in need of interpretation.

APPENDICES

FOR A
SMALL LITERATURE

(Kafka's Diary Entry for
December 25, 1911)

25 December. What I understand of contemporary Jewish literature in Warsaw through Löwy, and of contemporary Czech literature partly through my own insight, points to the fact that many of the benefits of literature—the stirring of minds, the coherence of national consciousness, often unrealized in public life and always tending to disintegrate, the pride which a nation gains from a literature of its own and the support it is afforded in the face of a hostile surrounding world, this keeping of a diary by a nation which is something entirely different from historiography and results in a more rapid (and yet always closely scrutinized) development, the spiritualization of the broad area of public life, the assimilation of dissatisfied elements that are immediately put to use precisely in this sphere where only stagnation can do harm, the constant integration of a people with respect to its whole that the incessant bustle of the magazines creates, the narrowing down of the attention of a nation upon itself and the accepting of what is foreign only in reflection, the birth of a respect for those active in literature, the transitory awakening in the younger generation of higher aspirations, which nevertheless leaves its permanent mark, the acknowledgment of literary events as

objects of political solicitude, the dignification of the antithesis between fathers and sons and the possibility of discussing this, the presentation of national faults in a manner that is very painful, to be
sure, but also liberating and deserving of forgiveness, the beginning
of a lively and therefore self-respecting book trade and the eagerness
for books—all these effects can be produced even by a literature
whose development is not in actual fact unusually broad in scope, but
seems to be, because it lacks outstanding talents. The liveliness of
such a literature exceeds even that of one rich in talent, for, as it has
no writer whose great gifts could silence at least the majority of cav-
illers, literary competition on the greatest scale has a real justification.

A literature not penetrated by a great talent has no gap through
which the irrelevant might force its way. Its claim to attention
thereby becomes more compelling. The independence of the individual writer, naturally only within the national boundaries, is better
preserved. The lack of irresistible national models keeps the completely untalented away from literature. But even mediocre talent
would not suffice for a writer to be influenced by the unstriking qualities of the fashionable writers of the moment, or to introduce the
works of foreign literatures, or to imitate the foreign literature that
has already been introduced; this is plain, for example, in a literature
rich in great talents, such as the German is, where the worst writers
limit their imitation to what they find at home. The creative and
beneficent force exerted in these directions by a literature poor in its
component parts proves especially effective when it begins to create a
literary history out of the records of its dead writers. These writers'
undeniable influence, past and present, becomes so matter-of-fact
that it can take the place of their writings. One speaks of the latter
and means the former, indeed, one even reads the latter and sees only
the former. But since that effect cannot be forgotten, and since the
writings themselves do not act independently upon the memory,
there is no forgetting and no remembering again. Literary history
offers an unchangeable, dependable whole that is hardly affected by
the taste of the day.

A small nation's memory is not smaller than the memory of a large
one and so can digest the existing material more thoroughly. There

are, to be sure, fewer experts in literary history employed, but literature is less a concern of literary history than of the people, and thus, if not purely, it is at least reliably preserved. For the claim that the national consciousness of a small people makes on the individual that is such that everyone must always be prepared to know that part of the literature which has come down to him, to support it, to defend it—to defend it even if he does not know it and support it.

The old writings acquire a multiplicity of interpretations; despite the mediocre material, this goes on with an energy that is restrained only by the fear that one may too easily exhaust them, and by the reverence they are accorded by common consent. Everything is done very honestly, only within a bias that is never resolved, that refuses to countenance any weariness, and is spread for miles around when a skilful hand is lifted up. But in the end bias interferes not only with a broad view but with a close insight as well—so that all these observations are cancelled out.

Since people lack a sense of context, their literary activities are out of context too. They depreciate something in order to be able to look down upon it from above, or they praise it to the skies in order to have a place up there beside it. (Wrong.) Even though something is often thought through calmly, one still does not reach the boundary where it connects up with similar things, one reaches this boundary soonest in politics, indeed, one even strives to see it before it is there, and often sees this limiting boundary everywhere. The narrowness of the field, the concern too for simplicity and uniformity, and, finally, the consideration that the inner independence of the literature makes the external connexion with politics harmless, result in the dissemination of literature without a country on the basis of political slogans.

There is universal delight in the literary treatment of petty themes whose scope is not permitted to exceed the capacity of small enthusiasms and which are sustained by their polemical possibilities. Insults, intended as literature, roll back and forth. What in great literature goes on down below, constituting a not indispensable cellar of the structure, here takes place in the full light of day, what is there a matter of passing interest for a few, here absorbs everyone no less than as a matter of life and death.

A character sketch of the literature of small peoples.
Good results in both cases.
Here the results in individual instances are even better.

1. Liveliness:
   a. Conflict.
   b. Schools.
   c. Magazines.

2. Less constraint:
   a. Absence of principles.
   b. Minor themes.
   c. Easy formation of symbols.
   d. Throwing off of the untalented.

3. Popularity:
   a. Connexion with politics.
   b. Literary history.
   c. Faith in literature, can make up their own laws.

It is difficult to readjust when one has felt this useful, happy life in all one's being.

[. . .]

Goethe probably retards the development of the German language by the force of his writing. Even though prose style has often traveled away from him in the interim, still, in the end, as at present, it returns to him with strengthened yearning and even adopts obsolete idioms found in Goethe but otherwise without any particular connexion with him, in order to rejoice in the completeness of its unlimited dependence.

[. . .]

AN INTRODUCTORY TALK ON THE YIDDISH LANGUAGE*

(Franz Kafka, 1912)

BEFORE we come to the first poems by our Eastern Jewish poets, I should like, ladies and gentlemen, just to say something about how much more Yiddish you understand than you think.

I am not really worried about the experience this evening holds in store for each of you, but I should like it to be universally comprehensible, if it merits it. Yet this cannot be the case so long as many of you are so frightened of Yiddish that one can almost see it in your faces. Of those who take an arrogant attitude to Yiddish I do not even speak. But dread of Yiddish, dread mingled with a certain fundamental distaste, is, after all, understandable, if one has the good will to understand it.

Our Western European conditions, if we glance at them only in a deliberately superficial way, appear so well ordered; everything takes its quiet course. We live in positively cheerful concord, understanding each other whenever necessary, getting along without each other whenever it suits us and understanding each other even then. From

* A speech given by Kafka as introduction to an evening of dramatic readings in Yiddish by the actor Yitzhak Löwy at the Jewish Town Hall in Prague on February 18, 1912.

263

within such an order of things who could possibly understand the tangle of Yiddish—indeed, who would even care to do so?

Yiddish is the youngest European language, only four hundred years old and actually a good deal younger even than that. It has not yet developed any linguistic forms of a lucidity such as we need. Its idiom is brief and rapid.

No grammars of the language exist. Devotees of the language try to write grammars, but Yiddish remains a spoken language that is in continuous flux. The people will not leave it to the grammarians.

It consists solely of foreign words. But these words are not firmly rooted in it, they retain the speed and liveliness with which they were adopted. Great migrations move through Yiddish, from one end to the other. All this German, Hebrew, French, English, Slavonic, Dutch, Rumanian, and even Latin, is seized with curiosity and frivolity once it is contained within Yiddish, and it takes a good deal of strength to hold all these languages together in this state. And this, too, is why no sensible person thinks of making Yiddish into an international language, obvious though the idea might seem. It is only thieves' cant that is in the habit of borrowing from it, because it needs linguistic complexes less than single words, and then too, because Yiddish was, after all, for a long time a despised language.

In this whirl of language there are, however, certain fragments of recognized linguistic laws which dominate it. For instance, Yiddish originated in the period when Middle High German was undergoing transition into Modern High German. At that time there was a choice of forms, and Middle High German took one course and Yiddish the other. Or Yiddish developed Middle High German forms more logically than even Modern High German did. For instance, the Yiddish *mir zeinen* (we are) is a more natural development from the Middle High German *sîn* than is the Modern German *wir sind.* Or Yiddish keeps to Middle High German forms in spite of Modern High German. Whatever once entered the ghetto had come to stay. And so we still find forms like *kerzlach, blümlach, liedlach.*

And now the dialects enter into this linguistic medley of whim and law. Indeed, Yiddish as a whole consists only of dialect, even the written language; though agreement has been largely reached as to its spelling.

With all this I think I have for the present convinced most of you, ladies and gentlemen, that you will not understand a word of Yiddish.

Do not expect any help from the explanation of the poems. If you happen to be unable to understand Yiddish, no explanation on the spur of the moment can be of any help to you. At best you will understand the explanation and become aware that something difficult is about to follow. That will be all. I can, for instance, tell you:

Herr Löwy will now—and this is indeed the case—recite three poems. First, "Die Grine" by Rosenfeld. *Grine* are the green ones, the greenhorns, the new arrivals in America. In this poem a little group of such Jewish immigrants are walking along a street in New York, carrying their seedy luggage. A crowd, of course, gathers, stares at them, follows them, and laughs. The poet, his emotion at this sight transcending the limits of his own personality, speaks across these street scenes to Jewry and to mankind. One has the feeling that the group of immigrants comes to a stop while the poet is speaking, in spite of the fact that they are far away and cannot hear him.

The second poem is by Frug and is called "Sand and Stars."

It is a bitter commentary on a promise in the Bible that we shall be as the sand which is upon the seashore and as the stars of the heaven. Well, we are trodden down like the sand. When will it come true that we are as the stars?

The third poem is by Frischmann and is called "The Night Is Still."

In the night two lovers meet with a devout and learned man who is going to the synagogue. They are startled, afraid of having given themselves away, but later they reassure each other.

Now you see, such explanations are quite useless.

Strait-jacketed in these explanations, when you hear the poems you will try to make out what you know already, and you will miss what is really there. Fortunately, however, everyone who speaks the German language is also capable of understanding Yiddish. For, seen from a distance, though of course only from a great distance, the superficial comprehensibility of Yiddish is a product of the German language; this is an advantage it has over all the other languages in the world. To make up for that, it is only fair that it should also have a disadvantage in comparison with all others. The fact is, Yiddish cannot be translated into German. The links between Yiddish and

German are too delicate and significant not to be torn to shreds the instant Yiddish is transformed back into German, that is to say, it is no longer Yiddish that is transformed, but something that has utterly lost its essential character. If it is translated into French, for instance, Yiddish can be conveyed to the French, but if it is translated into German it is destroyed. *Toit*, for instance, is not the same thing as *tot* (dead), and *blüt* is far from being *blut* (blood).

But it is not only at this distance from the German language that you yourselves speak, ladies and gentlemen, that you can understand Yiddish; you are even allowed to come a step closer. It is, to say the least of it, not so very long ago that the familiar colloquial language of German Jews, according to whether they lived in town or in the country, more in the East or in the West, seemed to be a remoter or a closer approximation to Yiddish, and many nuances remain to this day. For this reason the historical development of Yiddish could have been followed just as well on the surface of the present day as in the depths of history.

You begin to come quite close to Yiddish if you bear in mind that apart from what you know there are active in yourselves forces and associations with forces that enable you to understand Yiddish intuitively. It is only here that the interpreter can help, reassuring you, so that you no longer feel shut out from something and also that you may realize that you must cease to complain that you do not understand Yiddish. This is the most important point, for with every complaint understanding diminishes. But if you relax, you suddenly find yourselves in the midst of Yiddish. But once Yiddish has taken hold of you and moved you—and Yiddish is everything, the words, the Chasidic melody, and the essential character of this East European Jewish actor himself—you will have forgotten your former reserve. Then you will come to feel the true unity of Yiddish, and so strongly that it will frighten you, yet it will no longer be fear of Yiddish but of yourselves. You would not be capable of bearing this fear on its own, but Yiddish instantly gives you, besides, a self-confidence that can stand up to this fear and is even stronger than it is. Enjoy this self-confidence as much as you can! but then, when it fades out, tomorrow and later—for how could it last, fed only on the memory of a single evening's recitations!—then my wish for you is that you may also have forgotten the fear. For we did not set out to punish you.

NOTES

ANDERSON: *Introduction*

[1] Letter to Gershom Scholem of June 12, 1938.

[2] From Kafka's early prose piece in *Meditation*, "On the Tram."

[3] "I have vigorously absorbed the negative element of the age in which I live, an age that is, of course, very close to me, which I have no right ever to fight against, but as it were a right to represent" (DF 99).

[4] Hence the religious, allegorical interpretations of Kafka's first readers, including Max Brod, Margarete Susman, Kurt Tucholsky, Hans-Joachim Schoeps, Herbert Kraft and (in a different notion of allegory), Walter Benjamin, Gershom Scholem, and Theodor Adorno. The French Surrealists, who saw in Kafka's writings the objectification of an archetypal dreamworld, merely shifted this allegorical reading into the realm of the unconscious.

[5] See the early writings of Hannah Arendt, Albert Camus, Walter Emrich, Herbert Tauber, Heinz Politzer, and especially Günther Anders, whose *Kafka Pro and Contra* (Munich: Beck, 1951; English translation, New York: Hillary House, 1960) was conceived in exile in Paris and reworked into book form immediately after the war.

[6] *Kafka: Letteratura ed ebraismo* (Turin: Einaudi, 1984), pp. 3–6.

[7] *Franz Kafka: Eine Biographie seiner Jugend* (Bern: Francke, 1958).

[8] Among the most important are Marthe Robert's *As Lonely as Franz Kafka* (New York: Harcourt Brace Jovanovich, 1982), Ritchie Robertson's *Kafka: Judaism, Literature and Politics* (New York: Oxford University Press, 1982); cf. also Giuliano Baioni's *Kafka: Letteratura ed ebraismo* (Turin: Einaudi, 1984), and Hartmut Binder's numerous studies (note 15).

[9] A devoted reader of Buber's journal *Der Jude* ("The Jew"), Kafka published a number of his stories there in 1917 and 1918.

267

[10]*Kafkas böses Böhmen* (Munich: Text und Kritik, 1975).

[11]The term "Jewish self-hatred," introduced by Theodor Lessing to describe the Jew's alleged internalization of their antagonists' racial stereotypes and prejudices, is still controversial. For a recent, lucid overview of the problem, see Sander Gilman, *Jewish Self-Hatred* (Baltimore: Johns Hopkins Press, 1986).

[12]Kraus delivered his lecture "Heine and the Consequences" sometime in March 1911; Kafka's diary entry for March 26 speaks of "early lectures by Kraus and [Adolf] Loos." Loos's lecture was his famous defense of architectural purity, "Ornament and Crime."

[13]Evelyn Tornton Beck's *Kafka and the Yiddish Theater* (Madison: University of Wisconsin Press, 1971) first documented these relations.

[14]*Der junge Kafka* (ed. G. Kurz [Frankfurt a.M.: Suhrkamp, 1984) is the title of a recent anthology of critical essays devoted to Kafka's writing before "The Judgment" (1912).

[15]To questions of literary influence, as well as all other biographical problems, the German literary scholar Hartmut Binder has devoted numerous books and anthologies, none of which is available in English. See especially his *Motiv und Gestaltung bei Kafka* (Bonn: Bouvier, 1966), *Kafka-Handbuch* (Stuttgart: Kröner, 1979), *Kafka in neuer Sicht* (Stuttgart: Metzler, 1976), and *Kafka: Der Schaffensprozeß* (Frankfurt: Suhrkamp, 1983).

[16]See Wayne Burns, " 'In the Penal Colony': Variations on a Theme by Octave Mirbeau," *Accent*, 17 (1957) 45–51; and Franz Kuna, "Art as a Direct Vision: Kafka and Sacher-Masoch," *Journal of European Studies*, 2 (1972) 237–46.

[17]See the passage beginning "Every human being is peculiar . . ." (DF 201–6)

[18]Part of this success was due to Weininger's much-publicized suicide in 1903, at the age of twenty-three, shortly after converting from Judaism to Christianity and finishing his doctoral thesis. Published posthumously in the same year, *Sex and Character* met with immediate success, was reprinted twelve times in eight years, and was highly regarded by Strindberg, Kraus, and Wittgenstein. In 1930, Theodore Lessing referred to Weininger as one of the chief examples of "Jewish self-hatred."

[19]Max Brod's biography was written in the 1930s and first published in English in 1947 by Schocken Books. Since then Ronald Hayman's *Kafka* (1982), Ernst Pawel's *The Nightmare of Reason: A Life of Franz Kafka* (1984), and Peter Mailloux's *A Hesitation before Birth* (1982) have filled this gap in the English-speaking world.

WAGENBACH: *Prague at the Turn of the Century*

[1]Friedrich Thieberger, *Erinnerungen an Franz Kafka, Eckart* (October 1953), p. 49. [The present version does not include all of the author's notes; we have attempted, however, to preserve the essential notes.—TRANS.]

[2]Leo Perutz, *Nachts unter der steinernen Brücke. Ein Roman aus dem alten Prag* (Frankfurt a.M., 1953), p. 233 and 327f.

[3]Gustav Janouch, *Gespräche mit Kafka. Erinnerungen und Aufzeichnungen* (Frankfurt, 1951), p. 42.

[4]Franz Werfel, *Embezzled Heaven* (New York: Viking Press, 1940), pp. 213–14.

[5]R. M. Rilke, *Erzählungen und Skizzen aus der Frühzeit* (Leipzig, 1928), p. 301. From the story "Die Letzten" (1902).

[6]Max Brod, *Zauberreich der Liebe* (Berlin, 1928), p. 92. The *Kunstwart* illustration is "The Plower" by Hans Thoma.

[7]Egon Erwin Kisch, *Die Abenteuer in Prag* (Vienna, 1920), p. 69.

[8]Ernst Wodak, *Prag von gestern und vorgestern* (Tel Aviv, 1948), p. 16.

[9]Oskar Wiener, *Im Prager Dunstkreis* (Vienna, 1919), p. 104.

[10]Heinrich Rauchberg, "Nationale Haushaltungs-: und Familienstatistik von Prag," *Deutsche Arbeit* (January 1905).

[11]E. E. Kisch, *Jahrmarkt der Sensation* (Mexico, 1942), p. 85.

[12]Paul Leppin, "Prag," *Witiko II* (1929), p. 115.

[13]Fritz Mauthner, "Erinnerungen I," *Prager Jugendjahre* (Munich, 1918), p. 29.

[14]Willy Haas, "Begegnungen mit Kafka," *Neue Literarische Welt* 25 (January 1952).

[15]Willy Haas, "Werfels erster Lehrmeister," *Witiko II* (1929).

[16]Hermann Bahr, *Frana Sramek. Das bunte Buch* (Leipzig, 1914), p. 109f.

[17]R. M. Rilke, "König Bohusch," *Erzählungen*, p. 135.

[18]Heinz Politzer, "Prague and the Origins of Rainer Maria Rilke, Franz Kafka and Franz Werfel" in *Modern Language Quarterly*, vol. XVI, no. 1 (March 1955).

[19]Theodor Herzl, *Die entschwundenen Zeiten* (Vienna, 1897).

[20]Emil Utitz, *Kakfa a Praha*, ed. P. Demetz (Prague, 1947).

[21]Felix Weltsch, *Religion und Humor im Leben und Werk Franz Kafkas* (Berlin, 1957), p. 35.

[22]Felix Weltsch, "The Bohemian Jew: An Attempt at Characterization," in *Czechoslowak Jewry—Past and Future* (New York, 1943).

[23]Ibid.

[24]Oskar Wiener, *Deutsche Dichter aus Prag. Ein Sammelbuch* (Vienna, 1919), p. 5.

[25]Wiener, *Dunstkreis*, pp. 44–47 (abbreviated).

[26]Josef Mühlberger, *Franz Kafka, Witiko I* (1928), p. 106.

[27]Utitz, *Kafka a Praha*.

[28]Paul Leppin, *Daniel Jesus* (Leipzig, 1905), pp. 111 and 109.

[29]Ibid., p. 31.

[30]From "Giulietta," *Ausgewählte Romane und Novellen*, vol. 1 (Leipzig, 1919) p. 165.

[31]R. M. Rilke, *Die Aufzeichnungen des Malte Laurids Brigge* (Wiesbaden, 1951) pp. 50, 60.

[32]Mauthner, "Erinnerungen," p. 51.

[33]Heinrich Teweles, *Der Kampf um die Sprache* (Leipzig, 1884), p. 12.

[34]Mauthner, "Erinnerungen," p. 52.

[35]Max Brod, *Schloss Nornepygge* (Stuttgart, 1908), p. 239.

[36]Brod, "Werfels Sonnenbrand," *Die Zeit* (August 11, 1955).

[37]Kisch, *Abenteuer*, p. 280.

[38]Quoted in Demetz, *Rilke*.

[39]Rudolf Vasata, "Kafka—A Bohemian Writer?" in *The Central European Observer*, vol. XXIII, no. 18 (August 30, 1946).

[40]Heinz Politzer, "Problematik und Probleme der Kafka-Forschung," *Monatshefte* (Madison, Wisc.), vol. XLII, no. 6 (October 1950), p. 280.

[41]*Zeitgenössische Bildnisse* (Amsterdam, 1940).

[42]Franz Werfel, *Der Weltfreund* (Berlin, 1918), p. 97.

[43]To Robert Klopstock, October 2, 1934; in *Der Monat*, 1949, vol. 8/9.

[44]Brod, *Biographie*, p. 153.

[45]Paul Leppin in *Das jüdische Prag* (Prague, 1917), p. 5f. The book was a collective work published by editors of *Selbstwehr*.

[46]Paul Leppin, *Daniel Jesus*, pp. 19, 16, 20, 50.

[47]Paul Leppin, *Der Berg der Erlösung* (Berlin, 1908), p. 10.

48Werfel, *Weltfreund*, p. 20.
49Max Brod, "Notwehr," in *Arkadia* (Munich, 1913), p. 157.
50Werfel, "Das Opfer," *Arkadia* (Prague, 1913), p. 19f.
51R. M. Rilke, *Tagebücher aus der Frühzeit* (Leipzig, 1942).
52Janouch, *Gespräche mit Kafka*, p. 25.
53Werfel, *Der veruntreute Himmel*, p. 355f.
54Thieberger, *Erinnerungen*.
55Brod, *Schloss Nornepygge*, pp. 470, 471, 473.

STÖLZL: *Kafka: Jew, Anti-Semite, Zionist*

1Arthur Schnitzler, *Der Weg ins Freie* (1908); quoted from *Gesammelte Werke. Die erzählenden Schriften 1* (1961), p. 755.
2Hartmut Binder, "Franz Kafka und die Wochenschrift *Selbstwehr*," *Deutsche Vierteljahreschrift* 41 (1967), p. 290.
3Feuilleton of the *Berliner Tageblatt*, Christmas 1909; quoted in *Selbstwehr* (January 14, 1910).
4*Selbstwehr*, September 9, 1910.
5K. Krolop, "Zur Geschichte und Vorgeschichte der Prager deutschen Literatur des 'expressionistischen Jahrzehnts.' " In *Weltfreunde. Konferenz über die Prager deutsche Literatur* (Prague, 1967), p. 49.
6*Selbstwehr* (April 31, 1907). Though in 1907 Jews comprised approximately 4.68% of the entire Austro-Hungarian population (1.5% less in western provinces like Bohemia), they accounted for an average 7% of Austrian insane asylum inpatients.
7Quoted in M. Durzak, *Hermann Broch* (Reinbek, 1966), p. 11.
8Robert Musil, *The Man Without Qualities* (New York: G. P. Putnam's Sons, 1980), p. 244.
9Ibid., p. 34.
10Ibid.
11"Kommt der Jude in das Land gezogen / kaum fünf Jahre—sein die ganze Gegend / erst noch Bettler, nun voll Kraft gesogen / das jus noctis primae lusterwägend." Petr Bezruč, *Lieder eines schlesischen Bergmanns*, translated into German by Rudolf Fuchs (Munich, 1926).
12*Selbstwehr*, September 15, 1912.
13Ibid., December 9, 1912.
14Grete Fischer, *Dienstboten, Brecht und andere* (Frankfurt a.M., 1966), p. 57.
15Jan Münzer, *Neviditelné ghetto* [The Invisible Ghetto] (Prítomnost), p. 692.
16K. Krolop, "Zu den Erinnerungen Anna Lichtensterns an Franz Kafka," *Philologica Pragensia*, vol. 5 (1968), p. 21f.
17Hugo Bergmann, "Erinnerungen an Franz Kafka," *Universitas* 27 (1972), 744. Quoted here in Ernst Pawel's translation; see Pawel, *The Nightmare of Reason. A Life of Franz Kafka* (New York: Vintage Books, 1985), p. 205.—TRANS.
18H. Kohn in *Robert Weltsch zum 70. Geburtstag. Von seinen Freunden* (Tel Aviv 1961), p. 114.
19Max Brod, *Über Franz Kafka* (Frankfurt a.M.: Fischer, 1974), p. 73.
20*Ostdeutsche Post*, March 5, 1901.
21*Deutsche Volksbote*, March 7, 1897.
22Quoted in Binder, "Franz Kafka und die Wochenschrift," p. 290.
23Max Brod, "Ein menschlich-politisches Bekenntnis. Juden, Deutsche, Tschechen," *Neue Rundschau* (1918), p. 1580ff.

²⁴*Selbstwehr*, November 18, 1910.

²⁵F. Kittel, *Socialdemokratie und Bauernstand* (Vienna, 1894), p. 6.

²⁶See M. Glettler, *Sokol und Arbeiterturnvereine (D. T. J.) der Wiener Tschechen bis 1914* (Munich and Vienna: 1970), p. 64f.

²⁷Elias Canetti, *Kafka's Other Trial* (New York: Schocken Books, 1979), pp. 84, 101.

²⁸*Selbstwehr* (December 29, 1912). Quoted here in Ernst Pawel's translation; see Pawel, *Nightmare of Reason*, p. 205.—TRANS.

²⁹See Binder, "Franz Kafka und die Wochenschrift."

³⁰*Selbstwehr*, December 23, 1910.

³¹Quoted in Helmut Binder, "Der Aber-Mann," *Die Zeit* (May 31, 1974).

³²Robert Weltsch, "Die Jugend des jüdischen Prag," in *Das jüdische Prag* (Prague, 1917), p. 17f.

DELEUZE AND GUATTARI: *What Is a Minor Literature?*

¹See Kafka's letter to Brod of June 1921, *Letters to Friends, Family, and Editors*, p. 289, and commentaries in Wagenbach, *Franz Kafka. Eine Biographie seiner Jugend 1883–1912* (Bern: Francke, 1958), p. 84.

²Ibid., p. 149: "Literature is less a concern of literary history, than of the people."

³See "Wedding Preparations in the Country," in Kafka, *Complete Stories*: "And so long as you say 'one' instead of 'I,' there's nothing in it" (p. 53). And the two subjects appear several pages later: "I don't even need to go to the country msyelf, it isn't necessary. I'll send my clothed body," while the narrator stays in bed like a bug or a beetle (p. 55). No doubt, this is one of the origins of Gregor's becoming-beetle in *The Metamorphosis* (in the same way, Kafka will give up going to meet Felice and will prefer to stay in bed). But in *The Metamorphosis* the animal takes on all the value of a true becoming and no longer has any of the stagnancy of a subject of enunciation.

⁴See Michel Ragon, *Histoire de la littérature prolétarienne en France* (Paris: Albin Michel, 1974) on the difficulty of criteria and on the need to use a concept of a "secondary zone literature."

⁵Kafka, *Diaries*, December 25, 1911, p. 49: "A small nation's memory is not smaller than the memory of a large one and so can digest the existing material more thoroughly."

⁶See the excellent chapter "Prague at the Turn of the Century," [included in this volume.—ED.].

⁷Constancy of the theme of teeth in Kafka. A grandfather-butcher; a streetwise education at the butchershop; Felice's jaws; the refusal to eat meat except when he sleeps with Felice in Marienbad. See Michel Cournot's article, "Toi qui as de si grandes dents," *Nouvel Observateur*, April 17, 1972. This is one of the most beautiful texts on Kafka. One can find a similar opposition between eating and speaking in Lewis Carroll, and a comparable escape into non-sense.

⁸Franz Kafka, *The Trial*, trans. Willa and Edwin Muir (New York: Schocken Books, 1956): "He noticed that they were talking to him, but he could not make out what they were saying, he heard nothing but the din that filled the whole place, through which a shrill unchanging note like that of a siren seemed to sing."

⁹Kafka, *Diaries*: "Without gaining a sense, the phrase 'end of the month' held a terrible secret for me," especially since it was repeated every month—Kafka himself suggests that if this expression remained shorn of sense, this was due to laziness and

"weakened curiosity." A negative explication invoking lack or powerlessness, as taken by Wagenbach. It is well known that Kafka makes this sort of negative suggestion to present or to hide the objects of his passion.

[10]Kafka's fascination with proper names, beginning with those that he invented: see Kafka, Diaries, February 11, 1913 (à propos of the names in "The Judgment").

[11]Kafka commentators are at their worst in their interpretations in this respect when they regulate everything through metaphors: thus, Marthe Robert reminds us that the Jews are like dogs or, to take another example, that "since the artist is treated as someone starving to death Kafka makes him into a hunger artist; or since he is treated as a parasite, Kafka makes him into an enormous insect" (Oeuvres complètes, Cercle du livre precieux, 5:311). It seems to us that this is a simplistic conception of the literary machine—Robbe-Grillet has insisted on the destruction of all metaphors in Kafka.

[12]See, for example, the letter to Oskar Pollak in Kafka, Letters to Friends, Family, and Editors, February 4, 1902, pp. 1–2.

[13]See H. Vidal Sephiha, "Introduction à l'étude de l'intensif," in Langages, 18 (June 1970), pp. 104–20. We take the term tensor from J.-F. Lyotard who uses it to indicate the connection of intensity and libido.

[14]Sephiha, "Introduction," pp. 107 ("We can imagine that any phrase conveying a negative notion of pain, evil, fear, violence can cast off the notion in order to retain no more than its limit-value—that is, its intensive value": for example, the German word sehr, which comes from the Middle-High German word ser, meaning "painful").

[15]Wagenbach, Franz Kafka, 78–88 (especially 78, 81, 88).

[16]Henri Gobard, "De la vehicularité de la langue anglaise," Langues modernes (January 1972) (and L'Aliénation linguistique: analyse tetraglossique [Paris: Flammarion, 1976]).

[17]Michel Foucault insists on the importance of the distribution between what can be said in a language at a certain moment and what cannot be said (even if it can be done). Georges Devereux (cited by H. Gobard) analyzes the case of the young Mohave Indians who speak about sexuality with great ease in their vernacular language but who are incapable of doing so in that vehicular language that English constitutes for them; and this is so not only because the English instructor exercises a repressive function, but also because there is a problem of languages (see Essais d'ethnopsychiatrie générale [Paris: Gallimard, 1970], pp. 125–26).

[18]On the Prague School and its role in linguistics, see Change, nos. 3 (1969) and 10 (1972). (It is true that the Prague School was only formed in 1925. But in 1920, Jakobson came to Prague where there was already a Czech movement directed by Mathesius and connected with Anton Marty who had taught in the German university system. From 1902 to 1905, Kafka followed the courses given by Marty, a disciple of Brentano, and participated in Brentanoist meetings.)

[19]On Kafka's connections to Löwy and Yiddish theater, see Brod, Franz Kafka, pp. 110–16, and Wagenbach, Franz Kafka, pp. 163–67. In this mime theater, there must have been many bent heads and straightened heads.

[20]A magazine editor will declare that Kafka's prose has "the air of the cleanliness of a child who takes care of himself" (see Wagenbach, Franz Kafka, p. 82).

[21]"The Great Swimmer" is undoubtedly one of the most Beckettlike of Kafka's texts: "I have to well admit that I am in my own country and that, in spite of all my efforts, I don't understand a word of the language that you are speaking."

BAIONI: *Zionism, Literature, and the*
Yiddish Theater

[1]For a Zionist interpretation of Max Brod's novel see H. Herrmann's dialogue review in *Selbstwehr*, n. 20 (May 19, 1911) and Brod's reply in n. 21 (May 26, 1911). See also J. Rabinowitz, "Von westjüdischen Schriftstellern," *Der Jude*, vol. v (1921), pp. 165–66.

[2]But see also Binder's dissenting opinion in *Kafka-Handbuch* (Stuttgart, 1979), vol. I, p. 376.

[3]On October 1, three days before this performance, Kafka had been in the Altneu Synagogue where he observed three Orthodox Jews, obviously from Eastern Europe, during their prayers. In his diary he notes how they huddled beneath their prayer shawls, pronouncing each word in a delicate, beautiful chant. Nevertheless he was not particularly moved: "I was stirred immeasurably more deeply by Judaism in the Pinkas Synagogue" (D 59).

[4]*Stenographisches Protokoll der Verhandlungen des 5. Zionisten-Congresses in Basel* (Vienna, 1901), pp. 99–100.

[5]*Stenographisches Protokoll*, pp. 111–12.

[6]See Gershom Scholem, "Die jüdische Jugendbewegung," *Der Jude*, vol. i (1916), pp. 822–25. On Walter Benjamin's relation to the *Jugendbewegung*, see G. Schiavoni, *Walter Benjamin. Sopravvivere alla cultura* (Palermo, 1980), pp. 96–148.

[7]Christoph Stölzl, *Kafkas böses Böhmen* (Munich: Text und Kritik, 1974), p. 133.

[8]*Stenographisches Protokoll*, p. 102.

[9]See Buber's essay, "Die hebräische Sprache" (1909), in *Die jüdische Bewegung. Gesammelte Aufsätze und Ansprachen. 1900–1915* (Berlin, 1916), pp. 176–89, and the 1903 essay "Renaissance und Bewegung," ibid., pp. 95–108.

[10]See Kafka's diary entry for January 24, 1912, and *Selbstwehr*, nos. 1 (January 5, 1912), 2 (January 12, 1912), and 10 (March 8, 1912).

[11]*Selbstwehr* n. 2, op. cit.

[12]N. Birnbaum, *Ausgewählte Schriften zur jüdischen Frage* (Czernowitz, 1910), vol. I, pp. 71–73.

[13]Ibid., p. 273.

[14]Ibid., pp. 185–87.

[15]M. N. Silberroth, "Zionistische Romantik oder alljüdische Wirklichkeit?" *Selbstwehr*, n. 25 (June 20, 1913), pp. 4–5.

[16]Birnbaum, op. cit., p. 263.

[17]Ibid., p. 273.

[18]Ibid., pp. 268–69.

[19]Birnbaum, pp. 261–73.

[20]"Nationalbewusstsein und Stammesbewusstsein." On Oppenheimer, see Robert Weltsch's Introduction to *Year Book of the Leo Baeck Institute*, vol. ix (London, 1964), pp. xxiv–xxvii.

[21]See Oppenheimer, "Nationalbewusstsein und Stammesbewusstsein," in *Selbstwehr*, n. 9 (March 4, 1910).

[22]See *Selbstwehr*, nos. 1 (March 1, 1907) and 15 (April 15, 1910).

[23]See the summary of a performance of Yiddish folk songs in *Selbstwehr*, n. 5 (February 3, 1911).

[24]See Y. Löwy, *Selbstwehr*, n. 20 (May 20, 1910).

[25]Claudio Magris, *Lontano da dove* (Turin, 1971), pp. 21 and 23–26.

[26]Max Brod, *Streitbares Leben* (Munich, 1969), pp. 47–49.

[27]On Lateiner's *Meschumed* and on Kafka's relations with the actors from Lemberg, see Marthe Robert's incisive comments in *Seul comme Franz Kafka* (Paris: Calmann-Lévy, 1979), pp. 45–67.

[28]On the influence of the Yiddish theater on Kafka's writing, see E. T. Beck, *Kafka and the Yiddish Theater. Its Impact on His Work* (Madison, Milwaukee, London: 1971).

[29]*Selbstwehr*, n. 7 (February 16, 1912).

[30]"Ostjüdischer Rezitationsabend," n. 8 (February 23, 1912).

[31]Binder, *Kafka-Handbuch*, pp. 395–97.

[32]Ibid., p. 394.

[33]Ibid., p. 401.

LÖWY: *Libertarian Anarchism in* Amerika

[1]See, for example, their collection *Von Judentum* (1913), a copy of which can be found in Kafka's library. In a recent work, Ritchie Robertson labels Kafka's social vision "romantic anti-capitalist," citing my own definition of the concept, but interpreting it rather unilaterally as a synonym for "anti-industrialism" (cf. Robertson, *Kafka, Judaism, Politics and Literature* [Oxford: Clarendon Press, 1985], p. 141).

[2]W. Emrich, *Franz Kafka* (Frankfurt a.M.: Athenäeum, 1961), pp. 227–28.

[3]A. Holitscher, *Amerika heute und morgen* (Berlin: Fischer, 1912), p. 316. He also complains of the metallic din of the Chicago factories, with their sounds that are "cold and inconsolable like the whole modern world and its civilization, the most sinister enemy of the human species" (p. 321).

[4]Max Brod, "Verweiflung und Erlösung im Werk Franz Kafkas," *Über Franz Kafka* (Frankfurt a.M.: Fischer, 1966), p. 326.

[5]Alfred Wirkner, *Kafka und die Aussenwelt. Quellensstudien zum "Amerika"-Fragment* (Stuttgart, 1976), p. 81.

[6]Heinz Politzer, *Das Kafka Buch* (Frankfurt a.M.: Fischer, 1965), p. 151.

[7]Michal Mares, "How I Met Franz Kafka," in Klaus Wagenbach, *Franz Kafka. Années de jeunesse (1883–1912)* (Paris: Mercure de France, 1967), p. 254; and Max Brod, *Franz Kafka* (Paris: Gallimard, 1945), pp. 135–36.

[8]Mares, "How I Met Franz Kafka," p. 253; and Mares, "Setkanis Franzem Kafkou," *Literarni Noviny*, 15 (1946), in K. Wagenbach, *Kafka* (Hamburg: Rowohlt, 1964), p. 70.

[9]Mares, "How I Met Franz Kafka," p. 259.

[10]Max Brod, *Über Franz Kafka*, p. 76.

[11]As Marthe Robert justly notes (*Seul comme Franz Kafka* [Paris: Calmann-Lévy, 1979], p. 72), "*reserve* is an essential component of his art, the *stylistic principle* that insures his novelistic work against the triviality of the novel of ideas."

[12]"If any journal seemed tempting to me for any length of time . . . it was Dr. Gross's" (L 167). See also G. Baioni, *Kafka. Letteratura ed ebraismo* (Turin: Einaudi, 1984), pp. 203–5. On Otto Gross, see Arthur Mitzman, "Anarchism, Expressionism, and Psychoanalysis," *New German Critique*, 1 (winter, 1977).

[13]Kundera, "Quelque part là-derrière," *Le Débat*, 8 (June 1981), p. 58.

[14]Holitscher, *Amerika heute und morgen*, pp. 102–3.

KURZ: *Nietzsche, Freud, and Kafka*

(N.B. For reasons of space, not all of the author's notes could be reproduced.—
TRANS.)

[1] Freud, *Gesammelte Werke*, ed. A. Freud et. al., 3rd ed. (London, 1969), pp. 14, 86; cf. 10, 53. Freud's biographer Ernest Jones relates Freud's comment that no one had a more profound understanding of himself than Nietzsche: E. Jones *The Life and Work of Sigmund Freud* (New York: Basic Books, 1953–1957), vol. 2, p. 405 f. In Freud's circle Nietzsche was present primarily through Lou Andreas-Salomé, a close companion of Nietzsche, Rilke, and Freud. Compare her valuable study, *Nietzsche/Lou Salomé*, ed. and trans. Siegfried Mandel (Redding Ridge, Conn.: Black Swan Books, 1988).

[2] The archaeological approach is a historically oriented, transcendental formulation of philosophical problems: cf. W. Hogrebe, *Archäologische Bedeutungspostulate* (Freiburg and Munich: 1977), p. 36. Hogrebe refers to Kant's concept of a "philosophical archaeology." See also Paul Ricoeur, *Freud and Philosophy: An Essay on Interpretation*, trans. Denis Savage (New Haven: Yale University Press, 1970).

[3] Novalis, *Schriften*, eds. P. Kluckhohn, R. Samuel (2nd ed.: Stuttgart, 1954), vol. 3, p. 571, no. 107; cf. also "our own inner plurality," vol. 3, p. 662, no. 598. On Nietzsche's relation to Romanticism, cf. E. Behler, "Die Kunst der Reflexion. Das frühromantische Denken im Hinblick auf Nietzsche," in *Untersuchungen zur Literatur als Geschichte*, ed. V. J. Günther et. al. (Berlin,1973), pp. 219–48.

[4] Georg Lukács, *The Theory of the Novel* (Cambridge, Mass.: The MIT Press, 1971), p. 53 (translation emended).

[5] Ernst Mach denied the continuity of the self, defining it merely as an "expedient." Cf. E. Mach, *The Analysis of Sensations and the Relation of the Physical to the Psychical*, trans. C. M. Williams (New York: Dover, 1959). Mach had an enormous influence on the Young-Vienna movement. Hofmannsthal and Musil, for example, attended his lectures.

[6] See C. Schorske, *Fin-de-Siècle Vienna. Politics and Culture* (New York: Vintage, 1981); A. Janik and St. Toulmin, *Wittgenstein's Vienna* (New York: Simon & Schuster, 1973); *Critique*, vol. 31, no. 339–40 (1970), *Vienne: début d'un siècle;* G. Wunberg, *Der frühe Hofmannsthal* (Stuttgart, 1965), p. 15f.; R.-P. Janz and K. Laermann, *Arthur Schnitzler: Zur Diagnose des Wiener Bürgertums des Fin de siècle* (Stuttgart: Metzler, 1977). Of course, this experience is not limited to Vienna. Cf. also P. Szondi, *Theorie des modernen Dramas* (Frankfurt: Suhrkamp, 1963), p. 49, with reference to Strindberg's plays; M. Hamburger, *The Truth of Poetry: Tensions in Modern Poetry from Baudelaire to the 60's* (New York: Harcourt, Brace & World, 1970).

[7] Sigmund Freud, *Character and Culture*, ed. Philip Rieff (New York: Macmillan, 1963), p.41.

[8] Nietzsche, *Werke*, vol. 1, p. 1095. Anthony Wilden has also pointed to the affinity between these two questions in *The Language of the Self* (Baltimore: Johns Hopkins University Press, 1968), p. 184.

[9] Freud called Nietzsche's remark that an "ancient piece of humanity" is at work in our dreams "insightful" (*Werke*, vol. 2/3, p. 554; cf. Nietzsche, *Werke*, vol. 1, p. 455. Cf. also Freud, *Werke*, vol. 15, p. 83; vol. 11, p. 386).

[10] Walter Benjamin, *Reflections* (New York: Schocken Books, 1986), p. 157.

[11] Nietzsche, *Werke*, vol. 2, p. 73.

[12] As quoted by J. P. Hodin in "Erinnerungen an Franz Kafka," *Der Monat*, vols. 8 and 9, 1948–1949, p. 96.

[13] Samuel Lublinski, *Der Ausgang der Moderne* (Dresden, 1909), p. 65.

[14]M. Brod, *Über Franz Kafka* (Frankfurt a.M.: Fischer, 1976), p. 259. According to Brod, the thought of such a relation shows "a lack of instinct"; cf. also Claude David: "Max Brod n'avait pas tort: entre Nietzsche et Kafka il n'y a pas de rapport" ("Sur Kafka: quelques livres parmi beaucoup," *Etudes Germaniques*, vol. 30 [1975], p. 61).

[15]Cf. K. Wagenbach, *Franz Kafka, Eine Biographie seiner Jugend 1883–1912* (Bern: Francke, 1958), p. 103; Patrick Bridgwater, *Kafka and Nietzsche* (Bonn: Bouvier, 1974), p. 3f.; Brod, *Franz Kafka*, p. 57. Apparently, Kafka had come to know Nietzsche through his friend Oskar Pollak, who introduced him to the *Kunstwart*, one of the most influential cultural journals at the time, which identified itself with Nietzsche. Nietzsche criticized the *Kunstwart* for sounding the horn of Germanic nationalism (*Werke*, vol. 3, p. 1304); cf. also G. Kratzsch, *Kunstwart und Dürerbund* (Göttingen: Vandenhoeick & Ruprecht, 1969), p. 105. Kafka subscribed to the *Kunstwart* until 1904.

[16]*Werke*, vol. 1, p. 30.

[17]Both authors rely on classical sources, Kafka's formulation of the imperative being almost identical with Nietzsche's well-known phrase "Become what you are." Cf. Nietzsche, *Werke*, vol. 2, pp. 159, 197, 1063, 1094f. Their meanings, however, are not identical. For Nietzsche the imperative indicates "Preservation, development, elevation, support, expansion of power"—and thus mastery (ibid., vol. 2, p. 53). In this sense, Georg Simmel hoped in 1915 that the war would be the fulfillment of "what one has viewed as the formula of all morality: 'Become what you are!'" G. Simmel, *Zur Philosophie der Kunst* (Potsdam, 1922), p. 151.

[18]Issue 51 of *Aktion* (December 20, 1913) is entirely devoted to this incident. On Gross, cf. A. Mitzmann, "Anarchism, Expressionism and Psychoanalysis," *New German Critique*, 10 (1977), 77–104.

[19]Freud, *Werke*, vol. 13, p. 53.

STACH: *Kafka's Egoless Woman*

[1]Except for occasional emendations, all references are to *Sex and Character* (New York: AMS Press, 1975 [reprint of 6th edition, 1906, London: W. Heinemann; New York: Putnam]).

[2]Two examples: That women are fascinated by an erect penis, which represents "the most unpleasant thing of all," is for Weininger the "most decisive proof that women want from love not beauty, but rather—something else." On the relationship of the genius to his own sexuality, Weininger explains: "For there will never be, can never be, a truly significant person who sees in coitus more than an animalistic, piggish, disgusting act, or who would find in it the most profound divine mystery."

[3]Otto Weininger, *Gedanken Über Geschlechtsprobleme*, ed. Robert Saudek (2nd ed.: Berlin, 1907).

[4]The influence of Weininger on, among others, Arnold Schönberg, Ludwig Wittgenstein, Georg Trakl, Karl Kraus, August Strindberg, Gottfried Benn, Cioran . . . and Mussolini, is well established. Elias Canetti attests that in the twenties in Vienna *Sex and Character* was still to be counted among the most talked about books (*The Torch in My Ear* [New York: Farrar, Straus and Giroux, 1982], trans. by Joachim Neugroschel). On its reception, see J. Le Rider and N. Leser (eds.), *Otto Weininger. Werk und Wirkung* (Vienna: Österreichischer Bundesverlag, 1984). Further, Hans Mayer, *Outsiders: A Study in Life and Letters* (Cambridge, Mass.: The MIT Press, 1982).

[5]Gottfried Benn, "Doppelleben," *Prosa und Autobiographie* (Frankfurt a.M.,

1984), p. 397. The American edition of Benn's work *Primal Vision* (New York: New Directions), includes only excerpts from "A Double Life."

[6]The only document about Kafka's lasting interest in Weininger is a letter from the year 1921, in which he asks the writer Oskar Baum for the manuscript of his lecture on Weininger (L 276). The few surviving letters from Kafka's student years provide only sparse information about his participation in contemporary cultural currents. His notebooks from that time are lost. Nevertheless, around 1903 Kafka was very active in the literary section of the "Reading and Discussion Group of German Students in Prague," a liberal fraternity. Its well-stocked library, which he often consulted, subscribed to the most important literary journals, for example, Karl Kraus's *Die Fackel,* which devoted great space to the Weininger case.

[7]"Fear of woman is fear of senselessness . . . of the alluring abyss of nothingness" (*Sex and Character,* p. 298).

[8]Ernst Bloch writes of "the devaluation of woman here into a hetaira." "Weininger proceeded in this direction with total obsession . . . the most vehement misogyny known to history, a single anti-utopia of woman, in the middle of the Secession period" (*The Principle of Hope,* trans. Neville Plaice, Stephen Plaice, and Paul Knight [Cambridge, Mass.: The MIT Press, 1986], vol. II, pp. 593–94).

[9]*Die Fackel,* no. 229 (July 1907), p. 14: "One can imagine someone who abhors Weininger's conclusions (about the inferiority of women) and who cheers his premises (the otherness of women)" (*Die Fackel,* vol. 169 [November 1904], p. 7n. Freud found Weininger's work only "rather unconsidered."

[10]It is remarkable that this argument, stripped of polemical force, is today the basis for a possible sublation of sexual alienation: universal bisexuality as the basis for the communicability of sexual experiences. Cf. Christian David, "On Male Mythologies of Femininity," in J. Chasseguet-Smirgel (ed.), *Psychoanalyse der weiblichen Sexualität* (Frankfurt a.M., 1974), p. 71.

[11]Apparently, negation seems particularly obvious to Weininger's audience as the most concise formulation of patriarchal claims to power. With Robert Musil, femininity as an abstract deficiency is still a fact of general psychological formation: "he . . . sometimes sensed almost bodily the feminine nature of her deficiency as one among other sexual differences," *The Man Without Qualities.*

[12]Weininger does not mention the quality of material generosity that would have to follow here from this defect.

[13]Cf. pp. 287–88.

[14]Cf. pp. 288–89.

[15]Heinz Politzer, *Parable and Paradox* (Ithaca, N.Y.: Cornell University Press, 1962), pp. 197–200.

[16]"Sexual Types" is the title of the main section of *Sex and Character.* The concept of *type* is one of the frequent categories in the debate abut femininity at the turn of the century. Apparently, its ideological function is to sterilize and dull erotic experience, and is comparable to the medical nomenclature of sexual deviance. Max Brod noted correctly that the type "woman" corresponds to the type "ladies' man" ("Der Frauen-Nichtkenner," *Über die Schönheit häßlicher Bilder* [Leipzig, 1913], p. 24). Kafka used the word with extreme reluctance.

[17]Weininger writes: "And if all femininity is immoral, women must stop being women and become men." "Not affirmation and not denial, but the negation, the overcoming of femininity is what matters." "Women must fervently and truly and completely renounce coitus, which means, however: woman is doomed."

[18]See, for example, Bertha in *Comrades* (1886), Laura in *The Father* (1887), Thekla in *The Believers* (1888), Henriette in *Intoxication* (1899), the mother in *The Pelicans* (1907).

[19]"Woman is nothing; therefore, and only therefore, she can become everything, while man can only remain what he is" (294).

[20]Originally Brunelda was a singer, a private erotic allusion which refers to a medical lecture that Kafka attended in Jungborn in 1912. There, a doctor asserted "that breathing from the diaphragm contributes to the growth and stimulation of the sexual organs, for which reason female opera singers, for whom diaphragm breathing is requisite, are so immoral" (L 81; see also D 477).

[21]In the work of Franz Jung one finds a startling formulation which most concisely characterizes this terrible somatic dominance: a woman screams "coldly, as if from behind any core of humanity" (Das Trottelbuch [Berlin, 1918], p. 23).

[22]In a fragment to The Trial, a female figure (whose corporeality recalls Brunelda's, though in more subdued tones) appears and disappears—Helene, who for several weeks was the lover of state attorney Hasterer. "She was a fat female of uncertain age with yellowish skin and dark curls clustering round her forehead. At first K. never saw her except in bed, shamelessly sprawling, reading a serial novel. . . . Only when it was getting late, she would stretch and yawn or even throw one of her serial numbers at Hasterer if she could not attract his attention in any other way." "It was only misery and not malice which made her lean across the table, exposing her bare, fat, rounded back, in order to bring her face into close proximity with K.'s and force him to look at her" (243). This figure also reflects Kafka's voyeuristic interest in prostitutes. On November 19, 1913, about a year before writing this fragment, he notes in his diary: "I intentionally walk through the streets where there are whores. . . . I want only the stout, older ones, with outmoded clothes that have, however, a certain luxuriousness because of various adornments. One woman probably knows me by now" (D 238). This unusual "uniform," as it is described by Kafka, is also worn by Helene in The Trial: "generally in a dress which she doubtless thought highly becoming and stylish, actually an old ball-dress bedizened with trimmings and draped with several rows of conspicuously unsightly fringes. K. had no idea what this dress really looked like, for he could hardly bring himself to glance at her . . ." (243).

[23]Theodor Adorno, "Notes on Kafka," Prisms, trans. Samuel and Shierry Weber (Cambridge, Mass.: The MIT Press, 1981).

[24]Walter Benjamin, "Some Reflections on Kafka," Illuminations, ed. H. Arendt (New York: Schocken Books, 1969). See also the recent article on the connection between Leni and the Lilith of Jewish legend: Robert Kauf, "A Lilith Figure in Kafka's Prozess?" Monatshefte, 73 (1981), no. 1, pp. 63–66.

[25]All quotes are from Das Schloss, edited by M. Pasley (Frankfurt a.M.: Fischer, 1982), p. 154. See also p. 237 in the accompanying critical volume.

[26]The maids' disruptive function is interesting as a textual strategy. Kafka first writes: "There was hardly any peace and quiet in the room at all, the assistants. . . ." Here he apparently notices that the assistants already caused a commotion three sentences above; he then crosses out "the assistants" and continues: "often the maids came stomping in with their mens' boots."

[27]Here, and subsequently, the dating of fragments and short texts follows the conclusions of M. Pasley and K. Wagenbach: "Datierung sämtlicher Texte Franz Kafkas," in Kafka-Symposion, ed. J. Born et. al. (2nd ed.: Berlin, 1966). Kafka presumably began writing The Castle at the end of January 1922; cf. Hartmut Binder, Kafka. Der Schaffensprozess (Frankfurt a.M., 1983), p. 306f.

[28]Oswald Spengler, The Decline of the West, abridged edition by Helmut Werner (New York: The Modern Library, 1962), trans. Charles Francis Atkinson: "The feminine stands closer to the Cosmic. It is rooted deeper in the earth and it is immediately involved in the grand cyclic rhythms of Nature" (p. 354).

[29]Nietzsche, *Beyond Good and Evil*, trans. and ed. Walter Kaufmann (New York: Vintage Books/Random House, 1966), p. 169.

NORRIS: *Sadism and Masochism in "In the Penal Colony" and "A Hunger Artist"*

[1]"In the Penal Colony" and the first chapter of *Amerika* are sometimes treated as companion pieces because of Kafka's diary entry of February 9, 1915: "If the two elements—most conspicuous in the 'Stoker' and in the 'Penal Colony'—don't merge, I am finished" (D 330).

[2]Max Brod, *Franz Kafka: Eine Biographie* (Frankfurt a.M.: S. Fischer, 1968), p. 65.

[3]Gustav Janouch, *Gespräche mit Kafka* (Frankfurt a.M.: S. Fischer, 1968), p. 180.

[4]Franz Kafka, *In der Strafkolonie: Eine Geschichte aus dem Jahr 1914.* With original material and illustrations from the Workers' Accident Insurance Institute. Chronology and commentary by Klaus Wagenbach (Berlin: Verlag Klaus Wagenbach, 1975), pp. 65–94.

[5]Brod, p. 214.

[6]Lionel Trilling, "The Fate of Pleasure" in *Beyond Culture* (New York: Harcourt Brace Jovanovich, 1965), p. 63. (Trilling borrows "unpleasure" from Freud.) Sokel acknowledges his debt to Trilling in his work *Franz Kafka—Tragik und Ironie* (Munich: Albert Langen Georg Muller Verlag, 1964), p. 534.

[7]Sokel, p. 121.

[8]Franz Kafka, *Der Heizer, In der Strafcolonie, Der Bau*, introduction and notes by J. M. S. Pasley (Cambridge: Cambridge University Press, 1966), p. 17.

[9]Patrick Bridgwater, *Kafka and Nietzsche* (Bonn: Bouvier, 1974), pp. 41–46.

[10]Friedrich Nietzsche, *Genealogy of Morals*, in *Werke* vol. 3 (Frankfurt a.M.: Ullstein, 1976), p.266.

[11]Ibid., p. 289.

[12]Ibid., p. 315.

[13]Bridgwater, p. 42.

[14]Nietzsche, p. 345.

[15]Gilles Deleuze and Félix Guattari, *Kafka: Pour une Littérature mineure* (Paris: Les Editions de Minuit, 1975) contains no comparison of the two Kafka stories examined in this chapter.

[16]Ibid., p. 103.

[17]Barthes writes: "Throughout his life, the Marquis de Sade's passion was not erotic (eroticism is very different from passion); it was theatrical." Roland Barthes, *Sade/Fourier/Loyola*, trans. Richard Miller (New York: Hill and Wang, 1976), p. 181.

[18]Ibid., p. 36.

[19]Deleuze and Guattari, p. 19.

[20]Barthes, p. 20.

[21]Deleuze and Guattari, p. 66.

[22]Ibid., p. 23; Masoch has a novel by that title.

[23]Ibid., p. 18.

[24]Barthes, p. 31.

[25]Ibid., pp. 148, 164.

[26]Deleuze and Guattari, p. 66.

[27]Ibid., p. 21.

²⁸*Beyond the Pleasure Principle*, Sigmund Freud, *Gesammelte Werke* (London: Imago, 1948), 13: 3–69.

²⁹Deleuze and Guattari, p. 52.

³⁰Ibid., p. 109.

³¹Ibid., pp. 56–57.

³²*A Child Is Being Beaten*, Freud, *Gesammelte Werke*, 12: 97–226. For a discussion of the grammatical transformations of the fantasy, see Jean Laplanche, *Life and Death in Psychoanalysis*, trans. Jeffrey Mehlman (Baltimore: Johns Hopkins University Press, 1976), pp. 97–102.

³³Deleuze and Guattari, pp. 56–57.

³⁴Ibid., pp. 84–85.

³⁵Clemens Heselhaus, "Kafka's Erzählformen," *Deutsche Vierteljahresschrift für Literaturwissenschaft und Geistesgeschichte* 26, no. 3 (1952), pp. 353–76.

³⁶Deleuze and Guattari (p. 53) accuse Kafka of epistolary vampirism: "Il y a un vampirisme des lettres, un vampirisme proprement épistolaire. Dracula, le végétarien, le jeûneur qui suce le sang des humains carnivores, a son château pas loin. Il y a du Dracula dans Kafka, un Dracula par lettres, les lettres sont autant de chauves-souris."

³⁷A variant of this fantasy with a female "cutter" appears in a February 1913 letter to Felice: "To be a rough piece of wood, and to be braced against her body by the cook, who from the edge of this stiff piece of wood (approximately in the place of my hip) draws the knife toward her with both hands and powerfully slices off kindling for starting the fire" (F 202).

³⁸Kafka writes of the family dynamic, "Mother unconsciously played the part of a beater during a hunt" (DF 157).

MÜLLER: *Kafka, Casanova, and* The Trial

¹See Jürgen Born and Michael Müller, "Kafkas Briefe an Milena. Ihre Datierung," *Jahrbuch der Deutschen Schiller-Gesellschaft* 25 (1981), pp. 509–24; the quotation is taken from page 522.

²A thirteen-volume German edition, translated and introduced by Heinrich Conrad, was published from 1907 to 1909 by Georg Müller Verlag, Munich-Leipzig.

³See J. Rives Childs, *Casanoviana. An Annotated World Bibliography* (Vienna, 1956).

⁴Among the editions available to Kafka are the following: *Casanovas Gefangenschaft und Flucht aus den Bleikammern von Venedig* (Leipzig: Philipp Reclam, n.d. [1875?]); *Casanovas Gefangenschaft in den Bleikammern in Venedig und Flucht aus denselben* (Munich: Albert Medler, n.d. [1885?]); Jakob Casanova, *Meine Flucht aus den Bleikammern Venedigs* (Stuttgart: Literarisches Institut, n.d. [1907?]); *Des weltberühmten Liebeskünstlers Giacomo Casanova schmachvolle Gefangenschaft und tollkühne Flucht aus den Bleikammern Venedigs von ihm selbst erzählt und neu herausgegeben von Christian Kraus* (Berlin: Wilhelm Borngräber, n.d. [1911]).

⁵These and other literary sources are discussed by Hartmut Binder in his *Kafka-Kommentar zu den Romanen, Rezensionen, Aphorismen und zum Brief an den Vater* (Munich, 1976), p. 189.

⁶*The Memoirs of Jacques Casanova de Seingalt*, vol. 2, *To Paris and Prison*, trans. Arthur Machen, (New York: G. P. Putnam's Sons / London: Elek Books, n.d.), p. 547.

⁷Ibid., p. 549.

[8] Ibid., p. 551.
[9] Ibid., p. 563.
[10] Ibid., p. 554.
[11] Ibid., p. 567.
[12] Ibid., p. 553.
[13] Ibid., p. 558.
[14] Ibid., p. 587.
[15] Ibid., p. 571.
[16] Ibid., p. 574.

PASLEY: *The Act of Writing*

[1] See Erwin R. Steinberg, "The Judgment in Kafka's 'The Judgment,'" *Modern Fiction Studies* 8, no. 1 (1962), pp. 23–30.

[2] Hartmut Binder has argued that Kafka chose the octavo notebooks while working in the Alchimistengasse because he had to carry them home each evening. Even if such considerations influenced Kafka initially, these smaller notebooks were nevertheless, quite literally, the focus of his literary activity; as such, they certainly affected his literary form.

[3] Reference here is to Kleist's well-known essay, "Über die allmähliche Verfertigung der Gedanken beim Reden," literally, "On the Gradual Completion of Thoughts during Conversation."—TRANS.

[4] For a fuller treatment of this subject, see Hartmut Binder, "Kafkas Schaffensprozess, mit besonderer Berücksichtigung des 'Urteils,'" in *Euphorion* 70 (1976), pp. 129–74.

[5] Max Brod, "Uyttersprot korrigiert Kafka," *Forum* 43/44 (1957), p. 265.

[6] Friedrich Schiller, "Über naive und sentimentalische Dichtung," *Sämtliche Werke*, vol. 5, G. Fricke and H. G. Göpfert, eds. (Munich, 1959), p. 753.

[7] I quote from the handwritten manuscript of *The Castle* with the permission of Schocken Books, Inc., New York, and S. Fischer Verlag, Frankfurt a.M.

[8] One might except at most the four titles which appear in the "*Hochzeitsvorbereitungen*" ["The Synagogue Animal—Seligmann and Graubart—Has This Reached the Point of Being Serious?—The Bricklayer" (DF 368)]; but here too we can assume that the stories which belonged to the titles had already been completed.

[9] See M. Pasley, "Kafka's Semi-Private Games," *Oxford German Studies* 6 (1971–1972), pp. 128–31.

ANDERSON: *Unsigned Letters to Milena Jesenská*

[1] *Briefe an Milena*. Expanded new edition established by Jürgen Born and Michael Müller (Frankfurt a.M.: S. Fischer, 1983). An English translation of this edition is forthcoming from Schocken Books.

[2] Born and Müller, "Kafka's Briefe an Milena: Ihre Datierung," *Das Jahrbuch der Deutschen Schillergesellschaft* (Stuttgart: Alfred Kroner, 1981), p. 510.

[3] Three essays which deal with the Milena correspondence specifically are: Werner Vortriede, "Letters to Milena: The Writer as Advocate of Himself," in *Franz Kafka Today*, ed. A. Flores (Madison: University of Wisconsin Press, 1958); Hartmut Binder, "The Letters: Form and Context," and Hartmut Böhme, "Mutter Milena: On Kafka's Narcissism," both in *The Kafka Debate*, ed. A. Flores (New York:

Gordian Press, 1977). The first is the best essay, but despite early publication it has received little or no critical attention.

[4]Maurice Blanchot, *De Kafka à Kafka* (Paris: Gallimard, 1981). Félix Guattari and Gilles Deleuze, *Kafka: Toward a Minor Literature* (Minneapolis: University of Minnesota Press, 1986), chapter 3 of which is included in this volume. Elias Canetti, *Kafka's Other Trial* (New York: Schocken Books, 1974), a portion of which is also included here, treats the correspondence with Felice Bauer as a kind of variant of Kafka's novel.

[5]See Jacques Derrida, *The Post Card: From Socrates to Freud and Beyond* (Chicago: University of Chicago Press, 1987).

[6]Margot Norris, "Darwin, Nietzsche, Kafka and the Problem of Mimesis," *Modern Language Notes* (Baltimore: Johns Hopkins University Press, 1980), pp. 1232–53.

[7]Unsigned book-jacket copy on the German edition (Frankfurt a.M.: Fischer Taschenbuch, 1966).

[8]The first letter in the Haas edition.

[9]Freud, *Gesammelte Werke* vol. 17 (London: Imago, 1941), p. 47.

[10]With regard to identity fragmentation it is interesting to note Kafka's playful designation of names. Georg Bendemann is generally associated with Kafka in psychoanalytic or biographical readings of the story. Yet Georg's name isolates him from all the other characters, whose names begin with an F or an F sound: Freund, Vater, Frieda (Felice), Verlobte, all referring back to: Franz. Psychoanalytic criticism of "The Judgment" cannot simply isolate the subject in Georg; all the characters are projections of elements in Kafka's own self.

[11]Another image of castration, especially since Kafka associated the Medusa snakes with his own head.

ABOUT THE CONTRIBUTORS

Mark Anderson: Director of Deutsches Haus and Assistant Professor of German Literature at Columbia University; author of the forthcoming *Kafka's Clothes: Ornament and Aestheticism in the Hapsburg Fin de Siècle.*

Giuliano Baioni: Director of the Department of German at the Università Ca' Foscari, Venice; author of two books on Kafka, *Romanzo e parabola* and *Letteratura ed ebraismo.*

Elias Canetti: Nobel Prize Winner for Literature in 1981; lives in London and Zurich.

Gilles Deleuze: Emeritus Professor of Philosophy at the University of Paris VIII; author of books on Nietzsche, Leibniz, cinema, and psychoanalysis.

Félix Guattari: Psychoanalyst and co-author (with G. Deleuze) of *Anti-Oedipe.*

Gerhard Kurz: Professor of German literature at the University of Amsterdam; author of *Traum-Schrecken. Kafkas literarische Existenzanalyse* and editor of *Der junge Kafka.*

Michael Löwy: Director of a research group at the Centre National de Recherche Scientifique, Paris; author of *Rédemption et utopie.*

Michael Müller: Co-editor (with Jürgen Born) of the expanded edition of Kafka's *Briefe an Milena.*

Gerhard Neumann: Professor of German Literature at the University of Munich; co-editor of the German critical edition of Kafka; author of books on Lichtenberg, Goethe, Schnitzler, and Kafka.

Margot Norris: Professor of English at the University of California at Irvine; author of *Beasts of the Modern Imagination.*

Malcolm Pasley: Editor of the German critical editions of *The Castle* and *The Trial*; Professor of German at Magdalen College, Oxford University.

Reiner Stach: Professor of German at the University of Frankfurt; author of *Kafkas Erotischer Mythos.*

Chistoph Stölzl: Director of the German Historical Museum in Berlin; historian of Central Europe; author of *Kafkas böses Böhmen.*

Klaus Wagenbach: Author of the first critical biography of Kafka, *Eine Biographie seiner Jugend, 1883–1912*; director of his own publishing house in Berlin.

PERMISSION ACKNOWLEDGMENTS

Grateful acknowledgment is made to the following for permission to reprint or translate previously published material:

edition text + kritik: English translation of "Jude, Antisemit, Zionist Kafka" ("Kafka: Jew, Anti-Semite, Zionist") from *Kafkas Böses Bohmen* by Christoph Stölzl.

Fischer Taschenbuch Verlag GmbH: English translation of "Die Frau ohne Ich—Otto Weiningers 'Geschlecht und Charakter'" and "Das Ich der Frau ist ihr Körper" ("Kakfa's Egoless Woman: Otto Weininger's *Sex and Character*") from *Kafkas erotischer Mythos* by Reiner Stach. Copyright © 1987 by Fischer Taschenbuch Verlag GmbH, Frankfurt am Main.

Giulio Einaudi Editore: English translation of "Gli Attori di Lemberg" ("Zionism, Literature, and the Yiddish Theater") from *Kafka: Letteratura ed ebraismo* by Giuliano Baioni. Copyright © 1984 by Giulio Einaudi Editore, Turin.

Carl Hanser Verlag GmbH & Co.: English translation of "Das Urteil und der Brief an den Vater" ("'The Judgment,' 'Letter to His Father,' and the Bourgeois Family") from *Franz Kafka: Das Urteil: Text, Ma-*